Macmillan Literary Lives
General Editor: Richard Dutton, Pro
Lancaster University

This series offers stimulating accounts of the literary careers of the most widely-read British and Irish authors. Volumes follow the outline of writers' working lives, not in the spirit of traditional biography, but aiming to trace the professional, publishing and social contexts which shaped their writing. The role and status of 'the author' as the creator of literary texts is a vexed issue in current critical theory, where a variety of social, linguistic and psychological approaches have challenged the old concentration on writers as specially-gifted individuals. Yet reports of the 'death of the author' in literary studies are (as Mark Twain said of a premature obituary) an exaggeration. This series aims to demonstrate how an understanding of writers' careers can promote, for students and general readers alike, a more informed historical reading of their works.

Series Standing Order

If you would like to receive future titles in this series as they are published, you can make use of our standing order facility. To place a standing order please contact your bookseller or, in case of difficulty, write to us at the address below with your name and address and the name of the series. Please state with which title you wish to begin your standing order. (If you live outside the United Kingdom we may not have the rights for your area, in which case we will forward your order to the publisher concerned.)

Customer Services Department, Macmillan Distribution Ltd
Houndmills, Basingstoke, Hampshire RG21 2XS, England

Published titles

Morris Beja
JAMES JOYCE

Richard Dutton
WILLIAM SHAKESPEARE

Jan Fergus
JANE AUSTEN

Paul Hammond
JOHN DRYDEN

Joseph McMinn
JONATHAN SWIFT

Kerry McSweeney
GEORGE ELIOT (Marian Evans)

John Mepham
VIRGINIA WOOLF

Michael O'Neill
PERCY BYSSHE SHELLEY

Leonée Ormond
ALFRED TENNYSON

George Parfitt
JOHN DONNE

Gerald Roberts
GERARD MANLEY HOPKINS

Felicity Rosslyn
ALEXANDER POPE

Tony Sharpe
T. S. ELIOT

Cedric Watts
JOSEPH CONRAD

Tom Winnifrith and Edward Chitham
CHARLOTTE AND EMILY BRONTË

John Worthen
D. H. LAWRENCE

Forthcoming titles

Cedric Brown
JOHN MILTON

Deirdre Coleman
SAMUEL TAYLOR COLERIDGE

Peter Davison
GEORGE ORWELL

James Gibson
THOMAS HARDY

Kenneth Graham
HENRY JAMES

David Kay
BEN JONSON

Mary Lago
E. M. FORSTER

Alasdair MacRae
W. B. YEATS

Philip Mallett
RUDYARD KIPLING

Ira Nadel
EZRA POUND

David B. Pirie
JOHN KEATS

Grahame Smith
CHARLES DICKENS

John Williams
WILLIAM WORDSWORTH

Barry Windeatt
GEOFFREY CHAUCER

Edmund Spenser

A Literary Life

Gary Waller

Professor of English and Interdisciplinary Studies
Dean of Arts and Sciences
University of Hartford, Connecticut

MACMILLAN

First published 1994 by
MACMILLAN PRESS LTD
Houndmills, Basingstoke, Hampshire RG21 2XS
and London
Companies and representatives
throughout the world

ISBN 0–333–52357–1 hardcover
ISBN 0–333–52358–X paperback

A catalogue record for this book is available
from the British Library.

10   9   8   7   6   5   4   3   2   1
03 02 01 00 99 98 97 96 95 94

Printed and bound in Great Britain by
Antony Rowe Ltd
Chippenham, Wiltshire

For Philip
Goe, little book . . .

Contents

Preface

When Richard Dutton, the editor of this series, asked me to write a volume on Spenser, I was revising the Spenser chapter of the second edition of an earlier book on sixteenth-century poetry. To cover so intriguing a figure in a single chapter had necessarily meant some frustrating compression and reductiveness, so the opportunity provided by the Literary Lives series to read Spenser's life and works (both, in their different and interrelated ways, complex and contradictory texts) was an inviting one. The book has also, necessarily, taken shape against the broader background of a slow but deep revolution in Spenser studies, in studies of the sixteenth-century and the whole early modern period, in literary and cultural criticism and theory generally, and (not least) in biographical theory and practice. The changes and, not least, the contradictions of these wider critical movements have inevitably entered into its writing; in particular, they have influenced a central part of my argument that writing about any part of our cultural past necessitates writing about our own historical situatedness. To an open underestimated extent, the present is the subject (in many series) of the past it investigates.

In writing this book, I have accumulated many debts, institutional as well as personal. A fellowship from the John Simon Guggenheim Foundation in 1988 supported some of the research that has fed into it. The staffs of the Rosenbach Library, the Newberry Library, and the libraries of the University of Cambridge, Carnegie Mellon University, and the University of Hartford have been very helpful. The book has directly benefitted from the company, and occasionally the cuisine, of many annual luncheons of the Spenser Society, and even more meetings of Spenser-at-Kalamazoo. Especially helpful over the years have been Marion Campbell, Andrea Clough, Craig Dionne, A. C. Hamilton, Bob Hodge, Stuart Hunter, Roger Kuin, Ken Larsen, Gerald Rubio, Josephine Roberts, Ann Shaver, William Sessions, John Stevens, Robert Stillman and Suzanne Woods. In particular, Mary Ellen Lamb, Susan Green and Naomi Miller kindly offered many perceptive comments on a number of the chapters. My former colleagues at Carnegie Mellon gave me the leisure to undertake the book; my new colleagues at Hartford, especially President Humphrey Tonkin (himself one of our most distinguished Spenserians) and

Senior Vice President Jonathan Lawson, gave me the stimulus – an invitation to join them as Dean of Arts and Sciences – to (nearly) finish it before I joined them, and then not waste too much time doing the final bits and pieces. Lynne Kelly, Alan Hadad, Joel Kagan and Catherine Stevenson also played no small parts. My wife and colleague, Kathleen McCormick, has always been my best critic and provider of stimulation. Certainly not the least of the stimulants is the person to whom this book is dedicated and who, at the age of four, has been the perceptive listener to and actor of almost recognizable versions of some of the stories Spenser tells in *The Faerie Queene*. He likes the dragons and monsters best, not least because they mysteriously appear in C. S. Lewis's Narnia stories as well. I commenced my teaching career in Lewis's old rooms at Magdalene, which suggests that there is indeed some serendipitous connection in Faeryland (or Narnia) – even if, as Freud says, it is that of a profound fantasy. Philip knows that Freud's 'oceanic feeling' really refers to his bathtub, and Cape Cod, and beaches in New Zealand: he has helped keep me in the real.

The origins of various parts of Chapters 1, 2, 3 and 6 are to be found, in rearranged and compressed form, in *English Poetry of the Sixteenth Century* (Longman, 1986); versions of assorted paragraphs in Chapters 1, 2, 5 and 7 appeared in *The Sidney Family Romance* (Wayne State University Press, 1993). Prior publication, even where the similarities are generic rather than precise, is therefore acknowledged in these cases. Parts of Chapter 4 were written as a lecture at Victoria University of Wellington; the discussion of Petrarchism in Chapter 6 was presented at the conference on Love and Sexuality at the University of Toronto in 1991; parts of the discussion of masculinity were presented at the Shakespeare Association of America conference in Kansas City in 1992; the discussion of psychoanalysis, biography, and historical research in Chapters 1 and 7 was refined by some discussion of a paper I gave to the psychology colloquium at the University of Hartford in 1993 and at the 1993 University of Oklahoma conference on early modern cultural studies.

Quotations from Spenser's work are taken from the following editions:
The Faerie Queene, ed. A. C. Hamilton (1977), cited as Hamilton in the notes.
The Yale edition of the Shorter Poems of Edmund Spenser, ed. William A. Oram et al. (New Haven, 1989), cited as *Shorter Poems* in the notes.

A View of the Present State of Ireland, ed. W. R. Renwick (1970), cited
as Renwick in the notes.

In all cases original spelling is retained, except for the regularization
of i and j, f and s, u and v.

1

The Construction of a Literary Life

CONSTRUCTING THE SUBJECT

The writing of a 'literary life' of Edmund Spenser (c. 1552–98) is a project of which Spenser himself would have approved – indeed, it was a project to which he dedicated much of the energies of his adult life. Born in London in the early 1550s, Spenser grew up in the formative years of the early Elizabethan regime, and lived to within a few years of its end. His career and the beliefs he espoused throughout his adult life were closely bound up with the contradictory material practices and ideological struggles of the Elizabethan regime, including those over the nature and value of 'literary' experience and therefore of the whole concept of a 'literary life'.

Spenser was a prolific poet, whose career as a writer, unlike those of many other Elizabethan poets, lasted the whole of his adult lifetime. C. S. Lewis once remarked that everything that Spenser wrote outside *The Faerie Queene* was 'something of a diversion'. However much of an exaggeration that may be, nonetheless *The Faerie Queene* remains by far his most important work and it will receive most attention in the ensuing pages. Spenser's early work, written in the late 1560s, first flowered spectacularly in *The Shepheardes Calender* (1579) which was praised by Sidney in his *Defence of Poesie* (also written about 1579), although Lewis notes that Spenser 'was soon to write and perhaps had already written poetry which deprives the *Calender* of all importance'.[1] Spenser was certainly working on his epic during the 1580s; during that decade, also, he produced a tribute to Sidney, *Astrophel* (written c. 1586) which was published with *Colin Clouts Come Home Again* (1590). About the same time, he brought together a miscellaneous collection of old and recent poems which were published in 1591 as *Complaints*. Over the next five years, Spenser published a succession of volumes; these included the four *Hymns* (the first two perhaps written as early as the late 1570s, the latter two maybe fifteen years later); the *Amoretti*; and *Epithalamion*, the former an unusual (given the dominant English emphasis on secular erotic sonnets) Christianized Petrarchan sonnet sequence, the latter a poem celebrating an aristocratic marriage. But, unquestionably, his major achievement was *The Faerie Queene*, the first three Books of which were published in 1590, with a revised and expanded version in six Books appearing in 1596. The final poetry on which Spenser worked before his death may well have been the unfinished seventh book of *The Faerie Queene*, the so-called 'Cantos of Mutability'.

Although his origins are not well documented, Spenser was probably the son of a Lancashire merchant tailor. After his education at the Merchant Taylors School and Pembroke College, Cambridge, he sought advancement as a civil servant and courtier, and tried to cultivate what (by at least as early as the end of the 1570s) he saw as his primary vocation, that of a civil servant who was also, and not at all incidentally, a poet. In the late 1570s, he was in the employ of the Earl of Leicester (and thus became associated with at least the outskirts of the Sidney Circle) and then for some years worked under Lord Grey of Wilton, the Lord Deputy of Ireland. Spenser, in fact, spent most of the final twenty years of his life in Ireland and before his final return to England shortly before his death, made only two or three return visits, frustrating and disillusioning, to the land and specifically the court where his allegiances, political and literary, had remained centered. The work that constitutes his major claim to literary fame was therefore largely written in Ireland, and thus his poetical and literary career cannot be separated from the English occupation and attempted subjugation of that country.

While his primary vocation and source of income and position were political – as a secretary, landowner or 'planter' in occupied Ireland, Spenser also self-consciously tried to construct a literary life, that of the professional poet. He saw such a career as dedicated and, indeed, just as centrally important to the ideals and policies of the Elizabethan regime as that of Spenser the civil servant, the dedicated upholder of the Elizabethan rule of thorough in Ireland. Along with other late Elizabethan politicians, courtiers, and poets, including his patron Sir Walter Ralegh, Spenser attempted to sustain a myth of the poet as both the queen's, and the state's, most faithful servant. He thus has some claim to being regarded as England's first imperialist poet, with both terms having considerable if not necessarily equal weight (though which would bear the sway is something over which we may, as Spenser increasingly did, hesitate). It was a view of the poet – for reasons its advocates could not foresee – that anticipated a long and complex development in the history of attempts to define 'literature' and the shifting relations between that and other cultural practices.

In asserting that Spenser would have approved of the project of creating a · 'literary life', I of course do not want to claim that he would have approved of this one. He might have acknowledged that a 'literary life' is, as I will assert, never merely 'literary', but is always the product of complex cultural contradictions, many if not most of which are outside the individual writer's control; at other times, he might have asserted, as many others after him have – including many would-be faithful readers of his writings – that the 'literary' is in fact a relatively or even absolutely autonomous cultural practice, and while it may 'reflect' or 'reflect on' the broader cultural practices of its time, it gives us access to what Spenser, along with Sidney, might have termed an ideal or 'golden' world that is not to be explained away by other social or cultural phenomena. As Humphrey Tonkin affirms, articulating one of the articles of faith of the dominant tradition of traditional humanist criticism and biography, Spenser's poetry was 'a product of the age, but it was also the product of a particular individual'.[2] A 'literary' life, seen in those terms, might be conceived of as one that traces the seeds of such a belief and displays an author's attempts to realize it in the material details of his writings. Spenser, in fact, vacillates between the conceptions of the 'literary' – as autonomous or reflective – and, indeed it is in his vacillations, or as I prefer to put it, the ideological and material contradictions that underlie his 'personal' vacillations, in which the main interest of Spenser lies today. That opinion, of course, is not one with which Spenser or, indeed, many of his readers at the time, or perhaps many today, would have agreed. So it will be the burden of this particular 'literary life' to try, if not to prove that assertion, at least to suggest ways by which today's readers of Spenser might be led to construct their own readings not merely of the life and career of Spenser but of the broader cultural issues that they raise for us, one of the most important of which is precisely the relation of the 'literary' and a particular biography or 'life' to culture.

The contrast of the two models of a literary life I have just, somewhat crudely, enumerated, is complicated by a third model, which acknowledges the involvement of the historian or story-teller him- or herself. One of the commonplaces of contemporary criticism is that meanings are constructed by the interaction of texts and readers: they are not found solely 'in' the text or, in the case of a whole career, 'in' the details of that career. No reading of a text – whether the text of a poem or the text of a life – is, therefore, ever objective or disinterested; all readings are what Malcolm Evans calls 'readings-for' – readings supporting particular viewpoints – or what are sometimes called 'strong' or 'committed' readings.

Any literary life will therefore be constructed differently by different readers who will inevitably bring changing (and historically explicable) questions, interests, or anxieties to bear upon the past.[3] That is, however, not to say that a reading is merely subjective: all readings are the products of assumptions and expectations readers bring to their reading experiences; these interact – variously clashing with or matching – the repertoire of the text. But both text and readers are, in turn, produced by both the specifically literary ideology and the more general ideology of their societies.

Thus when today we read Spenser's writings, or contemporary documents that relate to his life, or the enormous amount of critical and scholarly material in the Variorum edition of Spenser or in the more recent *Spenser Encyclopedia*, we all bring particular ideologically produced repertoires – our expectations, preferences, beliefs, hopes, anxieties, our class, racial, gendered, or otherwise culturally specific assumptions – into dialogue with the particular repertoire of the text – its demands, pressures, its formal structure, conventions, the history of its productions, its current critical reception. Such interactions are inherent in all reading experiences; we could call it an ongoing 'dialogue' between text and reader, but we should perhaps talk of 'polylogue' since there are so many voices involved. There is, that is to say, no 'true' or authoritative reading of Spenser and his life that different biographies or critics have more or less adequately reproduced, one that we should somehow try to find or unearth. Rather, there is a continuing process of struggle and difference within the history of our culture to construct different histories within and for changing social formations. There are always historically or culturally dominant meanings, readings that we (or our teachers or powerful critics) prefer. The production of dominant readings is part of the mechanism by which 'Spenser' (in this sense a complex cultural construct not simply a historical person with definite, or more or less likely birth and death dates) has become part of the history of our culture, and without our fully realizing it.

I make this point emphatically because the first and intensely interesting fact about writing a literary life of Spenser is not just how intensely he himself tried to construct what would be accepted as an authentic and satisfying literary life for himself, but just how assiduously, for nearly three hundred years, the majority of scholars and critics have tried to stay within the boundaries of that conception. How to guide his readers to what he called a 'right' reading of a text was, as I shall show in Chapter 2, one of Spenser's recurring concerns as both a poet and a loyal Protestant Englishman, and even in their many disagreements, Spenser's admirers and commentators have overwhelmingly tried to be 'right' readers, far more so than the readers of his contemporaries, Sidney, Shakespeare, or Donne, whose lives and writings have often been cheerfully and frequently quite self-consciously inscribed within very different ideological frameworks in the course of what German reception-history theorists term their *Nachleben*, or after-life. Why, by and large, Spenser has been treated differently, and, why the many literary lives of Spenser that have been written over nearly 400 years at least until the 1980s have shared so many common assumptions and insisted so overwhelmingly on trying to reproduce the 'right' reading of his life and writings is a fascinating part not only of 'literary' history but of our broader cultural history. Janet MacArthur's recent survey of twentieth-century critical approaches to Sidney's and Spenser's sonnet collections makes it clear that while Sidney's *Astrophil and Stella* has been rewritten within diverse and contradictory paradigms of theory and criticism, the range of different approaches to Spenser's poems is much narrower. Spenser's announced ambitions to create what Coleridge termed a 'land of Faery . . . ignorant of all material obstacles' and the assumption that, in Sidney Lee's 1904 idealization of the poet's role, 'the poet's crown is alone worthy of the poet's winning', dominated Spenser scholarship until well into this century.[4]

Do we know what Spenser himself thought of such issues? From the writings (and related cultural practices) of most writers, we can construct a systematic, if no doubt changing and contradictory, account of the function of art, literature, and writing. But Spenser is relatively unusual in that the questions of the vocation of a poet and the social, even cosmic, importance of poetry were, quite explicitly, central ones for the whole of his literary career. Most of his writings either imply or openly argue for distinctive attributes for poetry and for the status of the poet. He was, in short, consciously and continuously constructing a literary life for himself. In order to find particular poems or other cultural practices provoking and admirable, we don't have to agree with their writer's view of them, any more than we do with any person's account of events in his or her life. But we should perhaps be curious, at the very least, why Spenser should have foregrounded such matters and made them such recurring concerns in his writings and life. Today, living in a culture where the writing and reading of poetry are somewhat marginal cultural practices but in which our dominant educational structures still insist that the poetry (along with novels, plays and other 'literary' forms) remain important, we might be intrigued to find just how seriously Spenser insisted he and his audience should take the function – one could almost say, using the religious term, the 'vocation' – of being a poet. And yet it is clear from reading his writings and those of others who comment upon him that however certain Spenser may have been about the importance of poets and poetry to society (and we can widen the discussion and talk about the importance of artists and art, generally), the detailed articulations of that importance not only change but contradict each other. At times Spenser appears uncompromising and confident; at others, uncertain or defensive. These vacillations are both inevitable and important: however marginal an activity it may be in any particular social formation, art usually constitutes a major site of ideological and material struggle, which may suggest that there is something worth struggling for. This awareness in itself makes the seriousness with which Spenser viewed poetry and the poetic vocation something to ponder.

The centrality to Spenser's life of the vocation of being a poet has been much commented upon in recent scholarship and criticism of Spenser. The most influential recent construction of Spenser's literary life is that of Richard Helgerson, whose New Historicist studies of Elizabethan poets have raised in compelling ways the issue of the self-consciousness of many English poets in the post-Reformation period about the poetic vocation.[5] Despite a long-standing, nostalgic picture of the Elizabethan age as one in which poetry flourished and was both a higher, 'spiritual' calling and materially rewarded, Elizabethan society, argues Helgerson, in fact marginalized literary writing, or what was generally termed 'poetry'; it was seen largely as an appropriate activity for juveniles, to be abandoned as the mature man (the gender needs to be noted) found his place in the adult world of public service and social responsibility. As a youthful accomplishment, the writing of poetry was therefore appropriate, even important, for an aspiring courtier, who might well find that to shine as a writer of lyrics and songs was an important part of his repertoire as a courtier and a means of his political advancement. Other courtiers found that music or dancing served similar functions.

What kinds of poetry were appropriate in the court, for an aspiring courtier or, in Spenser's case, someone from a lower social class, aspiring to employment in or near the court? In his survey of the Elizabethan court poets, and looking back as far back as what Thomas Nashe, with exuberant exaggeration, called the era of 'Chaucer, Lydgate, Gower, with such like, that lived under the tyrannie of ignorance', the Elizabethan courtier George Puttenham celebrated the court's role in establishing a new glory for poetry. In his treatise, *The Arte of English Poesie*, written probably in the 1580s, Puttenham asserts that the barbarous ignorance of the previous age had neglected poesie, but now its ancient dignity was being revived by 'many notable Gentlemen in the court'. He arranges both the subject-matter of poetry and its various kinds in a strict hierarchy. After the praise of the gods (or in a Christian country, matters of the Christian religion), the most important aim of poetry is to praise 'the worthy gests of noble Princes, the memorial and registry of all great fortunes'; this is followed by 'the praise of vertue and reproofe of vice, the instruction of morall doctrines, the revealing of sciences material and other profitable Arts, the redress of boisterous and sturdie courage'; finally, poetry is to be 'the common solace of mankind in all his travails and cares of this transitorie life'. Puttenham's account is strictly hierarchical, and rigidly subordinates poetry to public or, more accurately, class-specific interests. His emphasis is on the public responsibility of poetry: it should praise the great, reprove vice, and 'show the mutabilities of fortune, and the just punishment of God in revenge of a vicious and evil life'. Even the lowly pastoral is rendered publicly useful by its aim 'under the vaile of homely persons and in rude speeches to insinuate and glaunce at greater matters'. 'In everie degree and sort of men', Puttenham notes with blatant class bias, 'mens estates are unegall', and, by analogy, those kinds of poetry are preferred which serve the values and aims of the dominant power. It is a distinctively and unabashed drafting of poetry into the political, specifically the assimilation and appropriation of the 'divers' kinds of poetry into the centralizing hegemony of the Tudor court. Poetry is essentially decorative, even though many of the skills involved in writing it might be very useful when applied to more socially acceptable purposes. One such purpose was to gain access to influential members of the court either directly through what Puttenham terms the 'solace' afforded by poetry or by the poet's more utilitarian skills in writing and secretarial duties.[6]

But Spenser, Helgerson argues – and here, as a 'New' Historian, his views are in accord with most 'Old' Historical approaches to Spenser's career – challenged such a marginal role for the poet. He claimed that the poet, *qua* poet – not simply as a man whose rhetorical skills might be directed productively to other activities – had a serious and central role in the state. According to this view, Spenser's attempt to construct a more prestigious literary life for himself and for the figure of the poet generally was centered on the need for the skills and moral insights afforded to the monarch, the state, and humankind generally by poetry as such. Spenser did not totally abandon the lover-poet role that was felt to be appropriate for young men (though, as we shall see, his own love sonnets, the *Amoretti*, are unusual in the Petrarchan tradition for their explicit moral, even theological, interests), but rather he sought to show how it might mature by an exemplification of what Milton was later to term the 'sage and serious' role. Helgerson sees Spenser as a tragic figure: he was rewarded, belatedly but not entirely generously by the queen for his epic celebration of her regime (though it may have equally been a way of rewarding his loyal service as an oppressor of the Irish), but his elevated sense of the importance of the poet seemed to be matter of indifference to the court and, argues Helgerson, increasingly realizing this, Spenser lived the rest of his life disillusioned with what he saw as the betrayal of his (and the court's own) essential ideals, having fashioned an image of the poet and articulated political and even cosmic ideals to which he was to discover only lip-service was given. Helgerson's is an intriguing argument, all the more so because, despite its New Historicist caste, it remains very much in line with one of Spenser's own interpretations of his career that, as Helgerson puts it, he set out 'to redefine the limits of poetry, making it once again . . . a profession that might justifiably claim a man's life and not merely the idleness or excess of his life'. But Spenser was not consistent on this matter. Richard Rambuss has, by contrast, suggested that the single-minded pursuit of laureateship and a 'separation of the literary as a domain apart' over-simplifies Spenser's changing goals, and that at least early in his career it was secretaryship that he primarily pursued.[7]

My own attempt to construct a literary life for Spenser is largely in line with Helgerson's, although I take my account in very different directions. Not the least important of these is a foregrounding of gender, a matter about which recent New Historical criticism on the early modern period has generally been oddly uneasy. At other times, too, it attempts to replace the largely idealistic framework in which Helgerson casts his argument by means of an analysis of the material contradictions of Spenser's life and writings, not the least of which is what I term 'place', which includes the important fact that Spenser spent most of his adult life in Ireland. Finally, I acknowledge the place of the biographer in the story that (in this case) he constructs. Issues of class, race, gender, and unconscious and conscious agency invariably play crucial roles not just in the writing of the texts we study but in those we ourselves write, including biographies – a matter I shall take up in the final chapter. All were sites of major struggles in Spenser's attempts to define his own literary life and are also fundamental in the attempts of those who have followed him.

CLASS, RACE, GENDER, AGENCY

One commonplace way of constructing any life, literary or other, is chronological. Lives, are after all, lived chronologically, and so there may be a comforting sense of order to reading a life that starts, as our own do, from a birth or begetting and concludes with a death and some after effects. But despite the comfort of chronology, we all know that what the psychoanalyst Margaret Mahler termed the 'psychological birth'[8] of a human being does not usually coincide with the biological birth, and we all realize the significance of important episodes in our lives that seem to transcend or leap over chronology. More accurately, perhaps, we assign such events significances that may well, of course, change as our perspectives on them do – well after we enter into them, perhaps well after we apparently have lived through them. There will be a rough chronological structure to this literary life of Spenser: consecutive changes and chronological accumulation and disjunction did play major roles in his attempt to fashion a literary life. But I will supplement the chronological with more synchronic or synthetic interventions and overviews, especially of the factors that seem to me most crucial in understanding the significance of Spenser's career.

It seems 'natural' to want to know something of a writer's life. Why should that be? Different historical times may give different answers and favour varying understandings of what is 'natural'. Is it because of simple 'human' curiosity about a very different age? Perhaps because it helps us to understand the 'true' meaning of the author's writings? Or to understand ourselves and the ways we have been positioned by history? Because all human lives face recurring crises and dilemmas, and part of the 'genius' of the poet (or the artist generally) is an ability to put into moving language (or sound or shape) those crises and dilemmas? Because we think artists are uniquely creative personalities, individuals of genius, and carry the insights and highest aspirations of our civilisation? It is important to realise that before Spenser's time the notion of some kind of 'genius' associated with the artist would not have been a dominant one, and that the concepts of 'personality' or 'individuality' were predominantly understood in ways very different from today. Underlying the classic Freudian Oedipal drama – which in our century has so often been taken as the central myth of the unique personality, especially for the male, struggling to identify a 'real' self against the repression of his father, family, or country of origin – is the way crisis and identity get so irrevocably linked. With Spenser, as I shall show, an older sense of personality battles with this peculiarly modern sense and gives his career a distinctive shape. Modern writing in some senses dates from Spenser's time – 'modern' in the sense that identity, selfhood and 'individuality' are central issues. Perhaps only now, almost a century after Freud, can we understand the constructed nature of the personality, and realize that a literary life is itself a peculiarly modern cultural form. Initially, I want to look at three crucial aspects of his life that might be overlooked or marginalized by a standard chronological approach, but which are crucial to understanding his literary life: the nature of his class allegiances and aspirations; the fact that he was English and lived in an age when that was not a mere 'fact,' but was ideologically extremely heavily charged; and the seemingly trivial, but in fact crucial, issue of his gender-assignment as a man. An account of what these factors – class, race, and gender – meant to the shaping of Spenser's literary life may at times involve some chronological analysis, but to stand outside a simple chronological account can set up some fascinating connections and contradictions that provide fundamental keys to our understanding his career.

Class

On the occasion, in 1982, of the marriage of Lady Diana Spencer and

His Royal Highness Charles, Prince of Wales, Foster Provost, then the editor of the *Spenser Newsletter*, sent the following letter to her:

Madam:

On behalf of the *Spenser Newsletter*, and on behalf of the Spenser Society, whose president is Thomas P. Roche, Jr., of Princeton University, I am pleased to send you under separate cover a copy of *The Illustrated "Faerie Queene,"* a modernized and handsomely appointed version of Edmund Spenser's allegorical epic written to honor Queen Elizabeth I. The presentation copy has been donated by Mr Alvin Garfin of Newsweek Books, the publisher of the volume. As you know, Edmund Spenser claimed kin with the Spencers of Althorp, and in one of his poems entitled *Colin Clouts Come Home Again* he celebrated Lady Elizabeth Carey, Lady Anne Compton and Mounteagle, and Lady Alice Strange, the second, fifth, and sixth daughters of Sir John Spencer of Althorp. He called these ladies – who were presumably your aunts (with many "greats" prefixed) – by the names "Phyllis, Charillus, and sweet Amaryllis" respectively. I hope you will enjoy perusing this artistic visual treatment of the epic poem by "the prince of poets in his time," who may have been a relative of yours. I speak for Spenser scholars everywhere in wishing you the best of good fortune.[9]

Neither the appropriateness of a children's edition (as opposed, say, to a modern annotated edition) for the princess's reading pleasure nor the subsequent fate of the royal marriage are issues here. Touchingly, if slightly embarrassedly, gallant – it is especially striking that such a tribute should be written by a citizen of a republic that abolished the ancestors of the soon-to-be Princess Di's husband, root and branch, from dominion over it some two hundred years ago – the letter is an uncanny echo (as Provost himself notes) of Spenser's own aspirations and anxiety to be seen as related, even distantly, to the aristocracy. A. C. Judson's 1945 biography, which remains the fullest modern account of Spenser's life, is likewise concerned to give precedence to Spenser's supposed genteel connections. As Simon Shepherd notes, 'by giving primary place to the aristocratic Spencers, and to the poet's possible kinship with them', Judson and other biographers traditionally, almost universally, play down the 'inappropriateness' of Spenser's class origins, a move that echoes Spenser's own anxiety and ambition, 'rather than being a statement of his real place in the world'.[10]

What was Spenser's 'real' place in the world? The short answer is that we do not know, at least so far as his parentage is concerned, which makes it all the more interesting that so many biographers have been concerned to try to construct an 'appropriate' lineage for him. He was born in London, sometime between 1551 and 1554, possibly in West Smithfield, London, of parents whose identity is unknown, although there is much speculation, most of it deriving from his attendance at the Merchant Taylors' School, and much of it, as Shepherd notes, colored by the desire to find 'proper' ancestry for the 'prince of poets',[11] a desire that Spenser himself manifestly shared. The construction of an ancestry for one's life, literary and otherwise, was a common preoccupation among socially ambitious men at the time: Spenser shared his anxiety with the Sidneys and many other families who had a fake genealogy compiled for themselves. We know, in fact, very little of Spenser's 'real' social and familial foundations: his mother was named Elizabeth, but we do not know his father's name. While it is inferred that he was associated with the Merchant Taylors Company, there are records of a number of Spensers in the Company at the time. Some were prosperous and socially on the rise: one, John Spencer, became an alderman and later Lord Mayor of London, receiving a knighthood in 1594. Given Spenser's eagerness to point out his genteel connections, the lack of reference to such an honor in his writings suggests that this John Spencer is not the poet's father. Another, also John Spencer, was a journeyman in the Company, and so without any claims to gentility. We know nothing more of him. It is likely, as Ruth Mohl notes in her *Encyclopedia* entry on Spenser's biography, that 'Spenser was not born a gentleman (an important distinction at the time) but became one, without arms, by virtue of having studied at the university'.[12] It is clear that Spenser, like many later scholars, was reassured by that. As the editor of the *Spenser Newsletter* informed the future Princess of Wales some four hundred years later, Spenser himself claimed to be connected to an ancient family, the Despensers, and he dedicated three of the poems in *Complaints* (1591) to the three noble sisters of the family, *Mother Hubberds Tale* to Anne, Lady Compton and Mounteagle, *The Teares of the Muses* to Alice, Lady Strange, and *Muiopotmos* to Elizabeth, Lady Carey. Patronage, as I will note later, was a crucial institution in Spenser's construction of his career as a poet.

The connection with the Merchant Taylors is important regardless of the identity and status of Spenser's father. It enabled him to attend the Merchant Taylors' School in London, at least for a year, in 1569; and he was able also to attend Pembroke College, Cambridge, with the help of a bequest from the school. He matriculated in 1569 as a sizar, which is another useful clue to his likely class origins: as such, he earned his room and board by performing servants' duties. He took his BA in 1573, eleventh in a class of 120, and his MA in 1576, sixty-seventh in a class of seventy. His fellow students at Pembroke included Lancelot Andrewes, later a prominent Jacobean bishop and preacher, and Gabriel Harvey, two years his senior, who had a fellowship at Pembroke from 1570. Harvey and Spenser maintained a close friendship and literary collaboration for some years. Harvey was the son of a prosperous businessman, a ropemaker, from Saffron Walden, and it is likely that he provided Spenser with some worldly connections as well as recognizing the talents and ambitions of his younger friend. In 1580, a year after Spenser published his first work of poetry, *The Shepheardes Calender* – which starts with a dedication to 'the most excellent and learned both Orator and Poete, Mayster Gabriell Harvey' – Harvey and Spenser published five of their letters. These were concerned with a variety of literary topics, most especially the issue of quantitative verse. Since the issue of whether English versification, and indeed the English language generally, was appropriate for poetry, was a major one in Spenser's developing conception of his poetic vocation, we should pause a little over what today may seem an extremely arcane controversy, but which, at least to Spenser and some of his contemporaries was clearly an important issue, not least for its class base. Matters of race, class, and gender are not only great, motivating ideas; they are ways we describe the material details of our everyday existence, the lived experience of ideologies.

During the sixteenth-century and even well into the seventeenth, there were various attempts to adapt classical metres into English. Classically trained humanist scholars found syllabic and rhyming verse, which were characteristic of poetry written in the vernacular languages, barbarous. As part of the humanists' educational reforms, Elizabethan schoolchildren were brought up to accept and respond to quantity in scanning classical verse, and to recognize the harmony of quantitative metres from the way a poet manipulated the lines' oral qualities. Classical versification was one of the major interests of the European humanist movement, and Sturm, Ramus, Baif, Estienne, and Lipsius, among others, had written quantitative verse. The fundamental metrical pattern of classical scansion is based upon the duration of syllables, divided into short and long, and combined in different measures. The basic problem for the experimenters in English – as in Italian or French – was to adapt fixed syllabic rules to a language without established punctuation or spelling. Another crucial problem involved the adaptation of the movement of a line to ensure forceful and idiomatic movement. Hence the caesura was crucial in the handling of a line, permitting rhythmical breaks in the quantitative structure. The successful versifier thus had to be extraordinarily sensitive not only to a highly intellectual structure but to the cadence of his lines.

Given the distinctly pedagogical orientation of English humanism, it was an experiment that was inevitably going to be made, even if, with rare exceptions, it turned out to be a dead end. It also, one might suppose charitably, represents the willingness to simultaneously experiment and – where it was felt to be appropriate for political not just literary ends – to expunge ruthlessly any rival traditions, a combination that characterizes much of the Elizabethan poetic revolution. For the concern with classical verse forms was not merely a 'literary' matter. It was based on an unabashed appeal to a hierarchical view of language that saw it as analogous to the social hierarchy of the society. From Ascham onwards, pedagogues and poets attempted to wrestle the uncooperative vernacular into quantitative verse, finding, as classically trained scholars, the mere counting of syllables and the barbarity of rhyme somewhat simple alongside the sophistication of Latin verse, which appealed to the learned mind because of its difficulty and the technical skills required for its composition. 'The experiments were the natural result of the attitudes to verse and metre inculcated by the grammar schools', and were thus a typical expression of the age's beliefs not only in the value of education, but in the class basis of that education.[13]

It was a profoundly anti-democratic move that inevitably failed. Although Sidney, his sister the Countess of Pembroke, Fraunce, Campion, and much later Milton, and others produced workmanlike examples of quantitative verse, the rapid changes in spelling, idiom and flexibility that English was undergoing would simply not conform to any academically or socially pretentious desire to discipline a living and changing language. In the *Defence* Sidney argued that 'ryming and versing' did not make a poet, and in the *Arcadia*, the shepherds Dicus and Lalus argued along lines that would have been familiar to Sidney and his Circle, including Spenser. Dicus speaks of the 'secret music' and constant variety of poetry which can be achieved by appropriately measured words; Lalus argues that poetry must appeal to the intellect as well as to the musical sense and 'he that rhymes observes something the measure but much the rhyme, whereas the other attends only measure without all respect of rhyme; besides the accent which the rhymer regardeth, of which the former hath little or none'. Hamilton comments that 'the history of English poetry shows Lalus wins the debate. Quantitative verse failed because the English language is strongly and stubbornly stressed'. Sidney had said as much, commenting on English verse, that 'though we doo not observe quantitie, yet wee observe the Accent verie precisely'. Spenser had a part in this controversy. In October 1579 he wrote to Harvey that 'the two worthy Gentlemen, Master SIDNEY and Master DYER' have proclaimed 'a general surceasing and silence of balde Rymers . . . in steade whereof, they have, by autho[ri]tie of their whole Senate, prescribed certaine Lawes and rules of Quantities of English sillables for English Verse'. Later the same month he writes again requesting these 'Rules and Precepts of Arte' which Harvey has devised, or requesting his friend to 'followe mine, that M. Philip Sidney gave me, being the very same which M. Drant devised, but enlarged with M. Sidneys own judgment, and augmented with my Observations'. As the correspondence proceeded, Spenser came to have more doubts on the practicality of the scheme.[14]

In addition to their discussions of quantitative versifying, Spenser's and Harvey's letters are significant for their announcement of the explicit political interests as well as the literary ambitions of the authors. Such self-display was especially important for someone of Spenser's class and aspirations. He announces not just his literary ambitions, but his insecurity about his status when he notes that 'the twoo worthy Gentlemen, Master *Sidney*, and Master *Dyer* have me . . . in some use of familiarity [and] have proclaimed in their *arioipagoi*' the 'generall surceasing and silence of balde Rymers' which the quantitative movement was trying to supplant. By referring to Sidney and his friend Sir Edward Dyer, Spenser was making a claim for attention from two social superiors who were also deeply interested in poetry. Sidney repaid the compliment by an ambiguous though generally favorable mention of *The Shepheardes Calender* in his *Defence,* which he was writing about the same time as the Spenser/Harvey letters were published.[15] Spenser was by this time employed by the Earl of Leicester, Sidney's uncle, and there is a likelihood that he met regularly with members of the Leicester/Sidney circle to discuss literary as well as political and religious matters. There were

obvious benefits for Spenser in such an association, even if the
'Areopagus' did not have the formal characteristics of a literary and
scholarly academy like those commonly found at the time in France
or Italy. The Leicester/Sidney Circle, including the loosely organized group of poets and intellectuals centered on Sidney's sister, the
Countess of Pembroke, with which Spenser may have had some
occasional contact about a decade later, gave him important political
as well as literary connections. But his connections with Sidney, even
if they were at a respectable distance (there would be no reason why,
given their social differences, they would be close friends) meant
that he would have had his poetic as opposed to his political ambitions encouraged, at least by example and association. What distinguished the Sidneys' patronage was not only the inseparability of
political or literary interests, something most Renaissance patrons
shared, but a genuine love for poetry – indeed, on Sidney's part, a
concern, even an anxiety akin to Spenser's own, about the relative
autonomy of what in later centuries would be termed the 'aesthetic'
from other aspects of cultural practices. Spenser would have been
flattered to be associated with the genuine commitment to poetry in
the Sidney Circle, as well as by the political advantages of working
even on the margins of the Sidney/Leicester family and its faction.

Neither the class interests nor the specifically literary interests of
the Sidney circle can be underestimated when we consider Spenser's
own ambitions. Nor, indeed, as Jonathan Goldberg argues, should
the all-embracing homosocial caste of the patronage relationship,
and the multiple ways it intensified class and sexual bonds between
men. In Spenser's time, patronage was a major means by which the
powerful nobleman could exercise what a times appeared, even to
contemporaries, as a determinative degree of coercion over what
was written and published. However suspect in our own time (and
the pejorative associations of 'patronizing' are a register of the
change) it was one of the major apparatuses of cultural control of
pre-industrial Europe. It was a way by which the great and powerful
registered their authority. Its impact was not only economic but
ideological, affecting the most detailed material conditions and the
'inner lives' of men and women. As Robert C. Evans notes, it was 'a
psychological system, in the sense that the assumptions behind a
patronage culture inevitably affected how people thought about
themselves, others, and their mutual interactions'. For a writer like
Spenser, benefitting from the system meant the naturalization (or
toleration) of continual surveillance, and privileging hierarchical

rather than equal relationships. This matter of the class basis of patronage is important to mention since writers like Donne or Jonson were starting to make claims for 'friendship' as a way of leveling the hierarchy in patronage and it may be that there is an echo of such an emergent equality in the relationship between Spenser and Ralegh during the 1580s and early 1590s. But the dominant structures of patronage in the age, and those that dominate most of Spenser's working relationships, are ones that emphasized hierarchy and subordination within an unabashedly patriarchal structure of coercion. As Evans comments, 'literary patronage was not an isolated or peculiar arrangement, precisely because it reflected and replicated in one sphere the patterns of thinking and behavior dominant in society at large'.[16]

When *The Faerie Queene* was published, among the compliments to it expressed in the introductory commendatory poems by Ralegh, Harvey, and others, we can pick up the sentiment that Spenser was the protégé of Sir Philip Sidney. That would certainly have been a connection by which Spenser would have been pleased. Is there any evidence for it? In 'The Ruines of Time', published in 1591, Spenser looked back on his relations with the Dudley family – which included both Leicester and Sidney – and addressed Sidney's sister, the Countess of Pembroke. In the dedicatory note, Spenser describes the poem as a tribute to those who, a decade or more earlier, had promoted his career. Sidney was, he claims, 'the Patron of my young *Muses*'. About 1578, Spenser had certainly become acquainted with Sidney, possibly through Harvey. S. K. Heninger sees 1580 as a period in which both Sidney and Spenser reached their artistic maturity, a year in which each commenced an ambitious program designed to assert the potential of poetry as an instrument of social policy. But, he admits, the two likely had little direct contact, despite Spenser's employment by Leicester, Sidney's uncle.[17]

By the time he published the *Shepheardes Calender* and the letters exchanged with Harvey, then, Spenser had inserted himself into a respectable, but hardly highly placed, niche at the edge of the court. Rambus suggests that he seems to have thought of himself at this stage as pursuing two careers, that of a 'self-declared national poet', the other as a 'secretary and professional bureaucrat', and further comments, arguing against Helgerson, that 'the possibility of a singular career as a poet may never have occurred to him, and, given his social and financial ambitions' – and, we need to add, his class status and financial needs – 'could hardly have had much appeal for him'.[18] In that year, he was acting as secretary to John Young, Bishop of Rochester, who had been Master of Pembroke while Spenser was up at Cambridge. From that post, he moved into the employ of Leicester, and by 1580 – recently married, at St Margaret's, Westminster, to one Machabyas Chylde, of whom we know nothing else – he was appointed private secretary to Lord Grey of Wilton, the newly appointed Lord Deputy of Ireland. Instead of achieving a court post, close to the queen and influential nobles like Leicester or Sidney, he had to be content with becoming a civil servant beyond the margins of the court, accompanying one of the leading implementers of Elizabethan political and military policy in what became post-Reformation England's first major imperial expansion, the attempted re-conquest (for it had been attempted many times before) of Ireland.

Race

Spenser was English. He lived most of his adult life in Ireland. That juxtaposition of seemingly trivial facts in itself helps us to characterize his career in a very distinctive way. In Spenser's time, even a generation ago, many would have spoken of his 'nationality' as if that label were a neutral though not unimportant fact, but we have learnt that the term 'nation' is too ideologically charged to be comfortable. We might rather speak – again, more neutrally? – of Spenser's 'ethnicity'. Or we might use that highly charged and highly muddled term, 'race'. Or even 'racism'. Historically, such categories have been variously formed by means of conquest, colonization, and the consequent construction of mechanisms of inclusion and exclusion and participation in and exclusion from power. Anthias and Yuval-Davis speak usefully of 'racisms', modes of 'exclusion, inferiorization, subordination and exploitation' that are not referenced purely by ethnic or 'colour racism' phenomena. Racism is rather 'a discourse and practice of inferiorizing ethnic groups'.[19] This notion of race, to which we have become more sensitive today, or at least more awkward about, was starting to acquire some of its modern impact in Spenser's time, and his career and writings make distinctive contributions to those later developments.

Right across Europe, the early modern period sees the emergence of specifically racist understandings of the constitution of a nation. Though it waited until the nineteenth century to fully articulate itself as a mark of 'superiority' as opposed to 'lineage' or origins and destiny. Spenser's time is characterized by the sharp emergence of exclusionary ideologies and constitutive practices. Like most imperialist cultures, the England of Elizabeth's time claimed as universal values a set of ideologies that were both ineffably 'human', and mysteriously identified with being 'English' – a term which was, in its turn, an amalgam of values and practices approved by a small but dominant minority of people living in, or giving allegiance to, England. Such identification is, of course, further complicated in Spenser's case because, like later colonists, he defended Englishness and reviled the 'other' from outside England. He became not merely the apologist for a monarch and a court that, after 1580, he was to visit rarely, and then with a complex (and probably painful) sense of bewilderment and betrayal, but for a policy of such racist brutality that even C. S. Lewis, Protestant Ulsterman and admirer of Spenser only just this side of idolatry, summed up his views in these strong terms: 'Spenser was the instrument of detestable policy in Ireland, and in his fifth book [of *The Faerie Queene*] the wickedness he had shared begins to corrupt his imagination'.[20]

Racism, like imperialism, never leaves its perpetrator untouched. In *Culture and Imperialism*, Edward Said argues that the literature of an imperialist culture – whether or not it is explicitly 'about' the imperialist enterprise – nonetheless implies and in many senses relies upon it. We may believe that the source and center of cultural life exists in a metropolitan culture – Britain rather than its colonies; London rather than the regions; New York or Los Angeles rather than the industrial midwest or Norman, Oklahoma, say. The marginalized regions, especially when we consider the colonized world, may be considered, if at all, as derivative and clearly representing no independent or integral life – even though, as was clearly the case in the eighteenth and nineteenth centuries, the 'civilization' of the metropolitan world may have their very economic basis in them. Nonetheless, Said argues, a dependence upon the provincial or apparently powerless always lurks in the background, a marginalized, even absent, reminder of economic and ideological exploitation (and dependence) it may try to efface or naturalize. Metropolitan cultures effect this by means of narratives (what some would call 'myths') in which the 'natural' place for the conquered and colonized can only be an inferior one. Narratives like this are the primary ideological means by which these assumptions are engraved into a people. Said focuses on the nineteenth-century novel: its stories are ways of defining, indeed inventing, the political 'realities' of the triumph of British imperialism. A writer like Jane Austen may rarely mention the plantations and colonies 'overseas', but the values and prosperity of her characters depend on them. In other writers – Kipling is the most obvious example – the imperialist enterprise may receive direct treatment. Spenser, like Kipling, is an explicit celebrator: just as Kipling's portraits of India glamorize the imperialist enterprise, so Spenser makes no secret that the values of civility, justice temperance and (before all else) religious truth are embodied in the values of England and personified in the queen.[21] The English conquest of Ireland is not effaced (even though many of the detailed political realities may be): it is the work of a superior civilization, ultimately for the glory of God.

The Irish, however, despite (Spenser would have said 'because of') their Catholicism, had been stubbornly resistant to God's purposes long before Spenser was sent there, first visiting in 1577, in the service of Philip Sidney's father, Sir Henry, who was Lord Deputy of Ireland before Grey was given the post, one of the least desirable and unrewarding in the Elizabethan power structure. The English had not yet learnt to be efficient subjugators of another culture, let alone (a matter of more weight, given the history of colonialism in the following four hundred years) would-be humane ones. In accompanying Grey to Ireland, and remaining there, eventually becoming a settler, or 'planter', occupying and cultivating property seized from the Irish, Spenser was taking part in one of the inefficient and futile holocausts in the long history of what became imperialism. There is indeed a sense in which Spenser is the first and most prominent poet of British imperialism (though his main rival may be Kipling, so the competition is limited), and *The Faerie Queene* the great epic of the early history of that imperialism, just as Shakespeare's *The Tempest* may be seen as its first great poetic drama. Like Shakespeare's play, Spenser's epic registers some of the great contradictions that characterized imperialism; unlike Shakespeare, Spenser had a direct material stake in the racism that motivated the imperial enterprise, and his critiques of it are far less conscious and wide-ranging than Shakespeare's.

In Spenser's time, being 'English' was starting to acquire some distinctive ideological resonances. The consolidation of national states, part of a long-term political development throughout the Renaissance and early modern Europe, took a distinctive pattern in Britain. The union of England and Wales had been achieved by the domination of Wales by the English and the establishment of administrative units called 'marches' and the appointment of a lord deputy. The Welsh language and its tribal culture was progressively marginalized in what Raymond Williams termed a series of 'forced and acquired discontinuities', which he relates not to some submerged essence of Welsh 'identity', but rather to the material 'realities of subordination'. One of the most significant of these was language. Successive generations of a Welsh landowning class were anglicized and the Welsh language was made the 'object of systematic discrimination and, where necessary, repression'.[22] The union of Scotland was celebrated, but not completed in law under James (the First of England, Sixth of Scotland). But – as Spenser was to discover – Ireland was quite a different matter. The distance between London and Ireland was a not insignificant factor, particularly marked in a time when transport and communication were difficult. But for complex military, social and linguistic reasons, Ireland had long felt to be within the sphere of influence of whatever kings of England were strong or ambitious enough to try to assert their expansionist ambitions.

By the late sixteenth-century, the fervent nationalism of the Tudor regime (claims made on behalf of a 'nation' invariably serve the interests of a dominant class, which tries to mobilize the allegiances, and the bodies, of the less powerful around a notion of the state or nation) was centered upon a militaristic Protestantism. Like most successful revolutionary movements, the Protestantism of Spenser's time combined an impatient elitism with an energetic populism. Moreover, it articulated not just intellectual changes, but complex, deep-rooted shifts in the whole social formation. An English man or woman born a decade or so earlier than Spenser, in the reign of Henry VIII, might conceivably have lived through the reign of five other monarchs – and five changes in official religion. Religious controversy was, arguably, the most prolific literary form of the whole age: More against Tyndale, the Genevan exiles under Mary, Catholic and dissenting controversialists, Hooker and his great adversary Perkins, and the many popular controversialists including those who produced the so-called Marprelate Tracts of the late 1580s.

How did the theological controversies of his age impact on Spenser's life as a poet? Protestantism articulated the most insistent issue in sixteenth-century English poetic theory and practice by forcing poets and poetic theorists to justify or 'defend' poetry. The Protestant reformers themselves were neither exclusively negative nor monolithic in their views of poetry, and that whatever contradictions the idea of a 'Protestant poetic' may contain, it provided a major aspect of the theory and practice of poetry from the Reformation to the time of Milton. In their theological treatises, when the Reformers discussed the nature of man, they thought little of what the Romantics later would term the imagination, but they were willing to defend the artifice or images that poetry and other arts employed if they could be convinced religious truth was being served. Hence much sixteenth-century Protestant discussion of art and poetry focuses on the means of discriminating between true and false images. The fundamental question is: to what extent and through what mediating structures does language articulate individual feelings or thoughts? To what extent is poetry mimetic of the poet's inner states of feeling or those of its readers? What is the relationship between the state of salvation of the poet and the poem's 'truth' or integrity? Must the poet be morally good in order to write morally effective poems? The central issue behind such questions is the mediating (or what was suspected to be the distorting) power of 'images', including (most especially for a poet) language. We see the importance of the question in the vivid (and immediate) way Spenser deals with it in the first book of *The Faerie Queene*, where Red Crosse cannot distinguish between Una and the dream produced by the malevolent Archimago, the 'source of images'. At stake is the question that (as we shall see in succeeding chapters) throughout his career Spenser believed the faithful Christian always faces: how can one trust the products of the distorting human mind? Is not, to use Sidney's famous phrase, the 'erected wit' of the poet always undercut by the degraded and irredeemable 'infected will'?[23] How can a poet at once embrace theological truth and art, the piety and theological rigour of a Calvin and the worldliness of a Castiglione?

Of course, Protestantism set up a series of major ideological conflicts within the everyday material lives of sixteenth-century men and women, not only in the more arcane speculations about language and images for poets like Spenser. As Alan Sinfield notes, Protestantism created a universe of strife and tension: it demanded total allegiance in every aspect of life; it challenged the humanist belief in the educability of man; it created a stern, wrathful and determining god whose power reached into every moment of a man's life; and it focused relentlessly upon the inner coherence (or disparateness) of a person's sense of self.[24] One of the most powerful contradictions within Protestantism is, on the one hand, the privilege extended to the individual subject and, on the other, the precariousness of that subject before God. Whether chosen or rejected, saved or reprobate, the individual is isolated before God, constantly exhorted to look at the signs of salvation within, while knowing that his (or her) inward nature is evil. The elect Christian was constantly called upon to witness to God's truth while having to acknowledge that human nature was totally corrupt. The believer looked to God with his innermost being, while knowing that inner voice was able to call on God only by God's grace.

When the Protestant did turn to poetry, knowing it had biblical justification, he could find a powerful model for articulating the paradoxes of the created self. Here we come to a key aspect of what Philip Greven calls the 'inner life' of Protestantism.[25] The Protestant self is seemingly always in flux, continually changing even though it is built upon a theology of stasis. So the Protestant poet would inevitably find himself writing out his contradictions and anguish into his poetry, at once fascinated by words and aware of their untrustworthiness and suspicious of their promiscuous materiality, focusing uneasily upon specifically the relationship between God's Word and human words, between divine intentionality and the all too untrustworthy medium of expression. For Spenser, as a pious Protestant, a person's salvation, not merely a literary reputation, was at sake. Half a century later, Milton was to deal with the problem by imperiously invoking the Holy Spirit as his muse and praying (or assuming) he was being guided by Divine Inspiration; Spenser, as *The Faerie Queene* becomes seemingly more and more beyond his capacities to finish or control, rejects his own poetic creation as an example of the mistrustful promiscuity of worldly signification.

English Protestant nationalism, then, is a central factor in both Spenser's life and poetry. As an Englishman, he was committed to a distinctive reading of the world; as a Protestant, to a distinctive reading of God's purposes for the world; and as a poet, he saw his writing in terms of both Englishness and Godliness. Another aspect of English nationalism directly relevant to Spenser's conception of poetry is more narrowly linguistic. It revolves round the question of whether the English language was an appropriate medium for poetry of any kind, Protestant or other. The question of the appropriateness of the vernacular had been raised a century or two earlier by poets and politicians in the courts of Italy and France; it increasingly surfaces in English throughout the sixteenth-century. Puttenham's patriotic ideal of establishing 'an Art of our English Poesie, as well as there is of the Latine and Greeke' is a belated echo of Dante and Petrarch, Boccaccio or Ariosto. 'Our national tong is rude . . . our language is so rusty', bewailed Skelton, early in the century; in English, unlike Latin and Greek, everything is expressed in 'a manner so meanly, bothe for the matter and handelynge, that no man can do worse', is Ascham's similar opinion fifty years later. In *The Elementarie* (1582), Spenser's headmaster Mulcaster asks that the English develop 'the verie same treasur in our own tung', noting: 'I love the Latin but I worship the English.' The doubts about English were partly caused by its supposed lack of dignity. It was 'symple and rude' – again, we should note the class bias. And there were seemingly practical considerations. There was no standard form of English. Where Latin was the language of the learned, the vernacular was, seemingly, subject to change, variation, and (most reprehensible) vulgar usage. Many writers felt acutely that English lacked an aureate diction suitable for the ceremonial or complimentary poetry characteristic of an aristocratic society since, as Hawes put it in *The Pastyme of Pleasure*, 'elocucyon/doth ryght wel clarify/ The dulcet speche/frome the language rude', thereby making explicit the class bias of courtly diction. Nationalistic, political and religious pressures over the century brought more and more educationists and writers to try to improve the language, for instance by adopting archaisms, dialect words, or by imitating classical or Italian syntax – in short by augmenting vocabulary and syntax to make English more dignified or adaptable to high poetic purposes. Social order might be threatened by a language run riot. It is not merely a literary argument being advanced when Puttenham insists that the language of poetry is that of the court and its environs. Spenser took that invocation to reform and refinement very seriously.[26]

Puttenham's reference to the court as providing the appropriate model for high poetry makes very clear the identification of English nationalism with the dominant expression of class power. Even in Ireland, the ideological centre of Spenser's world always remained the English court. The court, of course, is a major cultural site of metaphorical, and therefore cultural, contradiction in the period, and I will discuss its influence over Spenser's life and writings in Chapter 2. But if Spenser's allegiances were centered on the English court, what influence did his career in Ireland have on his sense of being English? In subsequent chapters, I will consider the details of Spenser's Irish career in detail; here, it is sufficient to note both that for the first time outside the shores of its 'sceptred isle', the nationalistic English regime was exercising what came to be its imperialist ambitions and that Spenser's position in Ireland is intriguingly ambivalent. As a settler in an English colony, and one whose racial, political, religious and literary allegiances were elsewhere, he was an outsider in multiple ways. He lived in a country to whose culture he was a stranger; he owed allegiances to a regime that was increasingly indifferent to what he stood for. Hence the images he creates in his poetry of characters who inhabit alien worlds – women, savages, the rural, even the knights themselves as they battle against multiple embodiments of the 'other' – reflect back on his own ambivalence. Spenser articulates the first stirrings of what was becoming a pan-European imperialist ideology with all its alienation and contradictions. When we compare the early remarks of many explorers (and exploiters) of North America, what emerges is an uncanny sense that their reactions have been battle-tested before; looking back just a little, we can see that the site of the battle had (at least in the case of the English and their rivals, the Spanish) been Ireland. Thomas Harriott's famous description of Virginia contains many comparisons between the Indians and the Irish; John Smith compares Pocahantas's dress to the Irish mantle and 'trouses'; William Strachey observes that 'the married women wear their hair all of a length, shaven, as the Irish, by a dish' (an observation, incidentally, not borne out by pictures of Irish women at the time). What we see, in short, as D. B. Quinn notes, is the 'use of outlandish reference' to label the Irish as the quintessentially alien, the primordial 'other' of the civilized and elect English. Continuities and parallels in our own time are too numerous and painful to mention. Here, at the start of the history of imperialism is one of its essential psycho-cultural elements: the need to create a savage and despicable 'other', a 'no-self', as Greenblatt puts it, to embody (literally) 'all that lies outside, or resists, or threatens identity'.[27] The 'other' have strange customs, are savage, and speak a different language. Today, there are still tiny pockets of Ireland that are predominantly Gaelic-speaking, but most people speak English. In Spenser's time, the widespread speaking of the Gaelic was a striking sign of difference, and it is not surprising that language is one of the areas which Spenser and the other English planters wish to exterminate.

Yet, paradoxically, while Ireland was a place of savagery and alienation for Spenser, it was also increasingly where he was at home. It is significant that Book Six, which celebrates Courtesy, supposedly the central virtue of the Elizabethan court, is arguably the most ambivalent of *The Faerie Queene*'s Books, in the way that it radically calls into question not only offenders against courtesy, but its defenders as well. All the encounters between the knight of Courtesy and forest dwellers blur the distinction between courtesy and its opponents. If Calidore's quest to subdue the Blatant Beast is an attempt to establish the source of true courtesy and to continue to locate it in the English court, and especially the symbolic (and real) person, the Queen, we are never able to forget that his quest is unsuccessful, that his great enemy the Blatant Beast escapes, and seemingly can never be conquered.

Gender

Spenser was a man. That seeming triviality is in fact fundamental to our understanding of his career and a great deal besides in the period. Here we encounter another important consideration in our attempt to construct a literary life for Spenser today – the impact of feminism and today's heightened awareness of gender upon our rewritings of our intellectual and literary history. Gender, we have learnt, is not a characteristic with which one is born; nor is it a stable mode of categorization, either across history or within the life of an individual subject. The dominant ideologies of a society may indeed try to fix patterns by which individual subjects live their lives (it is, in a sense, their job to try to do so) and they thus try to arrange to have historically constructed characteristics seen as permanent or, worse, somehow justified by the universe or some deity. But in doing so, ideologies inevitably produce within themselves tensions and contradictions that we all spend our lives defining ourselves within and against, often with enormous pain and confusion. Our gender assignments are a fundamental factor in the ways we conceive of our lives. It is important, in writing of an age in which gender assignments were particularly rigidly conceived, that we should ask what difference did it make, not least to his poetry, that Spenser was a man.

'Being' a man (or a woman) is also a question-begging conception. My discussion of Spenser as a man is designed to open up some of the contradictory patterns that went into the constructing of the murky patterns of gender identity of his age. We should ask the question a little differently: What was it for Spenser to be born and socialized into assumptions and practices that were labeled as male? What did it mean to be interpellated as a male subject in the late sixteenth-century? Such matters have only recently started to surface in Spenser criticism and scholarship. And it is by no means irrelevant that most of Spenser's critics, at least until very recently, have been men. As Shepherd comments, this has led to an overwhelming assumption that gender is not relevant to the reading of Spenser. What he terms the 'primitive innocent world of male bonding' in Spenser criticism affects not only the values that were encoded in his poems but the ways in which they have been read in later times. Overwhelmingly, Shepherd claims, a 'male-authored poem has been serviced by male editors and critics "for a male readership." ' I, too, am a man.[28] As a man, I need to assume not the 'naturalness' of my readings but rather to ask what aspects of my own repertoire match (and mismatch) with Spenser's and so produce such readings. What affinities and alienations are there between our positions in what is often, in traditional literary study, constructed as a 'common' history and inheritance? In an age where most middle-class educated males are (we like to think) increasingly sensitive to issues of gender, class and race, certainly more so (we like to think) than those of Spenser and his time, are there more 'universal', or at least relatively stable, trans-historical aspects of our gender assignments than I should acknowledge? Are there, indeed, greater continuities within patriarchy in male behavior? Those are questions, in fact, that Spenser's poems should raise very compellingly and at times disturbingly, at least for a male critic. In traditional accounts of Spenser's life and works, matters of race and class have usually been given at least some cursory attention. But gender has rarely been considered. It is therefore important to stand back a little and consider it in some depth.

The interactions of sexuality and gender roles are many and inevitably contradictory, as the multiple sites of sex and gender interweave. Just as sexual identities may shift and blur, so gender roles could theoretically be organized by any number of categories: the assignments of 'man', 'male', 'son', 'husband' and 'father' are not absolute but are constituted by custom, routine, repetition, and the distribution of power, even though in many societies they may be identified with the presence or absence of supposedly fixed biological characteristics. 'Men' and 'women' themselves are categories that need not be limited by the dominant patriarchal heterosexism of our history. Seemingly inevitably, however, the social mechanisms by which sexual and gender roles are constructed tend to be mystified, as if they were indeed 'natural' categories. This was certainly the case in early modern England. Some will object that to impose what Goldberg terms 'modern sexualities' on 'Renaissance texts' and early modern lives is to unnecessarily privilege what may be only incipiently or pre-emergently found 'in' a text or an event.[29] But the narratives we enact are never those of which we or the dominant ideologies of our society may be aware or approve: other narratives than the most 'natural' or comforting lurk beneath the surfaces of our lives and our literatures.

What do we know of the development of gender assignments within Spenser's childhood? Although, as I noted above, discussing his class origins, we have almost nothing specific, we do know a great deal about the ideology of being a man in early modern England. And we can get very close to the embodiment of that ideology by examining the assumptions and practices that went into the upbringing of those men to whom Spenser looked as models for emulation. To take one example: in the 1620s, the dramatist Philip Massinger – whose father Arthur had been steward to Mary Sidney, Countess of Pembroke, at Wilton House, and who had the distinctive family first name – wrote a series of plays the heroes of which embody the ideal of benevolent aristocracy to which Spenser is committed throughout *The Faerie Queene*. Margot Heinemann argues that in these plays, Massinger, whose social rank and dependence on aristocratic patrons were much the same as Spenser's, 'saw the world in terms of a noble order of patrons and aristocratic rulers, as he had experienced it in his youth' on the Wilton estates.[30] If that is so, the gender politics of that order are blatant: aristocratic males, socially akin to Spenser's questing knights, embody the society's most heroic values and the seemingly inborn responsibilities of rank and birth.

What are these heroic values? The first is the assumption of the naturalness, indeed the virtue, of masculine dominance and aggression, most obviously seen in, though by no means confined to, military aggression. *The Faerie Queene* is one of our history's most blatant articulations of such an ethos. Camille Paglia even argues that 'Spenser is history's first theorist of aggression', with his questing knights embodying an Apollonian hostility to nature, and conquering the ever-threatening female, 'chthonian', urges of an unruly nature. The knights' armour is, she argues, 'a male exoskeleton' the embodiment of 'the hardness of Western will'. In turn, Spenser's heroines are most admirable when they become subjects of the male ethos and take on 'male fortitude and self-assertion . . . for male and female alike in *The Faerie Queene*, the psychological energy of aspiration and achievement is masculine'. Paglia's argument is an intriguing, even alarming, one, not least because it is put forward by a woman explicitly in the face of feminism's critique of Western patriachal gender stereotypes: 'feminists', asserts Paglia, 'seeking to drive power relations out of sex, have set themselves against nature. Sex is power. Identity is power. In western culture, there are no non-exploitative relationships.'[31]

Because it is so fundamental to constructing a satisfying shape to Spenser's career, and to understanding the dynamics of *The Faerie Queene* in particular, we must therefore consider in a little detail one of the most banal and yet arguably most destructive cultural metaphors of Western (some would say human, others patriarchal) culture: the intimate link between the Western male psyche and ideologies of virility and domination. Paglia clearly celebrates this link, seeing the 'testing and purification of the male will' through struggle, control and the violent imposition of intellect upon nature, especially as (literally) embodied in the female, as the triumph of our cultural history. For many of us today, men and women, this will seem unsupportable nonsense, but it may be persuasive to some, since the assumption that men are more naturally aggressive is deeply rooted in our culture. How 'naturally' aggressive are we? Are we, as some biogrammarians argue, 'wired' for aggression and the destruction of others, even of ourselves? And do we count as 'aggression' basic survival behaviors which restrict or threaten the survival of others? And who are the 'we' in my last three sentences? Freud claimed in *Civilization and its Discontents* that an 'inclination to aggression' was 'an indestructible feature of human nature': '*Homo homini lupus* . . . man [is] a savage beast to whom consideration towards his own kind is something alien.'[32] Freud's observations are probably at once too optimistic and too pessimistic: over-pessimistic in that he read a predominant Western cultural pattern as basic biological and psychic grammar, but over-optimistic in that he saw it as a matter of the 'individual' psyche rather than of a whole culture, and the product of historical processes in that culture. But it does articulate a seemingly unshakably dominant aspect of the ideology of masculinity that was central to *The Faerie Queene* and which remains so to the dominant pattern of Western gender identity.

A corrective to Freud's essentialism – and one of the most suggestive treatments of the structures, metaphors, and practices of Western masculinity in recent years – is Klaus Theweleit's *Male Fantasies*. It is a rambling mixture of brilliant insights, speculation, and minute textual analysis of the writings and fantasy world of the *Freikorps*, the proto-fascist mercenaries hired to put down incipient socialist revolution in Germany following the First World War. Theweleit denies constructing a history of Western patriarchial fantasies; nevertheless, his study is full of detours into the history of Western art, literature, and military and erotic history, many of which are directly relevant to our understanding Spenser. It leaves no doubt that the fascist personality is not merely an aberration of twentieth-century middle European history, but the inevitable outcome of post-Renaissance and to some extent Western patriarchal militarism. The importance of this study for my reading of Spenser is therefore both methodological and highly specific. Theweleit regrets that recent historians of Western culture have 'rejected the conventional history of 'kings and battles' for the 'hidden history' of everyday life, almost to the point of forgetting how much of everyday life has, century after century, been shaped by battles and dominated by kings or warrior elites', and specifically, by the ideologies that underpinned such elites. In his quest to 'find the desires and anxieties that are at the core' of the 'mystique of war and violence', he argues, following Deleuze and Guattari that 'the desiring-production of the unconscious' is cathected upon historically specific patterns, codes, conjunctions; and historical specifics must always be the locus for the playing out of patterns of human behavior, whether they are the products of culture or biology or a combination of the two.[33] This is an extraordinarily complex debate: to what extent do matters of relative size, shape, and hormonal constitution which seem more or less biological givens determine cultural meanings? Do they rather acquire meanings within culturally produced structures such as attitudes to 'proper' or appropriate activities, privileging even proper posture, movement, or particular physical skills, games, and pastimes? Regardless of origins and causes, the assignment of what is 'natural' to each gender articulates the characteristic metaphors of a culture, and these are observable not least in our distinctive gender choices and patterns.

Layered across these gendered roles (it seems natural to see the relationship as determinative rather than deconstructive, but that too is an articulation of ideological dominance) are both the multiple sexualities of being a man, and the shifting gender roles of masculinity. Where the bipolar gender ideology of Western society ensures a continuity and convenience, it distorts the lived realities (and livable possibilities) of individual human subjects and groups. As Alan Bray, Jonathan Goldberg and others have indicated, 'the hierarchies of Elizabethan society were oiled with sexual exchanges between men' – friendship, patronage, employment, pupilship, beds and living spaces shared – and yet there was not an adequate discourse available by which these relationships could be described.[34] There is a continuum of male/male relations which impact on the 'nature' of being a man. So far as the specifics for which Theweleit calls, in the England in which Spenser grew up and sought employment and advancement, there was a multitude of cultural experiences in which male aggression was reified as a seemingly natural process. The most obvious is perhaps what David Lee Miller calls 'the savage history of the state's primitive apparatus',[35] the unrelenting brutality of execution, judicial punishment and assault which was even more naturalized in the consciousness of Spenser's age than it is today. But beyond the obvious impact of the repressive state apparatuses of persecution and punishment, the structuring of a vast range of experience by a pattern of rivalry and conquest points to the dominant ideology – from which, of course, today we are hardly immune.

Spenser's poetry gives us one particular historical manifestation of this ideology in enormous, even obsessive, detail. It is chivalry – or more precisely, its Elizabethan revival. The longevity of chivalry, long after its military and political relevance were gone, has been widely commented upon by cultural historians. Throughout the sixteenth-century, English political organization and military technology altered drastically, rendering most of the specifically military aspects of chivalry obsolete, yet throughout the sixteenth-century, the trappings of chivalry, most visibly in the form of tournaments, like the annual tilts held on the anniversary of the monarch's Accession Day, greatly intensified. Chivalric tournaments, which are found throughout Spenser's epic, were in Elizabethan and Jacobean society major social events of the governing class designed to display what was seen as the essence of nobility, the ritualized expression of violence in the service of an ideal cause. We have no evidence that Spenser himself ever took part in a chivalric tournament, at least as a principal: after all, he was not an aristocrat or even a well-placed courtier. But Sidney, Greville, Ralegh and other courtiers of Spenser's acquaintance who embodied the masculine ideals celebrated in *The Faerie Queene* frequently took part in them. For such men, they were rituals that at once asserted a man's commitment to martial violence and allowed him to display himself to advantage within the usually less overtly physical aggression of the court's political and social rivalries. In *The Booke of Honor and Armes* (1590), Sir William Segar noted the continued dominance of at least the ideology of chivalric combat: 'each particular Gentleman or other person professing Honor and Armes, ought sufficientlie to bee moued thereunto for defence of his owne particular reputation'. As Richard McCoy points out, by the time Segar is writing the goal is clearly 'the regulation and containment of violence', so that the tourney became a form of 'conflict negotiation'. But the underlying ideology of masculinity as aggression is untouched. When an embassy from England visited the Landgrave of Hesse in 1596, a combat 'betwixt jest and earnest' was arranged, with the knights of Hesse announcing that they de-sired 'not to make devises, but to show their manhood'. The knight, tourneys, challenges, and skirmishes which make up such a over-whelming part of *The Faerie Queene* require to be read not merely as a part of the background of Spenser's life, but as a revelation of its gender and class politics. The chivalric ideal of the age might be summed up in the daring and gallantry of Spenser's friend Sir Walter Ralegh whom Spenser represents in Books Four and Six as Timias the squire who pines after the unapproachable Belphoebe; or in the Penshurst portrait of Philip Sidney, dressed in partial armor, one hand on hip, the other holding a sword, the essential heroic figure, 'untrammeled', as Maureen Quilligan points out, 'by any social con-text', as if the values he represents were absolute, unalterable by historical accident or even death.[36]

What psychological dynamics lie behind these masculinist values which are so unselfconsciously foregrounded in Spenser's career and his epic poem? Theweleit's key category to describe the mem-bers of the *Freikorps*, which he derives from Margaret Mahler, is 'the not-fully-born'. It is a concept worth pondering in some detail when we consider the primitive gender stereotypes in Spenser's work – both in his poetry and in his everyday life and work in Ireland. I make no apology here for what may appear to be a diversion from the 'facts' of Spenser's life: what I am concerned with is the signi-ficance of those apparent facts and Theweleit's and Mahler's ana-lyses offer us striking insights into that significance.

Mahler's work with children, especially with male children, gives us particular insight into a culturally produced personality structure that has, from all evidence, been remarkably (and depressingly) constant across the history of Western gender construction – and probably more intensely so in Spenser's time. In her work with children, Mahler isolated those who 'never attained the security of body boundaries libidinally', and having little sense of body bound-aries of their own, are never able to fully individuate. As they come to adulthood, they can achieve ego stability only in relation to the demands of outside authorities. They are violent and frequently destructive, and what impels their violence and destruction – however it may be transferred into socially approved activities – is this childhood failure to fully differentiate, and as a consequence, a simultaneous 'fear and longing for fusion' with some greater, authoritative power that might prevent their fragmentation. Such children, Mahler argues, develop only a social ego, one that is 'borrowed, painfully drilled into and fused onto the individual'.[33] The not-fully-born characteristically live out fantasies in which their incompletely formed egos have never adequately entered into object relations between a whole ego and a whole other. At times of stress, conflict and regression what such a personality has to fall back on for its stability are fantasies of incorporation into larger bodies. These bodies represent mother surrogates, idealized authority figures to replace and recall the mothering figures they both want to return to and separate from. In such circumstances, when we specifically consider male gender formation, 'the boy does not merely disidentify with the mother, he repudiates her and all her feminine attributes. The incipient split between mother as source of goodness and father as model for individuation is hardened into a polarity in which her goodness is redefined as a seductive threat to autonomy'. The boy who seeks his sense of autonomy 'must separate himself in the outside world from the mother's female body and in his inside world from his own already formed primary identification with femaleness and femininity. This great task is often not complete'. Indeed, the child 'seeks (its whole life long, if need be) its unification' with maternal bodies or maternal substitutes, by means of which it fantasizes it can become whole. Mahler's researches were carried out with mid twentieth-century children; Theweleit extends her concepts into tools of cultural analysis, suggesting that the 'not-fully-born' include the majority of Western men, and that even in the twentieth-century, 'only a handful of men . . . had the good fortune to be in some sense fully born'. Whether such characteristics become psychotic to the extent that members of the *Freikorps* demonstrate is presumably dependent upon the particular social formation in which they find themselves born and exercise their roles as males. But chivalry and the monarchistic state, which are so strongly celebrated in Spenser, clearly provided such a structure for men in early modern England.[37]

Northrop Frye noted that the battles and tourneys that permeate

romances like Spenser's are ritualized actions 'expressing the ascendancy of a horse-riding aristocracy', and 'express that aristocracy's dreams of its own social function, and the idealized acts of
protection and responsibility that it invokes to justify that function'.[38] They are not only fantasies of class, however; they are also
fantasies of gender. The stereotypes of romance have traditionally
been male: in Renaissance romance, the quests, adventures, battles,
heroic loves displayed the prototypical wish-fulfilments of the
'soldier-males' of the feudal and post-feudal aristocracy. The passionate celebration of ritual violence – seen in tourneys, jousts and
wars – were rituals of gender identification, conceived as spiritual as
well as physical rites of passage. As Shakespeare's *Troilus and Cressida*
dramatizes so effectively, the early seventeenth-century may have
seen the growing dominance of newer technologies of war and
different strategies of mass destruction from those of chivalry. But
the traditional view of the aristocratic male warrior as an innocent,
idealistic (and humanistically educated) youth lived on as both
an individual and collective fantasy.

Yet chivalric romance did not merely provide material for the
fantasies of its members; as in the case of Philip Sidney, chivalric
ideals frequently brought real, not just imagined, deaths. Destruction and domination are not merely fantasies. Male violence may, as
Theweleit argues, be seen in part as an attempt to cover over the
tragically self-destructive complex of gender stereotypes of the 'not-
yet-fully-born'. For men, the armored, near-anonymous body of a
combatant provided a challenge to imagine his own invulnerability,
which could be proven by subjugating and demolishing what is
vulnerable and different. The act of penetration of the enemy by
sword or lance is an obviously sexualized image: in the moment of
impact, the victor bears down on his weapon, which causes a spurt
of blood upon entry, as if the whole body has been turned into an
armored penis. Indeed, the warrior's sword or spear or dagger transcends the sexual, since they can do something that flesh and blood
cannot: they can penetrate, spurt, be withdrawn and remain as erect
as before (and if they break, be replaced by an erect alternative). The
loser is he who first loses all his capacity for erection. As Theweleit
notes of his warriors, 'they meet to kill; and the only one to "flow" '
(like a woman, one needs to add) is the man who dies. The holes and
gashes in his body are a signal of the enemy's reduction to the status
of a woman and the winner's transcendence of self.[39] The battles,
jousts and journeys in *The Faerie Queene* should therefore not simply

to be seen within 'literary' conventions. They are emblems of the desires and anxieties about gender that lie at the core of a culture's myths of violence and domination. The armed knights who thunder towards each other on horseback, or who hack at each other with swords, are metaphors for both a fantasy of invulnerability and a longing for fusion with a trans-individual force that they have been trained to repress in themselves and yet of which they are afraid.

This pattern of having recourse to domination and violence when faced with external threat and internal insecurity about gender identity has been so deeply ingrained in our cultural history that it seems to be natural and so outside gender. Spenser's epic, however masculinist its ethos, is also populated by a large number of women characters. But one of the striking aspects of the Third Book of *The Faerie Queene* is that the questing knight is a woman, Britomart. Usually, women were all too easily interpolated into male fantasies of power: they were, after all, 'naturally' the rewards, the prizes, for which the knights battled, objects on which the males of the chivalric caste could project their ego aggrandizement, their denial of the possibility of failure, their fear of annihilation repressed in the orgy of destruction and possession. Violence and war are primary male metaphors for conquest and control; the women are the calm oases or fertile fountains from which the men drink after the dangerous terrain of their adventures has been past through; the woman's passive, alluring, yet forbidden body waits as a reward after the men have slain the resisting, and therefore mutilated, bodies of dragons, monsters, or other enemies.

It is sometimes argued that the presence of a woman knight in *The Faerie Queene* establishes an overturning of patriarchy, and so a healthy alternative set of values. The desiring machine of erotic love that permeates the 'feminine' aspect of Spenser's epic might then be seen as the antithesis of the destructive machinery of militarism: it might be thought that if war and conquest represent the 'masculine' in heroic romance, love represents the 'feminine', and indeed it is often argued that the figure of Amoret in the middle books of *The Faerie Queene* represents this myth of women. Theweleit suggests that in asking the question, 'what was it to be a man?' we cannot neglect the question 'what was it to "be a woman?" ' – and that we should ask it not only from a woman's point of view, but from a man's. What were (and, for that matter, are) the 'male fantasies' by which men deal with the women in their lives? In early modern England, in order to maintain rigid gender stereotypes – at least on the level of the official ideology of what constituted 'men' and 'women' – just as women overwhelmingly learnt to disguise their forbidden masculine wishes behind a stereotype of female innocence, weakness and self-sacrifice, so men learnt to disguise their forbidden feminine wishes behind a stereotype of male virility. The result is a common pattern of fascination and alienation from the self as well as the 'other.' When a boy's own femininity must be repudiated, his adult attitudes toward women may easily be primarily ones of fear, mastery, distaste; ones which express a need of women but which seem unable to recognize them as different but like subjects. 'In such a society', all too often', Louise Kaplan notes, a boy's 'independence is founded on an infantile ideal of what a real man should be. He has very little opportunity to integrate the feminine and masculine aspects of his identity'. The consequence of such a pattern may be the early idealization of women as all-powerful objects to whom the boy looks for nurture and protection at the same time as he seeks to differentiate himself from them and becomes aware that what supposedly constitutes him as a man involves rejecting what Shakespeare terms the 'woman's part' in himself. In adult life, a pattern may be established whereby he continually tries to recreate this primitive maternal bond, and yet seek continually to break from it. In such a pattern, Kaplan argues, commenting on the preponderance of this pattern in the Renaissance, 'what boys seem to need most from the mother and continue to need and, as lovers and husbands, go on to get from other women is an all-present but unobtrusive Mother who is willing to stand by in the wings ready to rescue the mighty acrobat as he recklessly hurls his body through the open spaces', thus becoming one of Paglia's 'questing knights, isolated against empty panoramas' in *The Faerie Queene* (and indeed, she argues, throughout Western history), replaying the male's primitive struggle to tame (female) nature. As Paglia puts it, 'Men know they are sexual exiles. They wander the earth seeking satisfaction, craving and despising, never content. There is nothing in that anguished motion to envy'. As Freud writes in his essay on the Mona Lisa, men fear women's sexuality as 'ruthlessly demanding – consuming men as if they were alien beings'.[40] As we shall see when we look at Books Three and Four of *The Faerie Queene*, much of the eroticization of women in the Elizabethan court – its caste of erotic titillation, the language of Petrarchism, the casting of political rituals in terms of the erotic – can be linked to this pattern of fascination for and fear of women.

Predictably, given this analysis, the women characters who are most praised, like Britomart or Belphoebe, are those who also embrace the values of male struggle and violence. Overwhelmingly, love is coopted as part of the dominant masculine ethos. As Theweleit suggests, part of the warrior's simultaneous desire for and fear of fusion is directed towards the female – both within himself and in the society at large, because he feels he must keep women in subjection so that he need not acknowledge the woman in himself. Insofar as women were permitted any degree of agency, it was to support and succor men. But (even though we men sometimes find it difficult to accept this) women also exist outside male fantasies, in their real not just in their fantasized bodies; but the ideology of masculinity we have inherited prompts us all too often, insofar as these 'real' women threaten those fantasies, they have to be either controlled or escaped. *The Faerie Queene* plays out such patterns over and over, and the dominant metaphors for both escape and conquest are those of violence. The repeated confrontations of knights and adversaries represent part of the education of both men and women to accept violence and domination as the dominant means of dealing with gender difference. What Paglia celebrates as 'the sex and glamour of the armour-infatuated *Faerie Queene*' may be seen more gloomily, as the acme of Western patriarchy's fascination with violent rape as a metaphor for the norm of gender relations. But rape, asserts Paglia, is Spenser's metaphor for biology itself, and the 'sex war' in Spenser's epic is 'a Darwinian spectacle of nature red in tooth and claw, of the eaters and the eaten'.[41] *The Faerie Queene* has multiple examples: the pursuit of Florimell, Lust, Orgoglio, the molesting of Serena. But does Spenser simply reinforce such undisguised masulinist violence? Or are there instances in which a creative role is seen for desire to counterbalance the destructiveness of masculinism? This is a crux for much contemporary Spenserian scholarship, as I shall note in later chapters.

RESCUING MALFONT

In *The Faerie Queene* Book Five, Guyon and Artegall enter the palace of Mercilla, where they encounter the trial of 'foule Duessa', here representing Elizabeth's cousin and rival, the Catholic Mary Queen of Scots, who had been executed in 1588. They pass a poet, Malfont, whose tongue is nailed to a post (5. 9. 25). In Spenser's eyes, Malfont is the figure of both the poet whose gifts have been perverted by disagreement with the 'truth' and of the perverse reader who, for reasons of his or her deliberate agenda, has read and rewritten (or as Spenser would say, misread) the message of the poem. The image of the blaspheming poet is a warning to those who disagree with Spenser's own reading of Elizabethan history, and by and large, accounts of Spenser's life and writings, have overwhelmingly tried to avoid Malfont's fate. Malfont, however, may be seen very differently – even perhaps as the strong reader who has been persecuted by the dominant regime, and whose view of truth is too divergent from that of the dominant to be allowed to speak it.

There have been, however, a number of Malfonts in the history of Spenser criticism. While the history of Spenser scholarship and criticism from E.K.'s glosses on *The Shepheardes Calender* to the present have been largely reverential and (as the taste for Donne and the Metaphysical poets during the early and middle years of this century threatened to relegate Spenser to the archaic, has somewhat receded) the Spenserian text, if not his life, has been a major site of critical struggle. Indeed, a highly placed early reader suggested, in effect, that Spenser himself was the first Malfont, the heretical misreader of the material of his own poem: King James VI of Scotland (soon to become James I of England) had, according to one of Burghley's correspondents, 'conceaved great offence against Edward Spencer publishing in prynte in the second pt of the Faery Queene and sixth chapter some dishonorable effects (as the k. demeth thereof) against himself and his mother deceassed', and moreover that the king 'still desyreth that Edward Spencer for his faulte, may be dewly tryed and punished'. The reference is to the trial of Duessa in Book Five who, as noted above, represents James's mother, Mary Queen of Scots, who is accused of plotting to overthrow Mercilla, who stands for Queen Elizabeth. Although, on becoming king of England, James did not censure *The Faerie Queene*, it is intriguing to speculate what Spenser's fate would have been if he had lived into the new reign.[42]

According to the dominant tradition of establishing 'right' readers of Spenser, then, James was an early Malfont. He has, however, been vastly outnumbered. We can, indeed, trace a variety of ways in which Spenser's editors and commentators staked their claims as Bonfonts, right readers. Early commentaries on Spenser, including James's, tend to focus on historical and emblematic identifications of the allegory and to justify Spenser's poetic methods;

Warton's *Observations on the Fairy Queen* (1754) opened up the riches of Spenser's use of his medieval predecessors; nineteenth-century readers tended to see the poems in terms of Spenser's biography and his 'personal' vision; by the late nineteenth-century, as the professionalization of the discipline of literary studies intensified, Spenser's text became increasingly surrounded by notes and con-textual materials as the means by which 'right' readers – Bonfonts rather than Malfonts – would be produced. The start of a number of Malfontian traditions, however, can be seen surfacing in the nine-teenth century. One of the earliest appeared, appropriately enough, in the nationalist Irish journal the *Dublin Review* in 1843, which assailed Spenser as the willing agent of a repressive colonial power. Later in the century, Karl Marx termed Spenser *der Elizabeths Arschkissende Poet* (Elizabeth's arse-kissing poet), an epithet recently revived in Shepherd's more recent verdict that Spenser 'was a pen-pusher in the service of imperialism'. During the heyday of the New Critics and, in Britain, during the period of F. R. Leavis's greatest influence, Spenser's poetry suffered from another, less politically motivated group of Malfonts, who saw his poetry simply as archaic and abstract. In the first edition of the *Pelican Guide to English Liter-ature*, Derek Traversi writes – pointedly, his essay appears in the volume entitled *The Age of Chaucer* – of Spenser's archaism. In the *New Pelican Guide*, published in 1982, Spenser has been moved to *The Age of Shakespeare*, but W. W. Robson's essay likewise speaks of Spenser as difficult to penetrate, as an 'implied author, not a real historical person', and *The Faerie Queene* as enigmatic, voluminous, diverse, and long: 'it seems to be unpopular today', he observes, 'and is gradually being dropped from school syllabuses'. Yet he notes the extraordinary proliferation of Spenser scholarship: the world of Spenser studies 'is a world without a common reader', an escape-world for esoteric scholars, and *The Faerie Queene* merely a 'rich mine for symbol-seekers, allusion-spotters, and source-hunters . . . the crossword-puzzle appeal is strong'. More recently, Paglia's verdict is no less scornful of contemporary Spenserians: 'at the moment, *The Faerie Queene* is a great beached whale, marooned on the desert shores of English Departments'.[43]

Implied in all these accounts of Spenser, whether they are 'literary lives' or not, is that, no less than Milton and *Paradise Lost*, Spenser and his epic are part of the history not merely of 'English literature' (a category, after all, that was largely an ideological construct of the nineteenth and early twentieth centuries) but of something more powerful and permanent, the history of our attempts by means of art, and in particular through language, to assert ourselves in the face of impersonal, authoritarian, and repressive state and ideological apparatuses. Does art, does poetry, can a 'literary life', give us access to a realm of timeless beauty or truth? Probably not, at least not in the terms Spenser understood. Can they help us understand how we are constructed by contradictory histories, and thereby help us make both minute and large choices, personal and collective, in the present and directed towards a more just and fulfilling future? Perhaps. That may be a more limiting role for poetry than Spenser envisaged, and in the diminution may be seen not merely the rejection of his early ambitions but a betrayal of the very order he thought he was celebrating and upholding. His 'literary life' was a struggle to accommodate to these conflicting claims for poetry; it is thus not unlike some of the struggles we all live through as we consider the roles of art and poetry, artists and poets, in our own cultural moment. As Shepherd comments, 'in a sense it's an old story: distressed conservatives produce fascinatingly radical analyses that they themselves can't tolerate'.[44] The nature and contradictions of those analyses are the subjects of ensuing chapters.

2

The Poet's Three Worlds

Throughout our lives, certain places – usually geographical, though if we are even normally introspective, they can also be imaginary – accumulate emotional resonance for us. They may be places associated with our childhood, or with spectacular successes or losses; they may have acquired a familiarity because we lived or worked for many years there. Some of the associations we accumulate seem 'personal' or subjective: *here* I used to come when I wanted to be alone; *here* I met my wife or husband or lover; at this point some terrible tragedy – the death of a friend or loved one – occurred. But even these personal associations, which together help to give shape and meaning to a life, have a collective dimension, even while we may not at the time notice what it is. We may think of certain, especially very intimate, experiences as 'ours'; but the experiences of a particular history are inevitably forms and articulations of more general processes. Whether we speak of the shared dimension of such experiences as 'essential' parts of the permanent pattern of being human, or as archetypal, or as representing historically specific class or gender or ethnic constructions, there is no doubt that places – cities, countryside, names on a map, houses, vistas, imaginary worlds, activities in which we lose (or find) ourselves – are not merely neutral, but are heavily, complexly, metaphorical. In our metaphors for the places we inhabit and remember are our cultural values revealed.

In the opening chapter, I considered Spenser in relation to one such place that, by the sixteenth-century, had acquired – and in whatever changed ways retains – certain ideological resonances. That was England. Here I want to focus on three other 'places' within which or within the influence of which, Spenser spent his adult life. One is a specific geographical place; the second is an institution with specific material and enormous metaphorical resonance; the third is an activity by which he created, in a further, metaphorical sense, a 'place' or 'world' that was designed to reflect (to use his own recurring metaphor of the 'glas' or mirror) and reflect upon, the other two, but which increasingly, if never consistently, became its own world, at least in his mind. These three places are, respectively, Ireland, the court, and poetry. His life, literary and other, was dominated or – to use an appropriate metaphor for a writer – written by the often contradictory demands of these three worlds. In this chapter, I will look at each in turn.

THE COURT: A PLACE OF CONTROL

In speaking of the importance of 'place' in Spenser's life, I am suggesting that we must look not merely to the ideas that can be abstracted from his poetry, but to the events that determined the relationships between the poetry and his life, and also to ideas and feelings that play about (that existed in the vicinity of) both his life and writings. In many cases, Spenser will have been unaware of how his literary (and other) life was shaped as he struggled within the complex interplay of discursive structures, symbolic formations, and ideological systems of representation. The poem to which he devoted much of his energy, *The Faerie Queene*, was, like the rest of his life, coerced and compelled by political and wider cultural forces outside it, by networks of discourse in which it was caught or – to use Pierre Macherey's powerful metaphor – which haunt it, playing, encroaching, or teasing it from the edge of the text.

In his influential essay on 'Ideological State Apparatuses', Louis Althusser discusses the very concrete practices by which any society structures, even creates, the allegiances by which its members feel they 'belong' to it – the systems of education, characteristic lifestyles, patterns of religion, family organization, and so forth. It is by means of such institutions and structures, what Althusser called 'apparatuses', that ideology functions.[1] The major institution or social apparatus that dominates Spenser's, and indeed, sixteenth-century poetry generally, was the court. Looking back at his youth and attempting to make sense of those years which we now recognize as one of the cataclysmic eras of English history, Edward Hyde, Earl of Clarendon, focused on the institution in which he had spent his youth. The court, he wrote, was where 'as in a mirror, we may best see the face of that time, and the affections and temper of the people in general', for, he continued, 'the court measured the temper and affection of the country'.[2] Throughout Spenser's lifetime, 'court' was a powerful word as well as a powerful institution; it accumulated round itself ideas and feelings that were often contradictory or confusing, but always compelling. Spenser's early career is an instance of how men and women 'swarmed' to the court (the metaphor is a recurring one) for power, gain, gossip, titles, favours, rewards and entertainment. The court was more than merely the seat of government, or (a more accurate description, reflecting the peripatetic nature of royalty) wherever the monarch happened to be. Across Europe the idea of the court excited, far beyond its concrete existence, an intensity that indicates a rare concentration of power and cultural dominance. The court is Gabriel Harvey's 'only mart of preferment and honour'; it is what Spenser himself called the 'seat of Courtesy and civil conversation'; it is Donne's 'bladder of Vanitie'. In order to understand something of the importance of the court in Spenser's life and writings, we need to ask: what powers, real or reputed, did the court have over the destinies, tastes and allegiances of men and women? What recurring anxieties or affirmations are associated with the court? By whom are they voiced? With what special or covert interests? And with what degree of truth? What can they mediate to us of the court's influence on the ongoing and deep-rooted cultural changes of the period – the complex struggles for political and social ascendancy, the fundamental changes of ideology and material practice?

Such questions come down, perhaps, to this: how did the court's power operate upon the particular details of Spenser's life? How did this dominant social 'apparatus', the values of which were so compelling, control the specifics of his life, including the way his poetry was thought of, written, and received? I stress the word 'details' because, as Said explains, 'for power to work it must be able to manage, control, even create detail: the more detail, the more real power'. The court was one of the key places where, in the words of Foucault, 'power reaches into the very grain of individuals, touches their bodies and inserts itself into their actions and attitudes, their discourses, learning processes and everyday lives'.[3] The court produced, in all who came into contact with it, a set of expectations, anxieties, assumptions and habits, sometimes very explicitly, sometimes by unstated but very concrete pressures. Power is felt not simply in the ruling ideas of a society, but where ideology is located, in the particulars of our everyday lives, one area of which in this case is in the particularities of poetry.

What can Spenser's life and poetry tell us about how it was to be exposed to, fostered by, or exploited by the court? Throughout the early modern period, all European courts assumed the right to use the arts, including poetry, to control and in a very real sense create the tastes, habits, beliefs and allegiances of their subjects. In some cases this attempt was carried out through overt state apparatuses – through control and censorship of the theatre, imprisonment of playwrights, the discouraging of particular kinds of writing, and the active encouraging of others: by means of patronage or licensing laws. Before the invention of the mechanical mass media of today, Strong writes, 'the creation of monarchs as an 'image' to draw people's allegiance was the task of humanists, poets, writers and artists'.[4] Around the monarch was the court, and all over Europe, it was to the court that intellectuals, educators, artists, architects and poets were drawn. No less than the building of palaces or great houses, official state portraits, medallions or court fêtes, poetry was part of what Strong terms 'the politics of spectacle'. It was part of the increasing attempt – culminating in England in the reigns of James I and Charles I – to propagate a belief in the sacredness of the monarchy and the supportive but subservient role of the court and nobility. Just as, in Strong's words, 'the world of the court fête is an ideal one in which nature, ordered and controlled, has all dangerous potential removed', in which the court celebrated its wisdom and control over the world, time, and change, so poetry also became, as John Donne's friend Sir Henry Wotton put it, 'an instrument of state'.[5]

As Puttenham's potted history of the century's poetry makes very clear, there was implicitly and often quite blatantly a firm policy of binding poetry inextricably to the court. When he focuses on the 'new company of courtly makers' who 'sprong up' at the end of Henry VIII's reign, and 'greatly polished our rude and homely maner of vulgar Poesie', he is putting the court's imprimatur upon not merely a number of politically approved poets but also upon a certain function for poetry in the court. Briefly surveying the mid-Tudor poets, including Vaux, Sternhold, Heywood, Ferrys, Phaer, and Golding, he announces triumphantly that the tradition had not just continued under Elizabeth, but had been triumphantly surpassed:

> And in her Majesties time that now is are sprong up an other crew of Courtly makers Noble men and Gentlemen of her Majesties owne servauntes, who have written excellently well as it would appeare if their doings could be found out and made publicke

with the rest, of which number is first that noble Gentleman Edward Earle of Oxford. Thomas Lord of Bukhurst, when he was young, Henry Lord Paget, Sir Philip Sydney, Sir Walter Rawleigh, Master Edward Dyar, Maister Fulke Grevell, Gascon, Britton, Turberville and a great many other learned Gentlemen, whose names I do not omit for envie, but to avoyde tediousnesse, and who have deserved no little Commendation.

The men Puttenham mentions were all courtiers, and most were at a social rank above Spenser's. The poetry they wrote was rarely designed to be published. But even (or especially) if, Puttenham notes, 'many notable Gentlemen in the court . . . have written commendably, and suppressed it agayne, or else suffered it to be published without their own names to it', poetry was a common means for a courtier to display himself in the court. It was one of the colourful rituals by which a Ralegh or an Essex displayed his desirability for political favour or place (along with dancing, music and general self-display) and so advanced his political fortunes. Much of Ralegh's poetry was intended as a key to Elizabeth's political favour; Robert Sidney wrote most of his poetry while in exile in the Low Countries as an expression of his desire to be back in the centre of public affairs; while another of Puttenham's 'crew of courtly makers',[6] the Earl of Oxford, was writing incidental verse for over twenty years that had conventional erotic subjects yet which was clearly directed to his advancement in the court. It was a tradition that lasted well into the seventeenth-century. Frank Whigham has shown, furthermore, that when we look beyond the self-consciously 'literary', at other kinds of writing in the court, the same pattern can be observed. The rhetoric of Elizabethan courtiers' letters, for instance, shows the same hold of ideology over language as the rhetoric of poetry, the same desire to find a place within an already in-place discourse. The vocabulary, postures, and assumptions of the letters of Elizabethan courtiers are, like their poetry, essentially aimed at ceremonial display, while silently acknowledging the anxiety and insecurity of the court in their barely repressed concerns with competition from other courtiers, their fears of banishment and exclusion. It is the 'fictive ideologies' of a society, whether poetry or other kinds of writing, by which the court's power and privilege were expressed.[7]

But if poetry was a means of self-display for Puttenham's courtiers, it was an even more earnest means of self-promotion for those, like

Spenser, struggling to establish themselves within the court's orbit, not least as servants of the more privileged courtiers. A poet's success, Rambuss notes, was measured not by financial reward, let alone 'laurels', but specifically by 'gaining access to the privy chambers of lords and rulers'. When the court poets – whether aristocrats and court poets like Oxford or Sidney and the court employees like Spenser – thus found a pattern of discourse about the place of poetry already existing and a role waiting for them to fill. And they found it not simply as a 'literary' discourse, but rather as an all-embracing ideological and specifically material set of assumptions and practices. They inserted themselves into it in order to establish their places within a whole pattern of social discourse. The court poet's writing, therefore, tends to operate within a particular register of theme, syntax, grammar and vocabulary. Here Puttenham is once again our best spokesman. He writes of how the language of the poet must 'be naturall, pure, and the most usual of all of his country'. He identifies such language as 'that which is spoken in the kings court' rather than in the 'peevish affection' of the universities, let alone that spoken by the 'poore rusticall or uncivill people' or any 'of the inferiour sort' or regional speech. The acceptable language of poetry is 'the usual speech of the court, and that of London and the shires lying about london within ix myls, and not much above'.[8] Through such categorizations of exclusion and privilege, the dominant modes of poetry could be very precisely delimited. It thus became one of the regime's means of social stabilization and control. The 'social' text (the events under the pressure of which the poets wrote and of which they tried to be a part) and the 'literary' text (what they made of those events) are inseparable.

Note that Puttenham's list does not include Spenser, though he does mention some of the prominent Elizabethan courtiers who, at various times, gave Spenser support. Paradoxically, when we consider how his life was dominated by the court – and how obsessively his poetry returns to brood over the court, courtiers, and courtliness – in one sense, Spenser was not a 'court' poet at all. Certainly, he was not one of the aristocrats who Steven May classifies as Elizabethan court poets.[9] He was never at the centre of the court's activities. He hovered around it in two relatively short periods of time: first, in 1579–80, as an employee of Leicester when Leicester, Sidney and others were concerned that the queen might marry a French Catholic nobleman, Alençon; and second, on a visit he made to England in 1590–91 when, probably under the sponsorship of Ralegh, he was granted his pension by the queen. But he was drawn to the court, by allegiance and proximity and (when in Ireland) distance. He sought the court's approval and favor: it demanded his poetry and his loyalty.

Throughout his treatise Puttenham links the purpose and reception of poetry to the favour of courts and princes, repeatedly stressing the duty of the 'Civil Poet' to celebrate the values and acts of the court in the way 'the embroderer' sets 'stone and perle or passements of gold upon the stuff of a Princely garment'. Even if he was not among the aristocratic court poets, Spenser was, unquestionably, in Puttenham's terms, a 'Civil Poet'. But it is not only in his poetry that his 'civility' is displayed. While the *Arte of English Poesie* presents itself as a treatise on poetry, it is also setting out the ideal life-style of the courtier. The procedures of court poetry and court practice are built on the same values: indirection, dissimulation (what Puttenham terms *Beau semblant*), ornament, calculated ostentation, are characteristics that are simultaneously those of the poet and the courtier. The grace displayed by poet and courtier alike is inseparable from a training in the necessary courtly characteristics of dissimulation and indirection. When he discusses the use of allegory by the poet – 'Allegoria . . . the figure of false semblant' – Puttenham describes it pointedly as 'the Courtier'; and at the conclusion of his treatise, he echoes Castiglione's advice that the courtier should strive above all else 'to give entertainment to Princes, Ladies of honour, Gentlewomen and Gentleman', and to do so must 'dissemble' not only his 'countenances' and 'conceits' but also, all 'his ordinary actions of behaviour . . . whereby the better' to 'winne his purposes and good advantages'.[10] The terms are exactly those he uses to describe the making of poetry.

So we have a paradox: the institution, the place, that dominates Spenser's life and poetry was one in which he spent little time, and which relegated him to the margins of its activities. When Spenser treats directly of the court, his views predictably reflect the age's commonplaces, both positive and negative. The most detailed treatment of the court, and the virtue that purportedly lies behind it – courtesy – in *The Faerie Queene* is in Book Six (and I will consider that in detail in Chapter 6, in the context of the second three books of *The Faerie Queene* which were written in the 1590s). But the influence of the court permeates all of Spenser's work: early in his career, it was to the court, or at least to its margins, that he looked for employment. Inevitably, that meant relying on, and displaying his allegiance to,

one of the political-religious factions within the court. In his early
poems, especially in the *The Shepheardes Calender*, Spenser's allegiances within the court factions of the late 1570s are becoming very
clear. The poem, which I shall look at in detail in the next chapter, is
buoyantly critical of court and religious corruption: it has the icono-
clasm of the eager aspirant to court favour, one who is trying to
make his political beliefs and factional interests as clear as possible,
even to the point, on occasion, of a little tactlessness. In the *Calender*,
Spenser sees no contradiction between writing poetry and advocating a particular political agenda. Rambuss, indeed, sees him as setting out more than a poetic agenda, but rather staking a claim for
political employment, 'negotiating his own place in the world' in
what amounts to 'an advertisement of Spenser's qualifications for
secretariship'. His employer was John Young, the Bishop of Rochester,
himself a protégé of Archbishop Grindal, the maligned 'Algrin' of
the July eclogue, whose fall from favour clearly warns Thomalin that
he should perhaps seek a 'lowe degree.'[11] In the October eclogue, he
makes a plea for the court to support both poetry and the political
and religious policies favoured by Leicester: 'Advaunce the worthy
whome shee loveth best/ That first the white beare to the stake did
bring', he asserts, making a reference to Leicester's coat of arms. In
Mother Hubbards Tale, which (while not published until the *Complaints* volume of 1591) was probably written about the same time
and makes reference to some of that period's controversies, also
promotes the policies of the Leicester faction. In part three of the
poem (ll. 581–942), Spenser attacks backbiting, pretension and deceptive favorites. He alludes to Elizabeth's anger at Leicester's own
marriage, and later in the poem, once again to the issue of the
queen's proposed French marriage. Yet Spenser to some extent may
have hedged his bets. The work probably circulated among the
members of the Sidney/Leicester faction, and no doubt won him
applause for its political correctness, but if *Mother Hubbards Tale* was
indeed written about the time when Spenser was trying to display
his factional loyalties, nonetheless he did not publish the work for
over a decade. It may be that such satiric poetry was felt, by Spenser
or perhaps those in authority over him who may have read it, to be
somewhat tactless and potentially injurious to his career.

By the time, over a decade later, Spenser came to write his next
sustained poetic treatment of courts and courtiers, he was certainly
much more circumspect. In *Colin Clouts Come Home Again*, lines
660–770, his observations – that the court ought to be the model of

civil government and behaviour, on the opposition between court and country, and the dangers of court corruption – are the stock-in-trade of both anti-court polemic and pastoral literature. Spenser also takes the opportunity to make clear that, at least for his purposes, there remain examples of true courtly virtue. The list of court ladies who 'me graced goodly well' (ll. 485–583) include Lady Carew, some of the Spenser family, and a large group associated with the Sidney/Leicester Circle: Sidney's sister the Countess of Pembroke, Leicester's sister and sister-in-law, and Lady Rich. The lords to whom he wrote dedicatory sonnets include a number of courtiers, of greater or lesser importance at the time – Burghley, Cumberland, Hatton, Effingham, Buckhurst, Essex, Walsingham, Northumberland, Oxford, Hunsdon, and Ralegh himself. The list also includes some whom Spenser would have encountered in Ireland, like Grey, Ormond and Norris. Some Irish ladies are also praised in *Colin Clouts Come Home Again*, including the Countesses of Ormond and Kildare. And at the centre of this circle of lords and ladies is of course the queen herself, who, as Goldberg points out, herself played a number of ambiguously sexual and gendered roles.[12]

The most important court connection Spenser had was with Sir Walter Ralegh. An adventurer (in many senses), politician, poet, historian, freethinking intellectual, Ralegh probably met Spenser not in the court, where he probably would not have noticed him, but in Ireland: Ralegh was the commander of a military force deployed in 1580–81 by Grey to subdue Munster, and at the same time Spenser was one of Grey's secretaries. During that campaign, Ralegh directed the troops who tricked and slaughtered the Irish resistance forces at the siege of Smerwick, and as Grey's secretary, Spenser was responsible for writing up the official view of the incident. In 1589, after a number of years as the most glittering lord of the aging Elizabeth's court, Ralegh was again temporarily exiled to Ireland, and he visited the large land-holdings he had acquired as the spoils of his Irish service: some were near where Spenser was living, on the lands he had acquired as a planter, at Kilcolman. Spenser had an official position as clerk of the Council of Munster, and it is probable that not only was he associated with Ralegh on official business, but the two most likely visited each other.

At the shifting centre of the court was the queen. Elizabeth came to the English throne after twenty-five years of political (and undoubtedly personal) insecurity, and her motto *Taceo et video* (I see and am silent) probably sums up the most important lesson she learned about both personal and political survival. What she also learned, more positively, was the importance of what Stephen Greenblatt terms 'self-fashioning',[13] the need to present or form the political self in terms of image, what the Elizabethans termed (usually negatively, but with an eye on the political advantage it might afford) 'seeming'. At court, the men and women who surrounded the queen learned, as *Mother Hubbards Tale* puts it, 'To fawne, to crowche, to waite, to ride, to ronne,/To spend, to give, to want, to be undonne' (ll. 905–6). The stability of the regime came to depend heavily upon an extraordinarily wideranging and effective propaganda apparatus directed to create an image of the queen as the guarantor of stability and order in the commonwealth and an embodiment of the order of the whole universe. It was centered on the distinction between the queen as an ordinary mortal and the queen as the embodiment and guarantor of what was claimed to be national security and cosmic order. However farfetched such an analogy may seem to most of us today, it is sobering perhaps to find such ideological structures powerfully residual in the twentieth-century. For to find a modern equivalent, we have only to think of the systematic cults of personality associated with the dictatorships of Fascist Germany, Maoist China, or the right-wing despotisms of Haiti, Chile or Panama. Nor should we forget how in twentieth-century liberal democracies, similar cults have been systematically displaced onto figures of the capitalist consumer media, such as film stars, with, of course, not entirely dissimilar ideological effects.

The aim of any ideological apparatus is to control and even construct for the majority of the human subjects under its effective power a coherent presentation of reality. It needs to be sufficiently plausible and powerful to allow the dominant political power to justify not only its determinations of what it will desire to be labeled as 'common sense', but also to justify surveillance and repression in the name of the supposed realities that are represented by that label. We are dealing here with the mechanisms of ideology that are by no means confined to dictatorships, or to periods of repression like that of England in the sixteenth century. This is how ideology functions in all societies. By 'ideology', I do not mean a static set of false or partial ideas, but rather a complex of distinctive practices and social relations which are characteristic of any society and which are inscribed in its language and other material practices. Ideology applies to all the largely unconscious assumptions and acts by which men and women relate to their world; it is the system of images, attitudes, feelings, myths and gestures which are peculiar to a society, and which the members who make up that society habitually take for granted. In any society, especially in one as obsessed with order and control as the England and Ireland of Spenser's time, one of the functions of ideology is, as far as possible, to define and limit the linguistic and cultural practices by which members of that society function. If, as usually happens, a society likes to think of itself as harmonious, coherent, and consensual – an ideological construct to which *The Faerie Queene* was dedicated – then it is ideology that enables this to occur. In such a society, it tries to suggest the existing order of things (whatever that may be) is permanent, natural, universally acknowledged, embodying truths we would all agree with – and in so far as it persuades us that such 'truths' are not ideology. It provides seemingly coherent representations and explanations of our social practices, and in particular by giving us the language by which we describe and thus try to perpetuate them. Thus ideology acts as a kind of social glue, binding us all together, though, like most glues, it tends to be fast in some places and come undone in others.

How does ideology affect the writing and reading of literature? The impact of ideology upon the writings of a particular society – or, for that matter, on the conventions and strategies by which those writings are read – is no different from the way it influences any other cultural practice. In no case does a writer, as the producer of the text, manufacture the materials with which he (or she) works. The power of ideology is inscribed within the words, the rule-systems, and codes which constitute the text as and before it is written. Likewise, in the reading situation, we might imagine ideology as a powerful force hovering over us as we read a text; as we read it reminds us of what is apparently correct, commonsensical, or 'natural'. It tries, as it were, to guide both the writing and our subsequent readings of a text into coherence. When a text is written, ideology works to make some things more natural to write; when a text is read, it works to conceal struggles and repressions, to force language into conveying only those meanings reinforced by the dominant forces of our society. Part of the fascination of Spenser's poetry (and his conception of the life of the poet) is that oppositional voices are continually struggling to be heard. Even (or perhaps especially) a patriotic work like *The Faerie Queene*, which starts as a celebration of the Elizabethan monarchy, ruling class, and court ideals, incorporates ideas and practices that call their dominance into question. At certain points – as when Spenser criticizes the court of Elizabeth in *Colin Clouts Come Home Again* or Book Six of *The Faerie Queene*, he knew at least part of what he was voicing. That kind of opposition clearly operates on the level of very explicit ideas. But there are other kinds of opposition more subtly and profoundly encoded in the poetry. One important function of the literary text – perhaps, it is often argued, what constitutes 'the greatness' of a work – is precisely that of bringing out the multiplicity, contradictions and tensions that a dominant ideology tries to ignore or cover over. It does so not so much on the level of the explicit ideas to which a text points, but rather on the level of the text's 'unconscious', which we see both in the language and in the gaps and indeterminacies that accompany language. Poems are, after all, not ideas but words – words and the spaces around words – and it is on the level of words, on the level of the signifier, that we can read the strains, oppositions and struggles of an age. It is in language where the struggles for meaning and power take place – something all Protestants, including Spenser, felt very strongly.

Raymond Williams writes of how all societies consist of archaic, residual and emergent experiences, values, and practices.[14] The majority of any society's practices are inevitably residual, deriving from the past and closely identified with the historically dominant class of that society. A few are always archaic, the residuum of philosophical or religious ideas and practices from a previous age – an example in Spenser's poetry would be, as I indicated in Chapter 1, chivalry, largely abandoned as a material practice by the end of the sixteenth- century but still very powerful in its cultural implications and for commanding the allegiances of those participating in it. But within the inevitable flux and contradictions of any society, new experiences and practices are always emerging, always potential, and in periods of particular stress, like the last decade of Spenser's life, they may start to emerge more strongly. They are usually felt before they can be put into language, because there are, as yet no fully-formed structures of discourse by which they can be expressed. It is at such points of strain that certain forms of writing and other cultural practices are most revealing. In the late sixteenth-century we can look to the experimentation in the public theatre, the revival of verse satire, the unusual diversity of broken, mixed, unfinished works as indications that they are trying to articulate something which was already being felt but for which there were not yet adequate words. Williams terms 'pre-emergent' those cases where the structure of feeling that is tangible in particular writings is an articulation of an area of experience which still lies beyond full articulation – the significance of which may only become explicit years later as a more adequate language becomes available. Spenser was writing in a period where there was enormous pressure upon language to grapple with new experiences, new feelings and new social patterns. It was a time in which (as many poets themselves noted) language itself seemed to be simultaneously inadequate and overflowing. Although the poems may attempt to efface the struggle that has produced them, that struggle none the less leaves its invisible but indelible marks. What is not in the text is just as important as what seems to be there.

In later chapters I will show how *The Faerie Queene* is full of eloquent silences and half silences that betray deeply rooted ideological struggles. Its detours, silences, omissions, absences, faults and symptomatic dislocations – the places where, in Terry Eagleton's words, the text 'momentarily misses a beat, thins out or loses intensity, or makes a false move'[15] – are crucial for our understanding of this poet who wrote (and lived) so closely tied to, even though at a geographical distance from, the court. By any standards the ideological apparatuses of the Elizabethan regime were extraordinarily effective. I have commented on the tradition of Spenser's readers trying to align themselves as 'right' readers with the dominant reading of his poems. The same can in effect, be said of the Elizabethan regime in that its power to construct a narrative of its own history has lasted well into this century. Especially is this true of our residual conception of Elizabeth herself. As Thomas Cain notes, 'the traditional view' of Elizabeth was formulated in retrospect 'as Elizabethan history' in Camden's *Annales* (1615) and remained virtually unchallenged until this century, being notably elaborated in J. E. Neale's *Queen Elizabeth* (1934). It celebrates a golden age ruled over by 'an enigmatic Virgin Queen dexterously negotiating the perilous milieu of national and international politics, adored by her peaceful people, inspiring universal wonder'.[16] Voiced in homily, sermon, tract, proclamation, royal entertainment, ceremonial portraits, civic receptions, national holidays, pageants, and poems like *The Faerie Queene* inculcated into infinite details of everyday assumption and material practice, that picture of Elizabeth is one of our cultural history's most effective propagandist creations. There were, Cain suggests, four basic 'cults' of the queen that developed: to reinforce the ideology of monarchy: identifications of Elizabeth with Old Testament heroines such as Judith or Esther; with classical goddesses like Diana and Venus; the adaption of features from the Catholic veneration of the Virgin Mary; and the depiction of Elizabeth in terms of the unapproachable yet ever-alluring mistress of Petrarchan sonnets. In accord with Wotton's 'arte become a work of state', all these elements were used to fulfill a comprehensive ideological purpose, that of creating loyalty to the queen and the regime. Of fundamental importance in articulating these cults were the arts. In that sense, Spenser's dream of poetry fulfilling a public role was welcome to the queen and her court. In return, a central part of the role that Spenser was attempting to carve out for the poet was that of being an essential part of the order which he celebrated.

Ideological domination always involves more or less systematic attempts to control, marginalize or destroy rival depictions of reality. In Elizabethan England, the predominant 'other' was Catholicism, personified, at a distance, by the papacy, and near at home in the alluring figure of Mary Queen of Scots. Spenser's first-hand experience of Catholicism was limited to Ireland. He may have remembered from his childhood in the reign of Elizabeth's sister Mary some of the Catholic Church's ecclesiastical practices, and he may have read some Catholic theologians, but in fact he probably acquired most of his sense of Catholicism from Protestant polemical writers for whom Catholic doctrine was viewed as intellectually corrupt, its practices worldly, its clergy lazy, ignorant and venal. In the May eclogue of *The Shepheardes Calender*, Spenser's attacks on the 'lustihed and wanton meryment' of the shepherds who 'the right way forsake' are in line with conventional anti-Catholic propaganda. In the opening book of *The Faerie Queene*, the presentation of Catholicism and the papacy as the enemies of individual, national and cosmic order is consistent and vigorous. Archimago and the false anti-heroine Duessa attempt to undermine Una, who stands on this religio-political level of the poem for the English church, and Red Crosse, who represents England. Anti-Catholic polemic informs the major metaphorical details of the book: links between the papacy and the images of the Whore of Babylon in *Revelation*, and the assumption of duplicity, superstitions in Catholic ritual or practices like the rosary and the mass are consistent. The atmosphere of this level of entrenched polemic in Spenser's poetry reflects something of the siege mentality fostered in the English by Elizabeth's government from the start of the reign, but especially intensified after the excommunication, in 1570, of Elizabeth by Pius V. The excommunication of the queen meant that loyal Catholics were, as a consequence, released from their obligations to obey her and her government. Lay Catholics were under increased surveillance. They were often persecuted, especially if they harbored Catholic priests who were trained in increasing numbers in Europe, and sent secretly to England in an attempt to reclaim the English for the Church. John Wall notes that at one point over half the Catholic priests sent into England had been imprisoned and tortured, and many were publicly executed as a means of reminding the English of the cost of resisting the government. The priests were seen as agents of foreign powers, not only of the papacy, but also the Spanish and to some extent the French. Likewise, the struggles by the Irish against English occupation were widely seen as the spearhead of Catholic designs upon England, and the severity with which Ireland was treated was a similarly motivated brutality.[17]

The personal embodiment of this fear of Catholicism – the 'other' of Elizabeth in many senses – was her cousin, Mary Queen of Scots. As Michael O'Connell notes, Mary lies behind, even if she is not directly represented in, all the figures of female malevolence in *The Faerie Queene*.[18] Early readers of the poem, including, as I noted earlier, Mary's son, James VI of Scotland, made the identification between Duessa and Mary, which is certainly made very clear. In Book One, canto twelve, Fidessa, who is Duessa masquerading as Red Cross's 'true' betrothed, claims to be the 'wofull daughter, and forsaken heire/ Of that great Emperour of all the West.' In Book Five, Duessa is tried before Mercilla, who stands for Queen Elizabeth. The episode allegorizes the real life trial of Mary, at the conclusion of which she was executed: like Mary, Duessa is charged with treason and sexual corruption. Her very existence was a threat to Elizabeth, not least because she was a woman: younger, highly attractive even after years of imprisonment, and a mother; she was the political, religious, and sexual 'other' to the aging woman who had sacrificed herself and her sexuality to be the Virgin Queen, and the titular head and embodiment of the English national, Protestant state. In *The Faerie Queene*, Mercilla is depicted as torn between her compassion and an acceptance of the inevitability of Duessa's elimination: Artegall and Arthur both urge Duessa's guilt, and Mercilla leaves the court in tears. We learn of her execution only in passing, and after being told at length of Mercilla's tenderheartedness, a detail that Spenser clearly needed to insert to underline his loyalty to Elizabeth and his approval of the policy she enacted.

IRELAND: THE PLACE OF THE OTHER

Just as Mary Queen of Scots was the 'other' of Elizabeth herself, so Ireland was the 'other' of Elizabethan England. Spenser spent nearly twenty years in Ireland. He wrote most of his poems, including virtually the whole of *The Faerie Queene*, there. He also wrote a notoriously direct account of English policy towards the Irish, which over the years has had its defenders – who argue either that it is not atypical of other such analyses of policy in a ruthless age, or that we need to differentiate between Spenser the gentle poet and Spenser the practical planter and civil servant – but which is finally difficult to see other than racist and brutal, within its own much smaller scale akin to Hitler's 'final solution' or Mr Kurtz's exclamation in Conrad's *Heart of Darkness* to 'exterminate all the brutes'. Like Conrad's Kurtz, Spenser partakes of a rhetoric of that emphasizes exploration, conquest, overcoming any obstacle to achieve an end. It is, in the history of the West, a distinctively masculinist rhetoric that has characterized imperialism. It conflates military conquest, sexual pleasure, emotional distancing and the imposition of dominant values as universal rather than as historically contingent. In the late sixteenth century, poetry itself was co-opted as part of this world. Sidney's nationalism underlies his aesthetic and Kim Hall has linked the writing of sonnets to the national building and expansion that was effecting a rapid translation of a medieval economy to a nascent market one – with the inevitable expansion of markets into colonies and dominions. Spenser is likewise one of the earliest articulators through the medium of poetry of the aggressive imperialist dynamic.[19]

As centuries of the Irish have asked, 'why the English and us?'

Sixteenth-century Ireland was the nearest site to England of the struggle for European and, increasingly, global hegemony between Catholicism and Protestantism, and it was where the major parties in the struggle, Spain and England, developed and assessed expansionist and colonialist goals and strategies. Ireland had also long been a sphere of influence for English monarchs, who had for five hundred years or more tried, with only mixed success, to impose

English law, customs and rule upon it. During the sixteenth-century, especially after the Reformation, extra efforts were directed to conquer Ireland under Henry VIII and Elizabeth. It became an unenviable task to be appointed as Lord Deputy, a position Sir Henry Sidney (Philip, Mary, and Robert Sidney's father) held three times. Reading the official (English) accounts of the treatment of the sporadic Irish resistance is to open an appalling chapter of brutality, racism and genocide. It required all the landowners in the area to be declared rebels, attainted, and the land so acquired sold or systematically leased to colonists from England. The objections of the Irish landowners, some powerful and wealthy, proved the occasion, most notably a sustained 'rebellion' led by the earl of Desmond, who was killed in 1582. In 1580, the English generals Pelham and Ormond went into Munster, expressly to devastate the province by exterminating the populace. Pelham reported: 'My manner of prosecuting is thus: I give the rebels no breath to relieve themselves', so they become 'so distressed as they . . . offer themselves with their wives and children rather to be slain by the army than to suffer the famine that now in extremity beginneth to pinch them'. As we shall see Spenser's celebration of a brutal 'justice' in Book Five of *The Faerie Queene* is uncomfortably close to historical reality. The result was that by 1582, as MacCarthy-Morrogh notes, 'in Munster at least . . . human destruction was no longer a prerequisite for colonization. Since there were few [people] left in Munster, repopulation would have to come from England'.[20]

How did Spenser regard the offer of employment in Ireland? Instead of remaining at or near Elizabeth's court, serving Leicester and perhaps becoming a member of Sidney's circle, when he found himself, as Rambuss puts it, 'commissioned to a country that fiercely resisted the colonial government of which he was now a bureaucratic representative',[21] did he see it as an opportunity to forward his career or as a distraction from it? Do his writings give us an indication? Spenser had in fact probably visited Ireland first in 1577, as one of Sir Henry Sidney's secretaries, where he may have witnessed a particularly brutal scenes of execution and cannibalism described in the *View*. He arrived more permanently in mid 1580 to serve as chief secretary under Lord Grey of Wilton, a ruthless Puritan who had the support of the Sidney-Leicester faction in the queen's council. Certainly, Spenser's career as a writer flourished – but his writing was expressed not in poetry so much as in the duties of a secretary. What his removal to Ireland did provide were sights and experiences very different from those at court – though it might be said that they were the dark realities of the court.

Through both official documents and, not entirely indirectly, through *The Faerie Queene*, we learn of Spenser's involvement. It was not exactly that of a naive reporter. Spenser was not Pierre Bezukhov. He witnessed some of Grey's more thorough brutalizations of the Irish, such as repeated excursions into the Wicklow mountains where the rivers ran with blood, and the massacre of a surrendering garrison of Irish at Smerwick who were promised fair terms by Grey and then slaughtered, thus giving rise to a phrase still used in Ireland today, 'Grey's promise'. Spenser's report was faithful to Grey's convictions: that 'there was no other way but to make that short end of them which was made'. The English troops also carried out what was to become a staple of their policy in Ireland, one also commended by Spenser, a scorched-earth devastation of the Irish people and their lands, burning villages and crops, slaughtering and starving the inhabitants. Spenser's view was that the brutalization of the Irish was 'brought on themselves by their own wickedness'. On the way to across Ireland to its mission in the west, Grey's party stayed with the earl of Ormond, whose Countess is allegorized in *The Faerie Queene* Book Four as the courteous and learned nymph of the river Scir, a stark contrast with the barbarism being perpetrated by her guests and her husband, whose aim was to devastate Munster to make it 'as bare a country as ever Spaniard set his foot in' by consuming 'with fire all inhabitants and execut[ing] the people wherever we found them'.[22]

Following the success of Grey's campaign against the Irish resistance – which admittedly drew some criticism from the 'Old' English who lived mainly in the Pale around Dublin and who, much to the suspicion of the 'new' settlers, or 'planters', like Spenser, had for some centuries attempted a more reconciliatory policy towards the Irish – Spenser started to acquire land in Ireland, as part of Grey's policy of rewarding his followers with land confiscated from what were regarded as felons and traitors. The most important of these grants was Kilcolman Castle, in Munster, given in 1582. In the same year, Grey resigned as Lord Deputy and was replaced by the more conciliatory Perrot. Spenser, however, stayed in Ireland. His responsibilities had increased: he had acquired a clerkship in Chancery, by which post he was responsible for registering licences and grants in the archbishopric of Dublin. He was starting to acquire, probably far more easily than in England, a string of such positions, the most important of which was in 1584, that of clerk of the Council of Munster. Such involvement in the life of a planter and official drew him closer to the concerns of the 'New' English. Along with most of the planters, Spenser accused Perrot of being soft on rebellion, and of returning to the policy of favouring the 'Old' English who, the 'New' English believed, had sunk to or even below the level of barbarity displayed by the Irish themselves. Spenser and other Munster planters remained uneasy at any conciliation policy, and commenced what Canny calls 'an active program of propaganda to impress the validity of their case upon the government in England'.[23]

Spenser's *View of the Present State of Ireland* is the best known of these propaganda efforts. Registered for publication in 1596, but not actually published until 1633, it went through several drafts from about 1590 on, and argues for a vigorous program of final conquest and subjugation of Ireland and the Irish. In the opening section, Spenser attacks the pusillanimity of much earlier English policy which, in his view, had been over influenced by the 'Old' English preference for a degree of accommodation with the Irish chieftains, and their legal and tribal system. In the second section, he described, in terms that had been commonplace in English accounts for hundreds of years, Irish society: the Irish are barbarians, licentious (some commentators added that they were cannibals), and while there were certain admirable or charming aspects of ancient Irish life (Spenser's interest in Irish poetry and song is often mentioned by defenders of the *View* in this context), nothing short of force and thorough rooting out of the Irish identity would allow the rule of English law to be permanently established. Spenser saw this occurring in stages. Initially there would be an uncompromising military onslaught, involving either unconditional surrender or wholesale slaughter by military means or starvation. In advocating such a policy, Spenser praised the maligned Lord Grey whose military thoroughness he saw as both justifiable and extendible to the rest of the country. The second stage involved the establishment of complete military control and resettlement by the English. Those Irish remaining were to be integrated into an English system of government, education, and eventually law; they would swear loyalty to the English crown, annually assemble to detect any defectors, and abandon their Irish names and customs: an Irishman, he argued, would thus 'in short time learn quite to forget his Irish nation'.[24] Catholicism would be replaced by Protestantism, and finally the Irish would thereby be fit to live under English civil law. Spenser's proposals were not unusual by the standards of his fellow Munster planters. He is occasionally less extreme than some: Barnabe Rich, a fellow writer and planter, once suggested a program of general castration as a more effective policy than starvation. But the common assumption among the 'New' English like Spenser was that no reform of laws or accommodation with Irish ethnic identity could overcome the barbarism of the customs and structures of Irish society, and so any effective policy needed to be drastic: it is 'vain to speak of planting of new laws and plotting of policies till [the Irish] be altogether subdued'. But if Spenser's views were largely commonplace, and in part grew from years of discussion among the Munster planters, few advocated such a systematic, wholesale policy, combining a scorched-earth military conquest elimination or transplantation of the native population. The gradualist, 'Old' English policy of assimilation could only work after the Irish had been compelled by force and decimation to accept whatever solution the conquering English would impose on them. That is, of course, to assume that there would be many Irish remaining. As Ciaran Brady comments, 'should the ghastly operation prove successful, there would be few enough survivors ready to benefit from the delights of civility yet to come'.[25]

The arguments of the *View* grow from deeply held and aggressively asserted political convictions; they also grow from an increasing material stake in the land they advocate conquering. Here we can stand back and see Spenser in an emergent class of emigrants who saw themselves, whether by choice or in part reluctantly, as seeking to better themselves, from the late sixteenth century, we see the development of a central phenomenon of imperialism: the internal pressures to expel or exclude a proportion of the metropolitan population. The opportunity to become a 'planter' or 'undertaker' was afforded only to the educated class and by the 1580s is emerging the phenomenon that MacCarthy-Morrogh sees as highly evident a few decades later: 'the universities were turning out large numbers of graduates and quite simply there were not enough jobs to go round. This reservoir of 'alienated intellectuals' joined with the familiar younger son problem resulted in a number of over-educated and unemployed gentlemen kicking their heels in England. Spenser did not kick his heels. He was one of the earliest of the would-be gentlemen who saw that advancement might only come through taking employment in Ireland. As MacCarthy-Morrogh comments, many professional men 'would have crossed the Irish Sea intending only to mount the ladder of their profession and once settled transfer themselves home'.[26] Service meant cheap land, cheap labor, mounting social status. As he accumulated offices, so Spenser acquired land. As Rambuss comments, 'Spenser's university degree had already earned him the status of a gentleman, but he became a member of the landed gentry by virtue of the property he acquired in Ireland'. Would he have had the same opportunities in England? Would he have preferred to have been able to try? Did his supposed other career, the literary one, suffer because of his transplantation to the colonies, to adapt a phrase from later colonial history? He published nothing between the *Calender* and his return to England in 1590 – yet he must have been writing.

William Butler Yeats, of all people, tried to defend Spenser by drawing a distinction between the brutal civil servant and the delicate poet, an argument which, when we look at Book Five of *The Faerie Queene*, in which a policy of repression and terror over the enemies of Justice is also praised, seems specious.[27] Poet and civil servant are one. In fact, since more than half the poetry Spenser wrote, including more than half of *The Faerie Queene* was produced in his years in Munster, placing Spenser's literary and daily lives alongside each other greatly illuminates our reading of both. But there are, indeed, two Spensers to consider, as Berleith notes: one is 'the servant of the state, who writes a terrifying treatise called *A Vewe of the Present State of Ireland*, and the other is the Munster gentleman, who celebrates his marriage in the imagery of the Awbeg Vale and imagines himself a shepherd on the slopes of the Ballyhurst.'[28] The poet sees no contradiction between these two roles: the ruthlessness of the former makes the idyllic life of the latter possible. So rather than vaguely alluding to 'two' Spensers and so trying somehow to salvage one of them for moral approval, we might more usefully point to the cultural and perhaps moral schizophrenia of Spenser's life at this time.

It might – this suggestion is obviously made with heavy irony – even be possible to mount a case for Spenser as a major Irish poet, though few Irish would presumably make such a case. Homi Bhabha speaks of the inevitably changing boundaries of inherited discourses of 'national imagined communities' producing counter-discourses and counter-narratives out of living in more than one culture.

Spenser's assimilation into the life of a Munster country gentleman certainly took up much of his energies from 1582 until he was driven from his lands in 1598.[29] From 1585, he spent most of his time in Munster, initially working as a deputy to Lodowick Bryskett, the Clerk of Munster, under Sir John Norris, the president of the Council of Munster. His main business was surveying confiscated land, apportioning it into estates and adjudicating legal quarrels among the planters themselves. By 1588 he himself was in full possession of the Kilcolman estate which, after various legal battles with local Irish landowners, was formally given to him in 1590. Thereafter, for almost ten years, with the exception of two short and disillusioning trips to London, Spenser lived the life of a landowner, farmer and poet in Ireland. There was occasional danger from local Irish, and through the 1590s the planters watched with some apprehension the rise of an unusually well-organized leader for the Irish, O'Neill, while they increasingly pressed the government in London to take a harsher position towards the Irish. But for some years, the towns in the area were pacified, relatively prosperous, and there was no longer prolonged famine. The area, notes Berleith, 'showed signs of attaining the settled life of an English shire'.[30] The *View*, Books Five and Six of *The Faerie Queene*, and *Colin Clouts Come Home Again* were written at this time.

Colin Clouts Come Home Again nostalgically recalls events in 1588 and 1590 when Spenser met Ralegh, and the tone is one of admiration and gratitude to a fellow poet and landowner and of settled contentment, articulating what in later centuries became the partly nostalgic colonialist's call to a more robust life in the empire. Spenser also mentions his neighbour Ralegh's powerful unfinished poem, 'Ocean to Scynthia':

> His song was all a lamentable lay
> Of great unkindenesse, and of usage hard,
> Of *Cynthia* the Ladie of the sea,
> Which from her presence faultlesse him debard.
> And ever and anon with singulfs rife,
> He cryed out, to make his undersong
> Ah my loves queene, and goddesse of my life,
> Who shall me pittie, when thou doest me wrong.
>
> (164–77)

The poem's title is poignantly ambiguous. Where is 'home' for the poet? In the court? In Munster? Spenser's original readers would

identify 'home' with the civilized court to which the poet is returning after years in exile, but the Irish landscape and the community of
shepherd-poets is clearly where the poet is drawn. Yet we should
remember that this 'home' has been built at the expense, the waste,
the destruction, of many thousands of the homes (and lives) of the
Irish.

Sentimentally, one likes to think he returns, realizing at last where
his heart lies, his new 'home', but the material realities suggest that
he felt exiled once again in what he termed the 'barrein soyle' (*Colin
Clout*, l. 656) of Ireland because he has disappointed at court, and like
many colonists after him, in many places across the world, he returned with an energy and ambition fueled by his rejection by the
'mother' country for which he still yearns in confusion and bitterness. Three hundred years later he would have become a patron of
the local cricket club, complained of the wicket, drunk gin and
tonics, and waited for the bi-annual visit of the MCC. And praised
the local scenery. Something of the change – what Rambuss terms
'the second of his two pastoral beginnings' – can be seen in the
descriptions, recognizably Anglo-Irish-pastoral rather than simply
English-pastoral – in *Colin Clout*.

In the *Amoretti*, likewise, Spenser celebrates both his new marriage and the ordered domestic existence among Munster's hills and
valleys such that it has been claimed that 'no love poetry of the
period is comparable in its use of place and community'. *Epithalamion*
also mythologizes the landscape between Cork and Munster, and
the final four books of *The Faerie Queene* are full of references to the
Munster landscape: the Awbeg river appears as Mulla at the marriage of the Thames and Medway in Book Four; the judgement by
Nature on Mutability's case against the gods is set on what Spenser
calls Arlo Hill, which is Galtymore Mountain, just over 3000 feet
high, which would be clearly seen from Kilcolman. But bucolic as
the Irish setting of these poems may be, it is clear that Spenser, like
his poems, was torn by conflicting values. Brady suggests that even
in his pastoral haven he was undergoing a 'personal crisis' caused by
the relative neglect of the first three books of *The Faerie Queene*,
which had earned him a pension of £50 from the queen but no
preferment at court.[31] He was ill, his courtship of Elizabeth Boyle
went through difficulties, he was embroiled in a number of law suits
over his land, and the political situation was worsening, with increased rumours of Spanish threats and Irish resistance stirring again.
In 1596 Irish fighters led by O'Neill, now earl of Tyrone, rose and

a number of settlements in Munster were burnt and looted. On 16 October 1598, the fighting reached Kilcolman. Spenser and his wife had already fled, first to Mallow, then Cork, where he learnt, no doubt with some irony, that he had been promoted to be sheriff of Munster. His reaction was to write to the queen (probably in conjunction with others) a further account of Irish policy, sometimes referred to as *A Brief Note of Ireland*. His contribution is entitled 'Certain pointes to be considered of in the recovery of the Realme of Ireland'. Spenser reiterates that 'great force must be the instrument' and 'famine . . . the meane'. The queen's 'wonted milde courses' towards the Irish had resulted in the destruction of the dream of an English rural paradise in Ireland. The 'other' had returned to claim what it, at least, believed to be its own. It is a struggle that still continues.[32]

POETRY: THE PLACE OF AGENCY?

'O pierlesse Poesye, where is then thy place?', asks Spenser in the October eclogue of the *Calender* (l. 79). One of the much commented upon developments in our cultural history since the Renaissance has been the assumption of a natural distinction between 'private' and 'public' life. Our private lives, those activities and commitments which, it is often held, contain our deepest allegiances, are (or ought to be), it is assumed, built on values that we keep untouched by the tawdriness of the public world. Behind the distinction is an ideology of self-compartmentalization embodied in countless material details: in bourgeois family life, in the separation of marriage from the (predominantly male) workplace, or 'individual' values from those of the business world. Its presence is felt residually in the dichotomy of studying at a university and going out into the 'real' world, archaically expressed as 'town' and 'gown'. This dichotomy take very self-conscious shape in Spenser's lifetime. It seems to have increasingly been plain to him in many of the aspects of his life: between the court and the world, the queen and corrupt courtiers, his home at Kilcolman and the anarchic world of the rebellious Irish, and more consistently than all of these, between poetry and the very world for which it had some integral relation and for which it might speak. The question of poetry's power and place in the world troubled Spenser all his life. Was poetry the servant of the state? Or, as W. H. Auden once put it, does it 'do' nothing? Or, in Spenser's more elevated neoplatonic and Christian terms, does poetry offer an area of spiritual freedom and discovery that the world could not, ultimately, touch? Was it a realm, as we say today, of agency?

From his earliest published work, Spenser brooded over the relative autonomy of poetry. Indeed, we can trace much of those broodings to the education in the place and value of poetry that he would have received in his schooling. As Mary Ellen Lamb puts it, 'the suspicion that poetry (or fiction as it would now be called) was not an entirely masculine endeavor' was widespread in the educational ideology and practices of the time. It reappears in the widespread and at times virulent Protestant suspicion of the arts, including that of Stephen Gosson, to whose puritanical structures Sidney was in part replying in the *Defence*. Sidney himself acknowledged that poetry could be a 'nurse of abuse' and a 'mother of lies,' the gendered terms typically encoding the male suspicion of the seductiveness of the nurturing, overwhelming female. On the other hand, when rightly used, Sidney asserted, poetry could be 'sweet', and (in an extraordinarily revealing phrase) 'raise a leader from the Irish camps'. The gender and racial politics in that phrase are obvious, depressing, and looking at the age as a whole, ubiquitous. Masculinity is bound up with control of pleasure, and specifically of any pleasure associated with (or acknowledging an affinity for) what Shakespeare termed in *Cymbeline* 'the woman's part'. Poetry, like women, can be pleasing so long as the hierarchy of masculinist domination is maintained. Yet, as Lamb points out, at the same time as young boys were absorbing ideals of masculinity that involve the firm subordination of anything tending to effeminization, they were being introduced to the seductions of stories by mothers, nurses, and even (as in the case, in *The Faerie Queene*, Book Three, of Britomart's teacher, Merlin) other men: 'the pleasure elicited by the vernacular tales of childhood, the passions they aroused, and the affectionate bond they cemented between children and women, threatened the severe form of masculinity' inculcated through other child-rearing and educational practices, she suggests. Yet, presumably, the stories which 'holdeth children from play' so praised by Sidney could attempt to reinforce rather than subvert the ideals of masculine virtue. In a remark clearly germane to Spenser's epic ambitions, Sidney remarks that 'Orlando Furioso, or honest King Arthur, will never displease a soldier'. Hence, educationalists like Elyot and Ascham exhorted schoolboys to read Homer and Virgil to increase their courage as well as providing them with examples to emulate. Stories of a person's ancestors' bravery were, says Sidney, inspirational – they were the 'chiefest kindlers of brave courage' in the 'soldierlike nation' of Hungary, and in his own case, the ancient ballads of Percy and Douglas, Sidney attests, gave him more courage than a trumpet. Hence it is possible, despite its effeminizing tendencies, to describe poetry as the inspirer not of 'effeminateness but of a notable stirring of courage'. [33]

A case can easily made for Spenser's poetic career as the articulation of such values. Set within the tradition of Petrarchan love poems, Spenser's collection of sonnets, the *Amoretti*, is atypically moralistic, espousing a view of the relationship between poet/lover and his beloved that unambiguously advocates a Christian hierarchy of male control and female subordination. They reject the seductiveness of desire and poetry for the sober celebration of properly ordered religious duty, especially in marriage. Spenser's poetic ambitions culminate in an epic poem designed to celebrate the heroic ideals of heroic knights-at-arms, all of whom learn, in different ways to battle the seductiveness of error, self-indulgent pleasure, sensuality, independence, malice – all 'effeminate' characteristics that the misogenic tracts of the time attribute to women. Paglia's is the most sustained contemporary reading that relates Spenser's epic goals to the triumphant assertion of masculine will. *The Faerie Queene*, she proclaims, is a celebration of 'the mystical hieraticism of power', in which 'the hard edge of heroic male will is constantly fighting off the blurring of [the] female'.[34]

Yet there is another aspect of Spenser's commitment to poetry that complicates such a reading and makes what I have termed the 'place' of poetry so important in our assessment of his literary life. On the one hand, his stated goal was to enact for Elizabethan England, and in particular for the 'New' planters in Ireland, what he saw as the political as well as the literary responsibilities that a century of humanist educators had praised Virgil and Horace for performing for Rome. Language, the medium of the poet, was no less than statecraft the embodiment (and means of inculcation) of the moral order and even the religious foundations of the individual, the state and the universe. Such values are epitomized in the values of the questing knights of the epic: holiness, temperance, chastity, friendship, justice, courtesy, constancy. Together, they construct a process of education by which we are brought into conformity with our rightful natures and our place in the divinely ruled universe.

But what happens when these ideals are given, at best, only lip-service by the regime to which the poet has dedicated himself? And when the poet perceives that the ideals he continues to celebrate are less and less found in the very place in which they ought to be most obviously manifest? David Shore argues that Spenser's enactment of the poet's functions in the later books of *The Faerie Queene* and in the poems he wrote from about the late 1580s, are an 'unstable but necessary union of two ideas', the knight and the shepherd, Calidore and Colin Clout. In the figure of Colin, who appears in *The Shepheardes Calender*, *Colin Clout's Come Home Again* and *The Faerie Queene* Book Six, Shore sees a prolonged meditation on the 'nature and direction of [Spenser's] poetic career'.[35] In the *Calender*, Colin is the ambitious young poet who asserts his mastery of traditional poetic forms, the celebrator of love and the queen, and the aspirer to mature wisdom. Poetry is one of the means by which these goals will be achieved, along with good government, and the subjection of Catholicism to the truths of Protestantism. But where the *Calender* asserted with enormous confidence the public responsibilities of the poet, a decade or more later, Colin's lay of Bregog and Mulla and his list of the court's poets, the 'shepherds of the court', who have dedicated themselves to Cynthia without adequate acknowledgment or reward, all point to Spenser's sense of the disappointing powerlessness of the poet, most especially seen in the mistreatment of Ralegh mentioned by Thestylis. One consequence of this realization is a reversal, or at least a downplaying, of his lofty ambitions for poetry's public importance and impact. Book Six of *The Faerie Queene* reinforces such a retreat. In Canto ten, Calidore is presented with a vision of the triumph of Colin's art; his own beloved is 'advaunst to be another Grace' (6. 10. 16), a source of poetic and moral inspiration alongside the queen. Is Spenser substituting his own 'personal' source of inspiration for that of the public world? Is poetry an area of human agency only insofar as it withdraws from its political ambitions? Calidore is excluded from that world; Colin Clout may have no power, but he at least has the power of language, the power of storytelling.

So the poet may speak and write, just as the planter may attempt to build a rural paradise in Munster. How can each of them guarantee that such efforts will be rewarded? Or that their construction of poetry and domestic community will be acceptable to their peers? Of course, they cannot. But while the vicissitudes of worldly fortune that affected the worlds of politics and settlement was a traditional commonplace, Spenser was attempting to find something more permanent in the calling and the prophetic vision of poetry. How, then, does the poet guarantee that his readers will make the 'right' reading? Or must the poet – as Plato and some of the Elizabethan Protestants argued – be banished from the commonwealth, because he has no essential value to its functioning? This was a much debated issue in Spenser's circle. In the *Defence* – which can be seen as a kind of manifesto for English Protestant poets – Sidney confesses that poetry's ability to move its readers is not predictable or automatic; men may not be moved at all, or may not translate vision into praxis. Poetic power may be, as Margaret Ferguson has argued, 'viewed as a circuit of energy which goes from author to work to reader', and that energy can be diverted, adapted, or resisted, as well as used for illumination. Poetry, implies Sidney, directs us to self-study; it opens to us the possibility of discovering virtue in ourselves. Likewise, Montaigne, in his essay 'Of Experience', is also interested in the means by which reading changes a reader and he seems, as Sidney does, to oscillate between a belief that the reader is essentially passive in the reading process and an acceptance that the reader is creative.[36] What precisely that creativity consisted of is a major concern to the Protestant poet, for whom there was a very real danger of what Spenser in the opening book of *The Faerie Queene* depicts as the monster Errour, who spews forth a torrent of erroneous language and books. The very power of language, its inaugurating qualities, was both a matter of celebration and a matter of fear.

Hence the mixture of celebration and anxiety that many Elizabethan scholars and educators (and not only so-called 'Puritans') showed towards their language. Some complained that the Latin and Greek languages were too 'copious and plentiful' or criticized their 'inkhorn terms', just as they did dialect or archaism. Yet other writers perceived that the inrush of new experiences in the age meant, in Ralph Lever's plaintive but revealing phrase, that there were 'more things, then there are words to express things by', or in Spenser's schoolmaster Mulcaster's more reasoned judgement, that 'new occasions' bring 'furth new words'. But there was often a sense of alarm that language's multiplicity might get out of hand, and a desire that it should be disciplined and controlled, and so cleansed, as Nashe put it, 'from barbarisme'. To make the language 'gorgeous and delectable' was one thing; to make it a hodgepodge was plainly unacceptable, especially in a society where political and cultural control was paramount.[37]

So alongside the period's celebrations of the expansiveness of textuality, we must note as well the growing tide of hostility to Renaissance logophilia. Spenser's poetry is a clear example of the tension. In *The Shepheardes Calender* and *The Faerie Queene* he uses glosses and summary verses to summarize, point, or underline the 'message' of his poem. In doing so, he is not simply indulging in an archaic mode of annotation suitable for the 'antique' nature of his poems. Indeed, modern readers of Spenser's poems (and, indeed, of this book) may well be antipathetic to the archaism of his language – the self-consciously medieval diction as well as the alien and seemingly arbitrary spelling. The latter cannot quite be explained away by reference to the looseness of Elizabethan orthography; but the former is definitely deliberate. Thus modern editions of Spenser inevitably remain 'old spelling' editions: to modernize his language, except perhaps in a 'children's edition', let alone remove his archaisms, would be to distort one of his poetry's most distinctive effects. Indeed, many of his most characteristic verbal effects are achieved through variant spellings: like James Joyce, Spenser delights in wrestling with words to make them contain multiple or contradictory meanings, or underlining (often very heavily) their primary one. As Hamilton points out, Orgoglio is a 'Geant' (1. 7. 8) because he is the son of Gea, the earth; Duessa's breath smells 'abhominably' (1. 8. 47) because she is *ab homine*, from mankind and so beastly.[38]

Such plays on words are, interestingly, designed often to limit rather than expand the suggestiveness of language. Throughout Spenser's poems, the potential promiscuity of language is being confronted by an anxiety to find ways of limiting its meanings and power. The tireless repetition of commonplaces, the search for gnomic utterance, the popularity of emblem and referential allusion in allegory are features of the whole age. It is as if a plethora of expression were constantly being bullied into knots of meaning, much in the way that the Protestant propagandist marked the margins of his text by 'Mark ye this, ye hogges and dogges' or 'Here be sound doctrine'. What is at stake in Protestant attacks on poetry, romance, images, is ultimately a deep suspicion of language. Words let loose meaning, and as Protestantism tended to read the Bible, the word, preached, proclaimed and valorized in the authorized Word of the living God is acceptable only in that it is (if received by the Elect) unvarying and closed. But human words, over flowing in the materiality of signs into history let loose a promiscuity of writing that might end in damnation. By what miracle can words, black marks on a white page, become bearers of meaning? It is a question that haunts Protestant intellectuals and poets like Spenser. Throughout his work, there is a problematic relationship between words and meaning, writing and representation: every attempt to approximate truth is necessary yet feared because it will inevitably dissolve into an infinity of random signifiers.

How does Spenser try to handle this anxiety? A. Leigh DeNeef has shown how Spenser builds his concern with establishing the 'right' reading of his poem, and tries to 'guard his texts against the threat of wrong readings'. Not only do the poems contain pointed directions to 'the right speaker and right readers' within the narrative, but DeNeef argues, seeks to produce a kind of reading by which poet and readers are educated together. An illusion is created of meanings that are discovered, but are nonetheless the 'right' readings, which are what Foucault would have called 'within the true'. DeNeef indicates, however, that increasingly Spenser is distrustful of metaphorical language: the very ambivalence of language resists the degree of control the 'right' poet needs to create 'right' readers: 'even a Right Poet's writing can be "raced out" by a reader's wrong reading', and since the poet's job is to use language, 'not to define or emblematize. But to offer the opportunity to invent', the logical conclusion is to cease writing, to abandon the very vocation of poet to which Spenser felt that he had been called.[39] What then, does the poet do? If the message of his poem, the great design it is written to celebrate, is misread not only by Malfont and his kind, but even by those 'right' readers for whom it is primarily written and whom it celebrates, what does the poet do? In the neoplatonic terms that permeate both *The Faerie Queene* and the political ideology of the court itself, Spenser comes to see the poet's role as that of articulating the hints, however few and faint, of an eternal order behind, even if betrayed by, a fallen world. A nostalgia for a lost order, once apparently reflected in the universe and poetry alike, seems likewise to haunt many of those Spenser's critics most ferociously determined to be 'right' readers. Spenser, like most Renaissance intellectuals believed that God's purposes were reflected in the universe's order, proportion, and pattern, and that poetry could (and should) replicate that order. Seeking, in the words of the most assiduous of the numerological critics, Kent Hieatt, 'meaning, integrally expressed, below the surface of discourse', such would-be right readers have tried to turn criticism into description – the recognition of patterns and meanings over which the writer is in control, patterns that are ascertained by 'stringent standards of objectivity', and which 'must' be seen and acknowledged as the permanently and aesthetically valid possession for all readers'.[40] Even such readers however, have to admit (like Spenser) that there are precious few right readers and that, indeed, as is the case with all nostalgic ideology, their numbers grow smaller. Spenser may well have felt something like that about the true readers of poetry. Indeed, at the end of his epic, the implication is that the poet alone retains hints of such order. He must be sure to not betray his ideals, even if those whose power he supports do. Perhaps, finally – as we shall see in the Cantos of Mutability – only God possesses the agency, the sense of access to a reality that at least in his early poems Spenser saw poetry possessing.

3

The Making of a
Protestant Poet

The first two chapters have provided an overview of Spenser's 'literary life'. In this chapter I will trace his career chronologically through his early writings as far as *The Shepheardes Calender* (1579), which announced both his ambitions and such a level of poetic achievement that Sidney hailed him in the *Defence* as 'this, our new poet'.

What poetry written in English by near contemporaries would Spenser have known? Were there any native models to which he could turn? What theories of poetry were current as Spenser formed his self-understanding and ambitions as a poet? And, specifically, what place did poetry have in the England of his upbringing and education? Commentary on Spenser and on English poetry in the sixteenth-century generally has on the whole been embarrassed by what poetry there was in English before 1579, and preferred a picture of Spenser that sees him turning directly to the classics and contemporary French and Italians, reading Virgil, Mantuan, Tasso, Marot and others – and, of the English poets, only Chaucer and Langland. Yet most of Spenser's early poems, including *Virgil's Gnat*, the first version of *Mother Hubbard's Tale*, and *The Teares of the Muses*, are, in fact, very closely related to the typical poetical preoccupations of the mid-century period, in which an attempt was being made by a number of humanistically educated men to create a Protestant poetic and a Protestant poetry. For many God-fearing Protestants, 'Protestant' and 'poetry' were contradictory, and the leading intellectuals and educators of the sixteenth-century had somehow to work through that contradiction. Spenser's early work can be read as trying to wrestle with some of the issues of establishing a Protestant poetic, and *The Shepheardes Calender* is a momentarily triumphant achievement within the contradictions it sets up.

For most educated people in the middle of the sixteenth-century, the most obvious way of justifying poetry was that it was useful: for the pious Protestant that meant, specifically, it needed to be a tool for furthering the goals of the godly, and not be (as some detractors maintained it was) a hindrance and an incentive to sin. Its justification could not be separated from the aim of setting up and supporting a Protestant State. As part of the Reformation dynamic, there had grown up a body of devotional, propagandist, and polemical writing that helped spread the theological arguments that were the intellectual sustenance of the movement. In the early phase of the Reformation in England, Protestant poetry reflected such a view: it was strongly utilitarian, combining an insistence upon biblical themes and what was perceived as an appropriately unadorned poetic style. John N. King terms the poetic theory that underlay this movement a 'major shift in mimetic theory' within Renaissance poetics; he points out how the prolific 'gospellers' who wrote on biblical or devotional subjects in a variety of popular forms – ballads, fourteeners, poulter's measure – were deliberately rejecting the Italianate courtly forms like the sonnet and *ottava rima* of Wyatt and Surrey and developing alternative native forms.[1] Such a division is to oversimplify the way court poetry was permeated by Protestantism, but it does justice to the propagandist intents of Protestant poets and poetical theorists and it undoubtedly helps explain the ideological edge to what has traditionally been presented as Spenser's more sophisticated goals in *The Shepheardes Calender*. We can get some measure of the power of the Protestant poetical movement from glancing at both its theoretical statements and its practice: they deeply influenced Spenser in both his formal education and his religious avocation, and if as some readers have suggested, the dogmatic didacticism of Protestantism sits uneasily with his deep reading in both the classics and more recent European poets, that contradiction would not have seemed obvious, or even made sense, to the young Spenser. It may, of course, have laid down potential contradictions for later in his career.

In his *Defence of Poesy* (written about 1580 and first published in 1595) Sir Philip Sidney – like Spenser, who dedicated the *Calender* to him – was aiming at a very utilitarian goal, that of justifying poetry as a valuable activity within a Protestant state, and praised its ability to 'move men to take goodness in hand'.[2] Poetry could therefore (despite objections from some more extreme Protestants than Sidney or Spenser would have felt comfortable with) be seen as having a moral force, not least because it mixed didactic truth with what Sidney termed a 'delight' that enhanced its power to change our lives. Sidney's formulation is typical: poets, he writes, 'do merely make to imitate, and imitate both to delight and teach; and delight, to move men to take that goodness in hand, without which delight they would fly as from a stranger, and teach, to make them know that goodness whereunto they are moved'. The conclusion of the *Defence* likewise stresses that poetry is not 'an art of lies, but of true doctrine', and full of 'virtue-breeding delightfulness'. It is true that on occasion, Sidney affirms that poetry's role should be an opportunity for what today we would term wishfulfilment or fantasizing; for Spenser, however, it was strictly subordinate to the given meanings of the world – whether those meanings were conceived as given by God's Word, the order of Nature, or the need for civic responsibility. Poetry can help reform man's will: 'no learning is so good as that which teacheth and moveth to virtue', as Sidney writes.

From a post-Kantian perspective, if there are the beginnings of what later became an 'aesthetic' approach to poetry, hints of the treasured Romantic and modernist notion of the autonomy of the work of art, such elements are still subordinate to more obvious moralizing or utilitarian sentiments. Sidney writes of the poet's 'high flying liberty of conceit', the 'vigours' of the poet's 'invention' and, in one half of his most famous aphorism, asserts that 'our erected wit maketh us know what perfection is'. As usual, Sidney's is the most elegant English formulation of the poetical application of such an optimistic doctrine. Although his idea that the poet creates a new Nature is not original – it is derived from the Neoplatonic view of the artist as the vehicle of the Divine Ideas, popularized by such Italian critics as Landino or Scaliger – his formulation may have intrigued Spenser with its combination of Christian theology and Neoplatonic celebration:

> Only the poet, disdaining to be tied to any such subjection, lifted up with the vigour of his own invention, doth grow in effect another nature, in making things either better than nature bringeth forth, or, quite anew, forms such as never were in nature . . . so as he goeth hand in hand with nature, not enclosed within the narrow warrant of her gifts, but freely ranging only within the zodiac of his own wit.

Here the poet is celebrated as an autonomous maker. He takes the miraculous creation of the world by God, the divine poet, as his model, and draws down the magical powers of the universe into his own mind, 'the zodiac of his own wit'. The superiority of the poet's world is unabashedly celebrated in such a formulation since Nature's 'world is brazen, the poets only deliver a golden'. The poet's greatness is built upon his aspiring to encapsulate in his poem that beauty and splendour that shine in all natural things, and thus continuing God's divine creativity in his work. The poet is

> set . . . beyond and over all the works of that second nature: which in nothing he showeth so much as in poetry, when with the force of a divine breath he bringeth things forth surpassing her doings – with no small argument to the credulous of that first accursed fall of Adam, since our erected wit maketh us know what perfection is, and yet our infected will keepeth us from reaching unto it.

'Erected wit' and 'infected will': in these great opposites are epitomized the contradictory languages into which Spenser was attempting to insert himself. It is fascinating that here, at the end of his ecstatic sentence, Sidney comes right back to didacticism, and most particularly, in the Calvinist emphasis of the 'infected will', to man's radical inability to embody in action what poetry inspires him to perform. How did poets reconcile such oppositions? How can the erected wit and the infected will coexist? Whether or not Spenser actually read the *Defence* (it was not, after all, published until 1595) these contradictions surface throughout Spenser's poetry. They are the recurring issues for the construction of a Protestant civic poetry.

According to such a view (and here Sidney and Spenser would also have agreed) poetry is not only a moral teacher: it is the supreme moral teacher. It combines the conceptual advantages of philosophy with the concrete instances of history. Poetry will, so Sidney's argument goes, entice us into virtuous actions by imitating real virtue, not false illusion – by its imitation of what Sidney calls the 'golden' world, a world of moral inspiration of what may and should be, we learn more readily than from imitating the 'brazen' world of nature. The poet, Sidney argues, 'doth grow in effect another nature, in making things either better than nature bringeth forth, or, quite anew, forms such as never were in nature'. 'Poetry', therefore, he asserts, 'is an art of imitation, for so Aristotle termeth it in his word mimesis', not by simply reproducing the given world but by 'a representing, counterfeiting, or figuring forth to speak metaphorically'.[3] The main emphasis here is on metaphor as the primary way of speaking which brings about the effects of imitation, thus affecting the mind and the senses of the readers. Readers of poetry will thus be enticed towards the emulation of moral excellence by the power of poetry's mimesis, as it creates speaking pictures of how Nature might fulfill its potential. The final test of poetry is always in praxis: how it contributes to the moral improvement of its readers and to the wider society. The most triumphant creation of such a theory is unquestionably *The Faerie Queene*, perhaps the clearest and richest example of how the Elizabethan regime advanced its ideals through poetry. It is built on a desire to subdue language to power, to make signification transparent to meaning and to prevent the potential promiscuity of language from spreading unwanted meanings too far.

But the Protestant educators, not least Spenser's schoolmaster Richard Mulcaster, were also humanists, educated in the tradition of the Renaissance classical revival. They believed there were close affinities between Christianity and Neoplatonism, a suggestive accretion of ideas derived, at some distance, from Plato and remixed, from the late fifteenth-century onwards, by such thinkers as Ficino and Pico della Mirandola. After Christianity, Neoplatonism gave Spenser his most profound intellectual allegiances, including his typical syncretic belief that apparent intellectual opposites could be reconciled. According to the Neoplatonist model of reality, through his God-given power the poet creates 'another world' analogous to the way God himself created the world. The world is a rational universe created by a rational Creator who, in S. K. Heninger's words, followed the precepts of the Book of Wisdom, and made the universe 'according to number, weight, and measure'.[4]

The Neoplatonic affinities of Spenser's poetry is far more intense than with most Elizabethan poets. As Jon Quitslund has shown, the general interest in Platonism shown by Spenser's contemporaries is generally little more than a reverent and convenient lip service, a 'dilution of serious thought', but it did give their work a distinctively aesthetic aura which undermines the otherwise ubiquitous grey utilitarianism.[5] Their primary interest was in raiding Neoplatonism for compliments to the beauty of a mistress, or for tropes by which to express the enlightenment by which men might perceive God, or to make claims for the status of the poet as a prophetic articulator of truth, in Sidney's argument, as against the historian or philosopher or practical man of affairs. The poet can thus be presented as a creator, mediating between the world of transcendent forms and the brazen world of Nature. In the October Eclogue of *The Shepherdes Calender* and *The Tears of the Muses* Spenser combines neoplatonism and traditional Horatianism along with a Christian emphasis on divine inspiration.

We are now in a position to look specifically at the poetry written out of this contradictory amalgam of disparate intellectual traditions and cultural assumptions, about the time Spenser was starting his career in poetry, and which he was almost certainly familiar. Writing in the *Defence* of the stolidness of English poetry before Spenser's *Calender*, Sidney seems to be making an accurate judgement. Yet that view may not have been not Spenser's. He was, intellectually at any rate, in accord with such moralizing poets as Googe or Turberville who, writing as Spenser was starting his poetic apprenticeship, certainly saw pious and moral poetry as the natural outcome of the principles of humanist education. A poem for them is typically a well-modulated collection of sententiae. It is designed to show the universality of the human lot and to advance the moral and civic principles of the Tudor Protestant establishment. Like Spenser, too, these poets writing in mid century were by and large highly trained, public-minded public servants – statesmen, lawyers, scholars – who were primarily concerned with the pacification and reform of society and they directed their poetry (which was very much a minor part of their lives, and in that Spenser was to develop strikingly different ambitions) towards a readership of similar men. They shared the belief that poetry should inculcate an obedience to authority, a recognition of civic order, and could help reinforce doctrinal and moral stability. The quintessential didactic work of poetry – indeed the age's most ambitious poetical work before *The Faerie Queene* itself – which combined both the general moralistic caste of late medieval public poetry and the distinctive role of the new Protestant regime, was *A Mirror for Magistrates*. This was a collection of versified tragic tales taken from English history, first compiled by Thomas Baldwin under the reign of Mary, but not printed until 1559. It was very popular – perhaps the second most popular work of poetry (after Sternhold and Hopkins's lugubrious versifications of the *Psalms*, published in 1559) of the century. The *Mirror*'s authors included prominent nobles and courtiers, and the combination of medieval allegory, solemn moralistic tragedy, and public responsibility (all reinforced in a succession of additions) served the Elizabethan regime as a continually adapted reinforcement of its political aims. It went through nine editions by 1610, most with newly added tragedies 'all to be oftener read, and the better remembered' by 'the learned (for such all Magistrates are or should be)'. In the 1563 edition, written by one of Elizabeth's leading courtiers, Thomas Sackville, later Earl of Dorset, the figure of Sorrow appears and invites the reader to 'leave the playing, and the byter bale/ of worthy men, by Fortune overthrown', and after introducing a pageant of allegorical figures like Remorse, Maladie, and Warre, the first of those whose tales are to be told in the ensuing tragedies is introduced. The chronicle of tragedies taken as far as the War of the Roses. In the 1587 edition, the editor, Thomas Blennerhasset, included a tale of Uther Pendragon, taken from the Arthurian mythology on which Spenser was likewise drawing in *The Faerie Queene*, and in his introduction Blennerhasset described the additions as covering historical events 'from the conquest of Caeser unto the coming of Duke William the Conqueror'. The *Mirror* was a secular equivalent of the homilies that were read in churches each Sunday, giving detailed applications of its lessons, providing a 'mirror' for princes, governors, and soldiers. The collection was widely imitated, its basic formula adapted to other material, its political intent reinforced by many similar works. In contemplating writing *The Faerie Queene*, Spenser could clearly anticipate an audience accustomed to long moralistic epic.

The other poets King singles out as important in the emergence of Protestant poetry are today even less household (or even lecture-room) names than the *Mirror*, but these are the poets whose work lies behind, and in some cases alongside, Spenser's early writings. Luke Shepherd, for instance, was a popular gospeller and satirist, who wrote in rough Skeltonic verses and rambling alliterative verse. Robert Crowley was a printer and propagandist, who saw Langland's Piers Plowman (which he printed) as prophetic of the religious and social revolution of the time. Crowley's verse is awkward and rough, as in 'The Voyce of the Last Trumpet' which in thumping doggerel admonishes the godly:'Give easy awhyle/And marke my style/ You that hath wyt in store/For wyth wordes bare/ I wyll declare/ Thyngs done long time before'.[6] Nor should we forget the age's most popular work of poetry, the versification of the Psalms prepared for use in church by Sternhold and Hopkins, often known as the Old Version, the most famous of which is still to be heard in churches: 'Oh God our help in ages past /Our help in years to come: /Our shelter from the stormy blast / And our eternal home' (Psalm 100). The syntax of such poetry is generally wrenched, its idioms distorted, and its rhymes forced, in such masterpieces of bad taste as: 'Leave off therefore (saythe he) and know / I am a God most stout:

/ Among the heathen hye and low,/and all the earth throughout'.[7] Such verses, however unSpenserian they may sound, lead directly to the paraphrasical verse-tags at the head of each canto of *The Faerie Queene*.

With such poetry to choose from, it is not difficult to see why Protestant poetry, at least that written before Spenser's, has been neglected by modern readers. It is mainly versified Protestant and civic propaganda – moral commonplaces, precepts, encomia, epitaphs, expostulations on patriotism, moral dangers, or social evils, warnings against the dangers of life in court or the shortness of life in general. It is firmly in line with Ascham's requirement in *The Scholemaster* that literature 'gather examples' and 'give light and understanding' to good precepts.[8] But it is crucial to our understanding of the early phase of Spenser's literary life to set him in this dual context of mid-century 'theory' (if it can be dignified by that title) and practice. Writing as an earnest and politically ambitious Protestant loyalist, Spenser's early poems show not only the experimentation with stanzaic and metrical patterns that is characteristic of the 1560s and 1570s, but a similar taste for political allegory and moral didacticism. The poems he wrote before *The Shepheardes Calender* are still in the world of Googe and Turberville, and are closer in spirit to Crowley and the Old Version of the Psalms than Spenser's modern admirers like to admit. He may be a 'better' poet – more sensitive to tone and movement, more learned and more aware of multiple, especially politically well-placed, audiences – but Spenser was establishing himself within a recognizable tradition, as a serious Protestant poet. The publication of the *Calender* in 1579 is often seen as marking a turning-point in the age's poetry. But unlike *Astrophil and Stella*, the poem is not a courtly work: rather it continues in this tradition of the militant Protestant poets of mid century. The *Calender* is serious, moralistic, and satiric, all its elements incorporated into a firm Protestant didacticism. Spenser, in fact, was consistently indifferent to the Petrarchan fashions of his more courtly contemporaries. In part this was because he saw epic poetry as his ultimate poetic vocation, and the lyric as a diversion from his aims. As Helgerson points out, he was unique in his generation for presenting himself not as a courtly amateur but 'as a Poet, as a man who considered writing a duty rather than a distraction'.[9] But above all, he is self-consciously the Protestant Elizabethan regime's servant, in his poetry as much as he was (at that time) hoping to become in his political career.

EARLY POEMS

Discussions of Spenser's poetical career usually commence with his bursting onto the scene with *The Shepherdes Calender* in 1579. But we miss the direction and the careful, even precocious, preparation for his poetic vocation if we omit his poems of the decade before. In 1569 was published his translation of a series of illustrated poems by a Dutch Calvinist, Jan van der Noot, *A theatre wherein be represented as well the miseries and calamities that follow the voluptuous Worldlings, As also the greate joyes and pleasures which the faithfull do enjoy*. It is usually known as *A Theatre for Worldlings*. Spenser translated the sonnets and epigrams in this work from what is a lugubriously solemn collection of Protestant polemic, based on translations of Petrarch by the French Protestants Marot and du Bellay. He possibly undertook the translation as a school exercise, since it must have been done around the time he was ready to graduate from Merchant Taylors. In addition to the pious sentiments, what is noticeable about the translations is the way Spenser uses the occasion – acting very much like other mid-century poets – to experiment with various verse forms. He put four epigrams into rhyming twelve lines of iambic pentameter, and two others as fourteen-line 'Shakespearean' sonnets. What the original terms 'sonnets' he puts into blank verse, as if he were aware of the humanist desire to invent poetic forms equivalent to the Neoclassical forms that would no doubt have been approved by his schoolmasters.

Much later in his life, in 1591, revised versions of these poems appeared in the miscellaneous volume Spenser entitled *Complaints*. There they were described as *The Visions of Petrarch, formerly translated*, and *The Visions of Bellay*. The *Complaints* volume includes a variety of poems, some composed much earlier, others very close to the date of publication. Some of the early poems are clearly apprentice pieces, even though, twenty years later, they have been revised: much had happened in Elizabethan poetry between 1569 and the 1590s, some of it pioneered by Spenser himself, and in their later revisions the poems are rhetorically more sophisticated. But they retain their original didactic goals: the preface describes the volume as 'complaints and meditations of the worlds vanitie, verie grave and profitable'. The complaint was a poetic form that drew on medieval and Reformation didacticism, and was the poetic equivalent of the admonitions of sermon or homily. Typically, it moralized on such typical vicissitudes of worldly life as unrequited love, the unpredictability of fortune, and the miseries of mankind's fallen state. Like the long, moralistic verse narratives of the *Mirror*, the poems in *Complaints* focused on the unpredictability of the lives of princes and the need to abandon the temptations of the world.

Early in his career, then, as he was struggling to find a voice among the poetic experiments of the mid century, Spenser turned to these French and Italian poems with a classical setting, and, as Margaret Ferguson notes, 'used the discipline of translation to define himself against as well as through the voice of his French Catholic original'. The use of du Bellay is especially interesting: he was a Catholic but, Spenser must have recognized, also concerned to unite Classical and Christian modes of thinking through the medium of poetry. But where du Bellay is deeply pessimistic about Rome's fall and the lessons later civilizations might learn, and gloomy about the prospects of even high poetry achieving later fame, Spenser counters with an envoy in which he praises du Bellay himself, and then turns for even higher praise to the figure of the French Protestant du Bartas, whose 'heavenly muse' aimed at 'th'Almightie to adore'. As Ferguson comments, 'du Bellay's project of reviving the pagan Roman spirits may need to be supplemented – if not directly opposed – by faith in the Christian God and his promise of immortality for believers'.[10] The subject of all these poems is the vanity and unpredictability of human life. *Visions of Bellay* consists of fifteen sonnets dealing with the fall of Rome, displaying 'this worlds inconstancies', and proving that 'all is nought but flying vanitie'. The brilliant monuments of Rome have decayed, its symbols of beauty and triumph lie neglected or destroyed. *The Visions of Petrarch* is more personally focused, though once again the focus is on the 'vaine worlds glorie'. Based on some of Petrarch's sonnets on the death of Laura – by way of Marot – they use some vivid metaphors for disaster and contingency in human life.

The original versions of Spenser's *Bellay* and *Petrarch* date from the late 1560s; also collected in *Complaints* are three more substantial poems, two of them translations, that probably were originally written in the late 1570s, about the time Spenser was composing the *Calender*. Here too, he showed himself a serious experimenter with the growing technical possibilities of English verse, displaying a developing interest in emblematic and allegorical methods of fixing meaning, and above all, a commitment to what he conceived as the serious vocation of the Protestant poet. *Ruines of Rome* is another meditation on Rome's decay. A translation of a sonnet sequence by du Bellay, whose broodings over Rome were among the most pervasive of the Renaissance – Spenser returned often in his career to them, and it is clear that what Shakespeare in his sonnets termed his 'war' against time was also deeply affected by them – these poems focused on the inexplicability and, at times, despair before the inevitability of time's destruction of all human attempts to build something permanent, whether on a personal level or in civilization. This force is what Spenser calls, in *The Faerie Queene*, 'mutability'. I shall take up Spenser's obsession with time and mutability (which was certainly not atypical among Elizabethan poets or, for that matter, ordinary men and women in the period) in Chapter 6.

Another poem in the *Complaints* volume that was most likely written early, also perhaps around the same time as *The Shepheardes Calender*, was *Virgil's Gnat*, a translation of what was thought to be an early pastoral poem of Virgil's. A shepherd kills a gnat that is trying to warn him against a poisonous snake; the gnat's ghost comes to him in a dream and upbraids him for his hasty ingratitude. Spenser's tidy translation adds some typical moralizations, but is generally a little more than a playful workshop exercise in which some political intrigue and gossip are mentioned. There may be a reference to his being sent to Ireland:

> I carried am into waste wildernesse,
> Waste wildernes, amongst *Cymerian* shades,
> Where endles paines and hideous heavinesse
> Is round about me heapt in darksome glades.
>
> (*SP*, p. 313)

As Rambuss points out, the poem is dedicated to Leicester, described as 'the causer of my care' (prefatory sonnet, l. 2), and he insists that the poem – or, at least, perhaps, its right meaning, is for Leicester's eyes alone. But any references to Spenser's relations with Leicester or to his career seem highly unsystematic, and the cryptic secrets that Rambuss suggests lie in the poem amount to little more than the assertion of the importance of secrecy (and, by extension, privileged information) itself.[11]

The last of the poems collected in *Complaints* and also probably written ten or more years earlier, is *Prosopopoia, or Mother Hubbard's Tale*, which is a more substantial piece of work than those at which I have glanced, and directly related to Spenser's political as well as his poetical aspirations. In the dedication to the 1591 volume, he writes of the poem as 'long sithens composed in the raw conceipt of my youth', and it clearly grows from the events of his years in London, when he was searching for some court position. It starts as an account of romantic and chivalric tales:

> Some tolde of Ladies, and their Paramoures;
> Some of brave Knights, and their renowned Squires;
> Some of the Faeries and their strange attires;
> And of the Giaunts hard to be beleeved.
>
> (*SP*, p. 336)

But quickly the poem becomes a satiric fable of the adventures of a fox and an ape, each of four parts satirizing the four estates. The opening section shows how a simple rural 'husbandman' is cheated of his flock of sheep by the exploitative and greedy pair. In the second part, the fox and ape are disguised as clerks, become first beggars and then a parish priest and his assistant. The situation allows Spenser to indulge in some fairly blatant anti-Catholic satire. The third episode shifts the satiric focus to the court, where the pair become courtiers and expose the hypocrisy and deceit at court. The fourth episode involves a more elaborate political satire: the fox and ape steal a lion's crown and regalia and agree to divide political power, the ape wearing the trappings of royalty, and the fox actually exercising power. Here Spenser anticipates some of the material he will include in *The Faerie Queene*. The fox harks back to a golden age in which property was more equably divided as opposed to the corruption of the present in which 'without golde now nothing wilbe got'. The fox and the ape vow to 'walke about the world at pleasure/Like two free men' (ll. 153, 159–60), sentiments hardly designed to appeal to Spenser's political loyalties – and yet at least implicit in the individualistic tendencies of Protestantism. The fox's sentiments on property are echoed in *The Faerie Queene*, book five, by a naively egalitarian Giant, related to one of the giants here mentioned as 'hard to be beleeved'. They exploit the whole kingdom at will until the gods are alerted. 'High Jove, in whose almightie hand / The care of Kings, and power of Empires stand' despatches Mercury to unmask the pair. Their 'tailes' (and, one might add, their 'tales') are 'utterlie bereft' (l. 1384).

The title, *Prosopopeia*, is a rhetorical term that means, Puttenham explains, 'counterfait impersonation',[12] and the poem is full of political references to events in the late 1570s, when the Leicester circle, which included Sidney and with which Spenser had some connection by virtue of his employment, was battling for control over the queen's policies, against the more moderate Burghley, who may be satirized by Spenser in the figure of the fox. There may be some references to Burghley's support for the queen's short-lived proposal to marry the French Duc d'Alençon, an alliance strongly supported by the French ambassador Simier, who was referred to by Elizabeth as her 'ape', and bitterly opposed by Leicester, Sidney and their circle. Such references seem to have landed the poet in some trouble: a number of contemporary remarks suggest that the work was banned or 'called in' and it was omitted from Spenser's collected works of 1611, when Burghley's son, the Earl of Salisbury, was still alive, and only added in the edition of the following year, after his death. None of these early poems constitutes much of a case for Spenser's being regarded as any better than a dozen or more minor poets of the 1560s and 1570s. What they demonstrate – *Mother Hubbards Tale* in particular – is their author's unswerving commitment to the Protestant cause in religion and politics, and to furthering his career in their service. He has set himself for a career at court, and clearly saw his developing poetic gifts as part of that commitment.

If we pause over these minor pieces – only in hindsight could we see them as the apprentice pieces of someone who was to become a master poet – what emerges from them are the commonplaces of Protestant theology and a determination to find a place for his vocation as a poet within that vocation. There is, for instance, is a firm and seemingly unwavering belief that 'mutability', the insistent subject of Bellay's and Petrarch's sonnets, can be understood only in the context of the Christian doctrine of Providence. Time, mutability and contingency are interconnected subjects that stayed at the forefront of Spenser's obsessions throughout his career. To analyze the modifications of the ways in which he handled what in *The Faerie Queene* he termed the 'great enemy', Time, is, in fact, not only to point to one of Spenser's recurring obsessions but to chart a significant shift in the intellectual history of the age.

The key to the traditional Christian interpretation of time's nature and meaning is the doctrine of Providence. According to the dominant medieval theological tradition from Augustine to Aquinas, and well beyond, Providence is 'the divine plan of the order of all things, foreordained towards an end', operating either directly or through the free will of intermediaries which exist by God's abundance of goodness, in order that the dignity of causality may be imputed even to God's creation. By such a view, causality should not be so exclusively attributed to divine power as to abolish the causality belonging to creatures, especially to humans. Thus the dominant medieval emphasis, as represented by Aquinas, is on a doctrine of 'general' as opposed to 'particular' or 'special' Providence. Calvin's disciple John Veron, however, reviewing the various theories of Providence extant in the sixteenth-century, rejects the medieval theory of God's 'generall ruledome' over events which makes God ruler 'onelye in name and not in deede', and, returning to the great medieval mastermind of the reformation, Augustine's doctrine of double predestination, claims instead that God possesses the 'whole governemente of al thynges, bothe in heaven and in the earth'. For Calvin and Reformation theologians generally, Aquinas's doctrine made God the ruler of the world 'in name onely and not in dede . . . because it taketh from him the government of it'.

Such an emphasis, which was commonplace in Reformed theology, is remarkable on two main grounds: for its rejection of the dominant medieval 'general' doctrine of Providence, and for the way an emphasis on God's 'special' Providence is expressed in their treatment of the nature and meaning of time. Rather than a smooth sequential unfolding of God's general government of the universe, time becomes a series of disconnected revelations from God, with each moment of time a new and apparently arbitrary creation. Whereas in Aquinas' doctrine of general Providence God is said to allow certain natural events to happen fortuitously, Calvin eradicates any sense of fortuitousness so that every event, even the falling of a tree, is caused directly by God. God's sovereign will, argues Calvin, upholds and directs all temporal events, and man's role is to inexorably advance His glory. Believers, Calvin claims, 'would rather that the whole world should perish than that any part of God's glory should be lost'.[13] It was such a degree of revolutionary fervor that animated Spenser's theological commitments in his early poems, and which emerges strongly in the temporal pattern of *The Shepheardes Calender*.

THE SHEPHEARDES CALENDER

'Eclogues', Puttenham writes, in his taxonomy of poetical kinds, were poems which 'in base and humble stile . . . uttered the private and familiar talke of the meanest sort of men', using 'the vaile of homely persons to insinuate and glaunce matters'.[14] The propagandist intent of a didactic poem like the translations of du Bellay or *Mother Hubbards Tale* is clear enough; much more discrete and yet far more powerful are the didactic uses to which Spenser put the seemingly harmless escapism of the pastoral in the *Calender*. We may see this by concentrating on a major absence in most Elizabethan pastoral literature: the lack of connection, except in the most general and predominantly literary terms, with the economic and social realities of the countryside itself. Ironically, what is *not* found in Elizabethan pastorals, especially those that had as their primary audiences members of the court, are the real conditions of Elizabethan country life, which was, especially from mid century on, passing through disruptive and painful transitions as land was appropriated and exploited by such great families as the Sidneys or the Herberts. In the placid, sophisticated world of Elizabethan pastoral disturbances that might point to the real, material conditions of the countryside, or to the interelations of court and country – except in the most idealistic terms – rarely occur. Hardship is predominantly depicted in universal terms. Weather may be foul, the shepherd's life hard, but such hardships are in the nature of things and in no way attributable to underlying economic realities, class antagonisms, or (once Spenser moves the pastoral mode of his poetry to Ireland) colonial exploitation. As Louis Montrose has shown, the pastoral makes the 'country' presentable for service in the 'court,' and the shepherd-poet's plaints, however disguised, are the loyal expression of political aspirations.[15] This is the case even when the pastoral is used for satire. Later in his life, in *Colin Clouts Come Home Again* (1591), Spenser attacks court corruption, while praising the Queen and the noble ladies around her; within what he terms 'this simple pastorall' both sycophantic praise and stern moral satire coexist, and in this uneasy juxtaposition of flattery and satire we encounter pleas for personal advancement along with condemnation of those who seek 'with malice and with strife/To thrust downe other' and 'himselfe to raise'. Returning to his plantation in Ireland, Spenser is looking back at England, and sternly rebukes the court, but the poem is still motivated by his desire to advance in its good graces. Such tensions – the largely unacknowledged gaps and repressions of the poem – are among those that typically dislocate much of Spenser's poetry of the 1590s including, most importantly, the final books of his epic.

It was in the *Shepheardes Calender* that Spenser first announced himself as a poet in the pastoral mode. The 'new poet' appeared for the first time independently in print in 1579, anonymously, under the imprint of the Protestant printer Hugh Singleton, who issued a book entitled *the Shepperdes Calender conteyninge xii ecloges proportionable to the xii monthes*. Later editions were to appear in 1581, 1586, 1591 and 1597, and the work appeared in the 1611 collected edition. It was elaborately introduced, as if the author and some of his friends and associates were aware of the remarkable quality of the work alongside most poetry of the time. The author, signing himself 'Immerito' (he who is unworthy) contributes a dedicatory poem:

> Goe little booke: thy selfe present,
> As child whose parent is unkent:
> To him that is the president
> Of noblesse and of chevalree.

The work is dedicated to Sidney – which certainly reinforces Spenser's allegiances to and his aspirations to be noticed or employed by the Sidney/Leicester Circle. I noted in the opening chapter that Spenser's direct contacts with Sidney himself may have been minimal. What was Sidney's opinion of Spenser? The *Calender* is, in fact, the only contemporary work Sidney mentions approvingly in the *Defence*. 'The Shepherds' Calendar hath much poetry in his eclogues', he notes in his thumbnail sketch of English poetry. It is 'indeed worthy the reading, if I be not deceived'. The vagueness of the remark suggests that Sidney may have only skimmed Spenser's poem: as Heninger notes, Sidney did not even mention Spenser as the author of the poem, and his comments have a 'curiously detached air'. What does he mean by 'hath much poetry in it', as if it had something other than 'poetry'? Heninger shrewdly notes that Sidney's focus on the fictive or 'imaginative' aspects of a poem might lead him to respond well to the monologues, dialogues, and fables, but overall while 'he is as generous as possible', Heninger speculates, 'there's disappointment . . . that so many other things distract from the poetry – such as, probably, the fuss over metrical patterns, and perhaps even the obtrusive calendar form'.[16]

The dedicatory poem is followed by an epistle dedicatory to Spenser's friend Gabriel Harvey, signed by one E. K. This 'person' may be a friend of the author, perhaps (as was long thought) Edmund Kirke, a fellow student at Cambridge; but, far more likely, E. K. is a pseudonym for Spenser himself or a composite of Spenser and

Harvey. In any case, what E. K. calls 'this our new Poete' is hailed for reviving 'good and naturall English words' and for launching his poetic career with a pastoral, 'as young birdes, that be newly crept out of the nest, by little first to prove theyr tender wyngs, before they make a greater flyght. So flew Theocritus . . . So flew Virgil . . . So finally flyeth this our new Poete, as a bird, whose principals be scarce growen out, but yet as that in time shall be hable to keep wing with the best'. The poem's setting is the changing seasons, month by month, of an anglicized classical landscape, complete with the trappings of classical pastoral poems, such as Virgil's *Georgics*: shepherds, meadows, fountains, bewailing lovers, music (especially the pipes), hymns, singing competitions, allusions to current political events and personalities, and references to what are seen as universal human patterns and problems. The *Calender's* form reflects the order of seasonal universe: twelve eclogues correspond to the twelve months, and Colin Clout, the lover-poet-priest figure, is the center, human and poetic, of the poem's round of seasonal and cosmic experiences, and in some of the eclogues seems to articulate Spenser's developing and sometimes conflicting views on poetry. Colin Clout is, therefore, not simply an everyman, but more precisely, every poet. But though the pastoral landscape may vary according to the weather and seasons, and be populated by suffering shepherds, there is no sense of a locale other than that of the genre: if Spenser was aware of the sharp satiric particularity of the English medieval pastoral, Piers Plowman, which draws very particular attention to the economic and social injustices of England, he chooses a very different use of the pastoral.

E. K., whoever he is, certainly shares Spenser's anxiety about directing the poem's readers to a 'right' reading. He claims that he 'was made privie to' the author's 'counsell and secret meaning' in the eclogues, 'as also', he adds, as if in confidence, 'in sundry other works of his'. It is possibly E. K. also who contributes a short essay on 'The generall argument of the whole Booke'. To further underline the 'right' reading, each of the poem's twelve eclogues has both a woodcut illustrating the subject of the eclogue, a prose 'argument', one or more verbal tags or 'emblemes' at the end, detailed glosses on both the texts of the poems and the verbal tags. There is also a brief verse epilogue. The emblems are of special interest, not least because, like the glosses, they are means by which the poet could help to direct (or in some cases, misdirect) the poem's readers to either particular or general meanings. Thus Colin's emblem, in January, points to the Christian symbol of the anchor as hope; November's, an adaption of the personal motto of Clement Marot, suggests Spenser's own poetical and religious ambitions; and the emblem to the epilogue, 'Merce non mercede' (grace not wages), stresses that poetic inspiration and perhaps human truths generally are the product of divine grace, not human rewards.

The emblems, commentaries and glosses have tantalized and sometimes irritated readers. They mix literary, moral, and theological references, thus displaying the author's learning and intellectual allegiances, and provide Spenser (assuming that he had at least some part in writing them) with the opportunity to do a number of things: not only to display his learning and his dedication to poetic tradition, but to demonstrate his political principles and his religious commitments, and above all to direct his readers' interpretations. Sometimes when these different allegiances threaten to contradict one another, they also provide him a means of making his priorities clear: as in the gloss to the emblem of 'February', when we are firmly told that Jupiter is a false God; or in the gloss to May, line 54, that Pan signifies Christ, who is 'the onely and very Pan'. On May, line 247, we are informed that 'Sweete S. Charitie' is a common Catholic oath, but that Catholics may have 'charitye alwayes in their mouth, and sometime in their outward Actions, but never inwardly in fayth and godly zeale'. The September eclogue makes Spenser's theological agenda most explicit: it attacks corrupt clergy, the secret Catholic infiltration of England, and politicians who prefer comfort to thorough religious reform. A number of readers have objected that the glosses make over-explicit or simplify what in the body of the poem is more balanced or subtle. Such objections show precisely the dilemma of the Protestant poet, one to which Spenser was sensitive all his career: the more that is left to the reader's own participation, the more he or she may be drawn in and 'moved,' to use Sidney's phrase, but also the more likely that there could be misreadings.

As well as making clear his religious and political allegiances, Spenser uses the *Calender* to set forth his own literary ambitions. In the April and October eclogues both verse and commentary make it clear that he is setting forth a manifesto for his own poetry. In April, we are told the hymn that Colin Clout, 'the Southerne shepheardes boy' – so-called most probably because Spenser was at the time working as secretary to the Bishop of Rochester – has composed for Eliza, the queen of the shepherds. In October, he focuses on the social responsibilities of the poet. Even though both Cuddie, 'the

perfect paterne of a poet', and his friend Piers complains about
the neglect of poetry – 'O pierlesse Poesye, where is then thy place?/
If not in Princes pallace thou doe sitt:/And yet is Princes pallace the
most fitt' – the true poet has no choice: his calling is to be within the
public world, criticizing, celebrating, offering counsel and wisdom.
As E. K.'s gloss claims, somewhat optimistically, 'such honor have
Poetes always found in the sight of princes and noble men'. His
gloss may seem somewhat optimistic, but it does point to the coterie
nature of court poetry, and especially, as Goldberg indicates, to the
homosocial basis of power and patronage at the time. The opening
eclogue contains some coy jokes about the unresponsivenes of
Rosalind by comparison with the warmth of Hobbinol. E. K.'s gloss,
sternly discoursing against 'disorderly love' but praising that what
Goldberg terms 'a proper pederasty': 'And so is paederastice much
to be praeferred before gynerastice, that is the love whiche enflamet
men with lust toward woman kind'. Hobbinol, we are told, stands
for Harvey, and clearly, Spenser's friendship with Harvey had many
dimensions to it – political, affective, literary.[17]

   Commentators have often pointed out how simplistic the glosses
are alongside the poem, where often the theological or moral issues
seem to be not so absolute. But that is to misunderstand the rhetorical differences between poetry and prose commentary. The poem is
designed, as Sidney put it, to delight, but in order to 'move' its
readers to take the moral easily, it must provide what Sidney calls a
'medicine of cherries'.[18] The glosses, however, are designed to be
medicine unmixed with any cherries: they are there as antidotes for
any possible mistaken reading. Spenser himself would not have seen
the contradiction between the poet and the commentator, and insisted that each complements the other. But, especially given Spenser's
later career, we can certainly pause over the contradiction between
the evocative poet and the politically correct commentator. The two
voices of the *Calender* are the same that throughout Spenser's career
fought for mastery; they are the voices of the optimistic, courtly
Sidney for whom man's 'erected wit' might inspire men to seek and
discover goodness, and the Protestant Sidney, for whom the 'infected will' undermines every possibility of attaining that goodness.

   I will briefly summarize each eclogue. January is a brief, slightly
sentimental opening to the sequence, as the lovesick shepherd Colin
bewails the loss of his love Rosalind, the dreariness of the month
reflecting his own emotional deprivation. The 'barrein ground' and
'naked trees' reflect his feelings as well as the season:

All as the Sheepe, such was the shepeheardes looke,
For pale and wanne he was, (alas the while)
May seeme he lovd, or els some care he tooke:
Well couth he tune his pipe, and frame his stile . . .

January provides an easy introduction to the more complex eclogues
that follow. Its gloss sets up an identification between Colin and
the poet, but the unattainable object of the shepherd's affections,
Rosalind, who recurs throughout the poem, is almost certainly, at
least in this eclogue, no more than an idealized figure, with no
specific historical reference. February, 'morall and generall' we are
informed, is a dialogue between Thenot, an old shepherd, and Cuddie,
a shepherd boy. Thenot tells the old tale of the oak and the briar to
point to corruption and ambition in court or church. The oak

> had bene an auncient tree,
> Sacred with many a mysteree,
> And often crost with the priestes crewe,
> And often halowed with holy water dewe.
> But sike fancies weren foolerie . . .

In addition to this specific reference to Catholic superstition, the
complaint is also expressed in more general terms: 'For Youngth is a
bubble blown up with breath,/Whose witt is weakenesse, whose
wage is death'. March is another dialogue between two shepherds,
Thomalin and Willye, on 'the delights of Love, wherein wanton
youth walloweth', while April returns to the lovesick Colin's unrequited love: Hobbinol (who stands for Harvey) tells Thenot that
Colin has broken his pipes and will sing no more, but in order to
show the grieving shepherd's skill, recites Colin's elaborate and
fulsome panegyric of 'fayre Eliza, Queene of shepheardes all'. In
Maye, Spenser's theological agenda becomes more explicit: playing
on the traditional equation of the shepherd with the pastor, he contrasts the ascetic dedication of the Protestant with the lax hypocrisy
of the Catholic. The moral is underlined by a retelling of the old tale
of the fox and the kid. The kid is deceived by the fox:

> . . . for he nould warned be
> Of craft, coloured with simplicitie:
> And such end perdie does all hem remayne,
> That of such falsers freendship bene fayne.

'By the Foxe', we are informed in the gloss, is meant 'the false and faithlesse Papistes, to whom no credit is to be given, nor felowshippe to be used'. The 'morall of the whole tale', a gloss on the ending insists, 'is to warne the protestant beware, howe he geveth credit to the unfaythfull Catholique'.

June returns to the lovelorn Colin, who shares a dialogue with Hobbinol about his unsuccessful love and his discontent about his poetic vocation. In this eclogue, Colin's love, Rosalind, seems to represent the queen, and Menalcas, his rival in love, perhaps Alençon, the queen's French suitor, whose possible marriage to Elizabeth was highly disturbing to the Leicester/Sidney Circle. July is also a dialogue, between Morrell and Thomalin, and is written in part in a style that links Spenser closely with his predecessors like Googe, Whythorne or the Old Version of the Psalms:

> O blessed sheepe, O shepheard great,
> that bought his flocke so deare,
> And them did save with bloudy sweat
> from Wolves, that would them teare.

Once again the eclogue refers to current politics, this time to the state of the church: the two participants are thinly disguised representations of Bishop Aylmer of London, who was notoriously anti-Puritan, and Bishop Cooper of Lincoln; while Algrind, for whom both Morrell and Thomalin express support, is Archbishop Grindal, who in 1575 had been censured by the queen for refusing to prosecute Protestant 'prophecyings'. August, however, is less obviously an intervention in current affairs. It is a singing match between Willye and Perigot, allowing Spenser (or his persona, Colin) the opportunity to display some dazzling adeptness in poetic styles. By contrast, September is once again highly polemical. It brings in not only references to Harvey, but Bishop Davies of St David's (Diggon) and Bishop Young of Rochester (Ruffy); its subject is church corruption, and the threat of Catholic resurgence:

> Never was Woolfe seene many nor some,
> Nor in all Kent, nor in Christendome:
> But the fewer Woolves (the soth to sayne)
> The more bene the Foxes that here remaine.

> . . . they gang in more secrete wise,
> And with sheepes clothing doen hem disguise,
> They walke not widely as they were wont
> For feare of raungers, and the great hunt . . .

The eclogue also deals with the neglect of the church by high-placed officials, who represent Burghley and Leicester. E. K.'s glosses produce an appropriate smokescreen – Spenser was, after all, dependent on the Leicester connection at the time – by expressing ignorance of some of the meanings, as when on the story of Ruffy (patently Spenser's employer, the Bishop of Rochester), he states 'This tale of Roffy seemeth to coloure some particular Action of his. But what, I certeinlye know not'.

October is the most explicit treatment of Colin's poetic ambitions. Piers and Cuddie debate the poet's social responsibilities. Poetry 'little good hath got, and much lesse gaine', and generous patrons seem to be lacking:

> But ah Mecœnus is yclad in claye,
> And great *Augustus* long ygoe is dead:
> And all the worthies liggen wrapt in leade,
> That matter made for Poets on to play

The poet's vocation is to give moral counsel. Piers asks:

> O pierlesse Poesye, where is then thy place?
> If nor in Princes pallace thou doe sit:
> (And yet is Princes pallace the most fitt)
> Ne brest of baser birth doth thee embrace.

In November, Thenot and Colin debate the loss of youth and beauty; Colin sings a dirge in honor of the lady Dido, whose identity is difficult to establish, however appropriate for the month her death might be. The eclogue's emblem underlines the Christian moral: 'For though the trespase of the first man brought death into the world, as the guerdon of sinne, yet being overcome by the death of one, that dyed for al, it is now made (as Chaucer sayth) the grene path way to lyfe. So that it agreeth well with that was sayd, that Death byteth not (that is) hurteth not at all.' December is likewise sombre, a hymn by Colin to the god Pan, and a repetition of his complaint about the loss of Rosalind's love. It is followed by an epilogue to the whole *Calender*, in which Spenser sends his poem out into the world, confident in its power – even though he modestly denies (as yet) matching Chaucer or the author of *Piers Plowman*:

> Loe I have made a Calender for every yeare,
> That steele in strength, and time in durance shall outweare:
> And if I marked well the starres revolution,
>   It shall continewe till the worlds dissolution.
> To teach the ruder shepheard how to feede his sheepe,
> And from the falsers fraud his folded flocke to keepe.
>   Goe lyttle Calender, thou hast a free passeporte,
> Goe but a lowly gate emongste the meaner sorte.
> Dare not to match thy pype with Tityrus hys style,
>   Nor with the Pilgrim that the Ploughman playde a whyle:
> But folowe them farre off, and their high steppes adore,
> The better please, the worse despise, I aske nomore.

Spenser was clearly very confident in the quality of his poem and in the impact the *Calender* would have. The roles of poet, pastor, and committed Protestant propagandist are firmly held together. The poem is written with a gusto and rhetorical confidence that marks the rising young poet, confident in attracting the attention or even the support of an influential group of patrons who will appreciate his gifts, not simply as an entertainer, but as a committed contributor to a common social, political and religious agenda. Even though much of the poem is cast in terms of universals – notably the monthly and seasonal patterns, what is presented as the eternal battle of good and evil, and the recurring contrast of Edenic innocence and the fallen human world – the poem has very specific connections to the world in which Spenser was setting out on his intertwined careers as poet and public servant. Helgerson, as I have noted, argues that Spenser is the first post-Reformation poet to consider writing as a politically useful vocation, and that we can see already a tension between the love poet and the prophetic or propagandist poet. There is no doubt that Spenser wants to take both parts of this dual vocation seriously, and at this point in his career he certainly saw no incompatibility. As we read back from later points in his literary life, we may well see the shadows of later fissures. But when it appeared, *The Shepheardes Calender* must have gratified both the poet and those among his patrons and supporters who cared about poetry. Whether, of course, there were many of those is another question, and one that will loom larger over Spenser's later career.

4

'Consorted in one Harmonee': *The Faerie Queene*, 1590, Books One to Three

In 1590 the first three books of *The Faerie Queene* were published. It was not only the culmination of its author's literary life but arguably, more than any other poem of its age, epitomizes the ambitions, failures and contradictions of the Elizabethan political and religious establishment and its poetry. In 1596 the poem was reissued, with some revisions, including a major change made to the ending the poem had been given in 1590, and with three additional books. The contradictions of both the poem and the age are especially evident in the books added in 1596, which will be the topic of the following chapter; in the 1590 *Faerie Queene*, despite what in retrospect can also be seen as major intellectual contradictions, there is a buoyancy and confidence about the role of poetry (and Spenser's own career as a poet) within the Elizabethan court, the English state, and within Spenser's life itself that the second group of three books blur. Like the *Shepheardes Calender*, which launched Spenser's career as a poet, the 1590 *Faerie Queene* is a product of a confidence that art can, without an loss of integrity, become a 'work of state', that a poet may pursue his literary vocation as well as being recognized as central to the well-being of the society. In this chapter, I will first consider the production of *The Faerie Queene* as a whole: the ways in which it responded to the demands not only of genre and poetic tradition, but of occasion, as Spenser considered his career and the role of the poet in the Elizabethan court, and then focus specifically on the books published in 1590.

The Faerie Queene was, very self-consciously, an attempt to write a great epic poem – for Elizabeth, for England, for Spenser himself, and also for the glory of English poetry. Those goals in themselves no doubt did not appear to be contradictory in Spenser's view of his own literary life, as he completed the *Calender* and, probably quite soon after, considered in detail the plan for what would be his epic. But as the next decade unfolded, an enormous fissure appears to have opened between the 'personal' and the 'public' roles and responsibilities that Spenser took on, which makes the largeness of the claims he makes for his epic and his epic ambitions all the more intriguing. Indeed, of all the age's poetry, *The Faerie Queene* is at once the most grandiose in its claims for wholeness of vision and at the same time the most dislocated and disrupted. To speak of 'contradictions' or 'dislocations' is, of course, not to play down a poem's importance or, to use the traditional term, its 'greatness'. Spenser's epic is the most important single poem of the early modern period – and one of the most intriguing in our literary history – precisely because it brings so compellingly to our attention the conflicting voices by and against which it was written; it allows us more richly than any other poem of the age to construct those voices which spoke so powerfully in support of the Elizabethan regime. Part of the 'greatness' of *The Faerie Queene* is not that it is triumphantly complete or all-encompassing, but that it emerges in a cultural space radically crossed by impulses and structures which it vainly tries to discipline, and which over and over at key moments in its unfolding, articulate the ideological struggles of late Elizabethan society, not the least of which was the place of poetry in that society.

As we have seen, Spenser's epic ambitions were announced in the epilogue to the *Calender*. It may be that he was working on what became *The Faerie Queene* as he finished that work. In one of Harvey's letters there is a reference to 'your *Faerie Queene*', and a comparison with Orlando Furioso which, Harvey comments, 'you wil needes seeme to emulate, and hope to overgo'. So *The Faerie Queene* may have been taking its earliest shape at least as early as the time Sidney was experimenting with *Astrophil and Stella* and writing the *Defence of Poetry*. By the mid 1580s, parts of the poem were circulating in England; in 1589 Spenser journeyed from his plantation in Ireland to be presented at court by Sir Walter Ralegh. In 1590 the first three books were published, and the following year Spenser was rewarded by the Queen by a lifetime pension of fifty pounds a year. So the poem was written not in the court that it was intended to celebrate, but in Ireland. As Spenser served the Elizabethan regime, accompanying Grey's forces in their series of brutal, even genocidal, attacks on the Irish; as the English invaders' scorched earth and ethnic cleansing policies took effect; as English settlers, including Spenser himself, moved into lands taken from the Irish in Munster and elsewhere, he was writing and assembling what became the Books of Holiness, Temperance, Chastity, and (although they were not published until 1596) parts of the Books of Friendship and Justice – where Spenser's vigorous defence of the English colonization of Ireland comes most explicitly to the surface – and Courtesy.

Traditional Spenser criticism – characterized for the most part by what Goldberg, following Barthes, terms 'theological' readings of both Spenser's life and works – has not always acknowledged that the poem could have been affected so intimately by the place where and the circumstances under which it was written. Spenser couches much of his poem in terms of universals, and much traditional Spenser criticism has assumed likewise that the poem 'in some way . . . gains stability and order from replicating verbally the assumed harmony of the universe' it works to valorize.[1] The case for such a view of the poem is certainly at its strongest in the opening three books. There is a sureness of touch, a confidence that poetic vision is replicated in the order of the state and the cosmos generally, and in the integrity, even the irrefutability, of the vision the poem wants to embody.

We need therefore, in fairness, to ask initially: what vision is it that Spenser himself wants – at least when he first planned and wrote the poem and probably throughout the writing of at least the first book – his 'right' reader to gain. I use the archaic word 'vision' advisedly, precisely because the poem is designed to exemplify a poetic and a metaphysic of stasis; ultimately the poem does try to reproduce the ideological universe of which it is a constituent part. But the material conditions of the poem's production – including the place in which it was written as well as the recurring issues of race, class, gender and agency that provided the conditions for the poem's writing – provided the material for the cultural unconscious underlying Spenser's writing of the poem, and a set of identifiable connections between the poem and the life Spenser was leading while he wrote it emerge, often despite his wishes.

The vision which Spenser's 'right' reader is asked to embrace is essentially in continuity with that of his early poems. Throughout these early books, Spenser's militant Protestant humanism is insistently foregrounded. Book One, the Book of Holiness, is built on a theologically cautious but firm outline of the Reformed doctrines of justification by faith, the division of mankind into those chosen by

God to be saved (the elect) and to be damned (the reprobate), and the quest to find true salvation. While Spenser does not write as a systematic theologian, the theological implications of the poem are in accord with those of the moderate left wing of the Elizabethan Church on such doctrines as Providence, Predestination, the Fall, Grace, Free Will and Election. Men and women are created by God as elect or reprobate, and all history is equally set under the judgement of the Word of God, and so some people or nations are likewise chosen as elect and reprobate. The allegory is directed to demonstrating God's purposes through his chosen people, individually and collectively. Later books play down such explicit theologizing, but when Book One was written, Spenser's theological allegiances are very clear.

Similarly clear is the intention, often announced quite explicitly, of the poem as a celebration of the universe's manifestation of harmony. It is built upon the traditional belief that reality is indivisible, and embraces the whole of creation. The different facets of an indivisible reality, which is often represented in the poem as a dance, circle, or pageant, or in emblems of reciprocity, symmetry, and harmony, are expressed in the structure of the whole poem – in the parallel and symmetrical quests of the knights with their 'like' races 'to run', the graceful and continuous replenishment of the world from the Garden of Adonis in Book Three and the pageant of Mutability, or the dance of the Graces on Mount Acidale in Book Six. With such recurring metaphors, *The Faerie Queene* – like Sidney's *Arcadia*, the only work of the period to rival it in scope and sophistication – attempts to stop the all too obvious flux and unpredictability of history by the assertion of timeless myths of origin, explanation and cosmic destiny.

The poem uses the trappings of chivalry – knights, ladies, tournaments, dragons, talking trees – with which modern children are familiar in comic books or television programmes, including that died-in-the-wool Spenserian C. S. Lewis's Narnia stories. In the Elizabethan Age, chivalry was obviously taken seriously by adults as well as children. Before dismissing it as arcane (and interestingly, there were, in fact, quite a few Elizabethans who did just that), we should acknowledge that chivalry, as I noted in the opening chapter, remained residually powerful for most Elizabethans, not least the aristocracy and their hangers-on. Chivalry was built upon a reassuringly traditional emphasis on hierarchy, as well as incorporating intense competitiveness and struggle; it insisted on a deference to the Queen's untouchable supremacy and yet encouraged her subject's individual prowess and ambitions. Its heraldic pageantry both helped to define the idealized history of the regime and gave rules for its nervous competitiveness. In the court, chivalry was a cultural mechanism designed at once to encourage and contain criticism and opposition – as we can see in Sidney's pageant *The Lady of May* or that staged by Sidney, Greville, and other courtiers in 1581, *The Four Foster Children of Desire*, where antagonistic political positions were articulated and then reconciled. Chivalric rituals, progresses, and tournaments likewise occupy key roles in Spenser's poem, often providing mechanisms for the battles between good and evil or for the apparent reconciliation of contention. By presenting harmony as something achieved through often violent struggle producing a stasis or harmony, the poem affirms a belief that the values it celebrates are beyond challenge, even beyond history, and that its own order both reflects and is valorized by the whole cosmic order. To read the poem in accord with such beliefs would be, in Spenser's view, to read it rightly, and the poem thrusts at its readers a formidable repertoire of strategies designed to produce such a reading.

This dual role of celebrating the ideal while warning against breaches of it is one that Spenser had adopted early in his career, when he similarly juxtaposed his criticism of corrupt courtiers with a radiant vision of Elizabeth in the April eclogue of the *Calender*. He saw the role of the court poet as that of reconciling ideological antagonisms and replacing the possibility of debating real alternatives by an assertion of their ultimate harmony. It is the role he confidently continues in the first three Books of *The Faerie Queene* and which also informs Book Four and most of Book Five, one able to countenance and even give voice to attacks on the Elizabethan court while celebrating unambiguously its glory and place in the cosmic order.

Thus Spenser combines the role of Protestant humanist moral critic – which, as we have seen, he shared with most English poets of the preceding quarter century – with what he perceives as the Virgilian role of the poet's moral power in a society he at once loyally celebrates and judiciously criticizes. In these early books, his confidence in his role is seen as analogous to the tolerant plenitude with which the queen herself embodies those same ideals. As he asserts at the start of Book II:

And thou, O fairest Princesse under sky,
In this faire mirrhour maist behold thy face,
And thine owne realmes in lond of Faery,
And in this antique Image thy great auncestry.

(2, proem 4)

In her allegorical role of Belphoebe, the Queen attacks and defeats challenges to her power with the same confidence that Spenser himself attacks them in the poem as a whole. When, in Book Two, Braggadocchio flatters Belphoebe (2. 3. 39) she sternly rejects his view of the court as a place of frivolity, just as Spenser himself did in *Mother Hubbards Tale*, in *Colin Clouts Come Home Again*, and throughout the early books of *The Faerie Queene* itself. What is noticeable in such passages is not only the absolute distinctions made between the dedicated, active life and the frivolous life of pleasure, but the poem's confidence in moral absolutes, and in the power of the poet to articulate them. Spenser appropriates the Virgilian role of celebrating the nation: he is both the prophet justifying a providential reading of history, and the Protestant nationalist assuming the public good can be served in the order, harmony, and wonder of the most serious kind of poetry, the epic. Classical epic, Arthurian legend and Italian romance are combined to justify Christian heroism in an assimilation of the same elements of the past used throughout the century by educators, propagandists, and poets to create and uphold the Tudor regime. Thus, in a letter he purportedly wrote to Ralegh, dated 23 January 1589/90, in which he explains the scheme of the poem, Spenser claims to be following Homer, Virgil, Ariosto and Tasso; he echoes the *Aeneid* in the poem's opening, he alludes to Italian romance epic throughout the poem; he speaks of magnificence as the ethical basis of the poem, and he continuously directs his reader to the central tenets of Christian theology. He wants, as well, to root these somewhat contradictory ideals in the concrete particulars of the Elizabethan court. As he put it in his Letter to Ralegh, the poem was designed 'to fashion a gentleman or noble person in vertuous and gentle discipline'. He writes as follows:

Sir knowing how doubtfully all Allegories may be construed, and this booke of mine, which I have entituled the Faery Queene, being a continued Allegory, or darke conceit, I have thought good aswell for avoyding of gealous opinions and misconstructions, as also for your better light in reading therof, (being so by you commanded,) to discover unto you the general intention and meaning, which in the whole course thereof I have fashioned, without expressing of any particular purposes or by-accidents therein occasioned. The generall end therefore of all the booke is to fashion a gentleman or noble person in vertuous and gentle discipline . . . By ensample of which excellente Poets, I labour to pourtraict in Arthure, before he was king, the image of a brave knight, perfected in the twelve private morall vertues, as Aristotle hath devised, the which is the purpose of these first twelve bookes: which if I finde to be well accepted, I may be perhaps encoraged, to frame the other part of polliticke vertues in his person, after that hee came to be king. . . . In that Faery Queene I meane glory in my generall intention, but in my particular I conceive the most excellent and glorious person of our soveraine the Queene, and her kingdome in Faery land. And yet in some places els, I doe otherwise shadow her. For considering she beareth two persons, the one of a most royall Queene or Empresse, the other of a most vertuous and beautifull Lady, this latter part in some places I doe expresse in Belphoebe, fashioning her name according to your owne excellent conceipt of Cynthia, (Phoebe and Cynthia being both names of Diana.) So in the person of Prince Arthure I sette forth magnificence in particular, which vertue for that (according to Aristotle and the rest) it is the perfection of all the rest, and conteineth in it them all, therefore in the whole course I mention the deedes of Arthure applyable to that vertue, which I write of in that booke. Bot of the xii. other vertues, I make xii. other knights the patrones . . . Of which these three bookes contayn three, The first of the knight of the Redcrosse, in whome I expresse Holynes: The seconde of Sir Guyon, in whome I sette forth Temperaunce: The third of Britomartis a Lady knight, in whome I picture Chastity. . . . But by occasion hereof, many other adventures are intermedled, but rather as Accidents, then intendments. As the love of Britomart, the overthrow of Marinell, the misery of Florimell, the vertuousnes of Belphoebe, the lasciviousnes of Hellenora, and many the like.[2]

Tonkin comments on the Letter that it 'raises so many questions that it is tempting to discard it altogether'. But its account of the poem is useful to show some of Spenser's intentions, at least at the time he wrote it. Nevertheless, the outline he gives is certainly not reflected in the poem as it was eventually written. It does not account for why he (apparently) chose a twelve-book structure. He does not confine himself to 'Aristotles twelve morall virtues'; the relationships between individual knights and their particular virtues are not simple: they do not simply stand for their particular virtue; and while Arthur frequently enters the poem, he never acquires the central place Spenser claims in the letter. In short, the letter to Ralegh cannot, except in the most general terms, account for the poem's growth or suggest how it could be read satisfactorily. *The Faerie Queene* is, in fact, such a rambling, open-ended, disrupted work that it suggests its author's intention changed, sometimes quite substantially, over the course of its writing. Even more important is the way what we can loosely call Spenser's 'unconscious' intentions change the poem very radically. We can see this in the ways the poem starts plot strands it cannot finish; characters metamorphose continually; instead of giving us the reassuring pleasures of a finished text which would (as Spenser wanted) reflect and teach about a stable world of universal values, *The Faerie Queene* is the quintessential example of what Elizabethan rhetorical theorists termed *copia*, or copiousness: the poem is a flow of textuality which undergoes what Goldberg terms 'continuous reconstitution'.[3]

In an important phrase in the letter to Ralegh, Spenser writes of his poem as a 'continued Allegory or darke conceit'. We need to spend a little time on allegory. In particular, it should not be seen simply as a 'literary' device; we need to root it in the material practices of the day, the 'social text' of late sixteenth-century England and Ireland. Allegory is a rhetorical device by which moral, philosophical or even psychological abstractions – such as Holiness or Temperance or Courtesy – may be represented or personified in characters in order to simplify and dramatize a complex experience. Thus, if an allegorical writer wishes to show that John is hesitating between his desire for an extra helping of chocolate mousse and his desire to fit into his suit, the writer may say that 'Greed and Vanity contended for mastery'; and the conflict might be represented in terms of a battle, or a wrestling match, or a football game. Today, allegorical writing tends to be an archaic form, and even in Spenser's time, it was becoming increasingly so, however strong the interest in it at the Elizabethan court remained. A century later it was to be laughed at: 'It was the vice of those Times to affect superstitiously the Allegory', whereby 'nothing would then be current without a mystical meaning,' wrote Rymer in 1674, in an age that was operating with quite different assumptions about the relation of signifier to meaning.[4] But for Spenser, allegory still seemed to grow naturally from a residual order of discourse whereby individual parts of the material world were given significance as parts of an interconnected universe of meanings. It looked back to increasingly archaic modes of thought – to Piers Plowman, Lydgate, or to A Mirror for Magistrates – and, interestingly, it was Spenser's fellow Protestants who were most scornful of it, perhaps because of the point Puttenham makes when he writes that both poet and courtier, use allegory when 'we speake one thing and think another' and when 'our wordes and our meanings meete not'.[5]

Indeed, it is intriguing that given the Protestant suspicion of it, allegory did not strike the pious Protestant Spenser as a peculiar form for a self-consciously Reformed poet to use. Yet he showed himself more shrewd than his fellow Protestants, at least in his poetic practices if not in his own comments and glosses on his poem. His choice to write The Faerie Queene as an allegory meant that the poem focused on a central poetic issue of the age, the relationship of meaning to language. Allegory is characterized by a deliberate and radical subordination of the signifier to what the poet wishes to be signified; typically, it incorporates comments upon the process by which language works, by what is implied by the relation between icon and metaphor, and so raises the fundamental question, in Isabel MacCaffery's phrase, of 'how far we may trust the basic medium, language'.[6] Hence Spenser frequently intervenes in his poem, directing his readers to the underlying meaning of his allegory.

Associated with the need to establish an authorial or extraverbal authority is the need about which, as a Protestant poet, Spenser felt strongly: to repress aberrant readings of the text. Donald Cheney speaks of the 'strong universal compulsion of readers . . . to master books and every day experience by imposing order and coherence where mere random circumstance is felt to be intolerable and threatening'.[7] How ironical it is, therefore, that the seeming endlessness of modern interpretations of Spenserian allegory does precisely the opposite of what he consciously intended – multiplying in a promiscuity of signification the signs, whereby rightly read, the poem will (it is assumed) point to permanent, ahistorical truths. But Cheney's point is a crucial one. Allegory represents an absolute desire to bring writing, and in one sense history, to an end. It tries rigorously to exclude anything that might disturb and challenge the monolithic readings the poet intended (as distinct, as we shall see, from those the poem articulated). Allegory tries to create and position a reader who, educated correctly, will read not necessarily simply or singly but certainly to find consistent and unified meanings and repress undesirable ones. A 'right' reader would never imagine, in Book One, that Errour might stand for Protestant (rather than Catholic) heresy or that (as in James of Scotland's 'erroneous' reading) Mercilla in Book Five, representing Mary Queen of Scots, is mistreated. Spenser's formidable control of rhetoric, structure, and above all of the poem's atmosphere tries to pressure the reader to accept the poet's interpretations. Yet what a poet may intend does not necessarily transfer into the slippery medium of language. So any reading of *The Faerie Queene* is determined not only by Spenser's intention – what Sidney termed its 'fore-conceit' – but rather by its status as powerful language. And, paradoxically, the language-density of the poem itself continually expands and thereby subverts the author's attempt to control meaning. As Goldberg argues, the endless quality of the poem as text denies the 'hermeneutic closure' that the poet so clearly wants. Continually, the text invites us, lures us, pressures us, to desire a particular meaning, 'and then obliterates the possibility' of fixing it. *The Faerie Queene* encourages what it deliberately tries to avoid; despite its language being selected with what Eagleton calls the 'fetishistic' force of allegory, the promiscuity of its language 'spreads infinitely'.[8]

Spenser's dilemma is not only that of the allegorist, but specifically of the Protestant allegorist: he is anxious about how fallen man's words might embody God's truths. One means by which he tries to limit a reader's possible meanings by an insistence that allegory is what he tells Ralegh, a 'darke' conceit, and that a correct reading is accessible only by arduous study by the subordination of textual ambiguity to authorial intention, and the recognition that the hidden 'true' meaning was available only to right readers. As Murrin has argued, the Renaissance allegorist wanted his text at once to open the truth to the properly subordinate reader, but to remain inaccessible to the undisciplined one. Thus Spenser works hard to direct us to his meanings by prefacing each canto with quaintly archaic quatrains, as if to underline the required readings and limit undesirable readings. As Quilligan notes, however, the quatrains only prove 'that Spenser, however great an allegorical poet, was not the best reader of his own poem when he had to resort to being an allegorical critic of it'.[9] It is there, in the quatrains, where Spenser's affinities with the Protestant anxieties over the promiscuity of language become very clear. In their simplicity, they reveal the impossibility of summarizing the intellectual richness of the poem, and the futility of trying to limit its meanings to 'right' ones.

If the quatrains fail to be of much use as signposts, the poem itself is rich with subtle structural and stylistic directions. To read the most successful parts of the poem is to enter not a geographical landscape which provides a background to abstract moralizing but a landscape full of richly suggestive stories. The poet, Sidney says, comes to seduce us with a 'tale'. The underlying meanings we are 'intended' to learn are designed to aid us in our battles with evil, and so be medicinal to our souls. Sidney speaks of poetry as a 'medicine of cherries';[10] one of Spenser's favourite metaphors is that his poem is a 'mirror', or an 'antique image': it is designed to let us see and explore the significance of the material world in the way dreams momentarily explore the displaced or repressed significances of our waking world. But those significances are not random or arbitrary. Spenser's tales are designed to reflect what he believes to be an atemporal, mythic world where quests, conquests, fears and tensions are occurring all the time, where we are always (it is assumed) like Red Crosse, engaged in a quest for perfection; like Guyon, in a quest for the appropriate and rational action; like Britomart, in our sexual relations, always faced with choices among different demands on our emotional and moral allegiances. In short, the world of Faeryland is meant to be a world of complex psychological and cultural discoveries. We are not given insights into the 'characters' of Belphoebe or Britomart or Florimel; rather, they are mirrors by which we, the poem's readers, learn about ourselves. The characters in whom Spenser is interested are, primarily, ourselves. Not that his characters are somehow representations of 'universals', or transhistorical figures. Indeed, they might have seemed very contemporary to his earliest readers – just as today, some of us may recognize parts of ourselves in them. But that is because notwithstanding enormous historical differences over the past four hundred years, in terms of historical continuity, we share a enormous and rich culture. But to say we recognize and somehow 'identify' with these characters would be to over-simplify. Identity comes from sameness, but knowledge comes from difference.

Since the early eighteenth century – at least until the recent emergent hegemony of the cinema – the dominant narrative form of our culture has been the novel, in which characters and their actions become part of an effaced illusion of realism, suppressing the contradictions of how those realistic effects are, in fact, constructed. Realism attempts to exclude any shifting in this involvement of reader, writer and textual surface: we are asked to judge character and action by consistency and fidelity to a socially dominant norm. No such constraints are demanded by *The Faerie Queene*: what is fore-grounded is rather a desire for rigorous ideological, not narrative or character consistency. Character, landscape and setting, action and motive, are all manipulated without regard for verisimilitude or consistency. It makes no sense (except as revealing our own literary presuppositions) to ask: 'where' in the forest is Belphoebe's pavilion? Is it close to the Bower of Blisse? Could Busyrane drive over to the House of Pride for the afternoon? Or to ask whether Amoret 'really' loved Scudamour? Nor is narrative consistency especially important. Magic and coincidence are part of the given of the poem. So, instead of having the pleasures of the classic realist novel, we are thrust into a text populated with figures 'moving in flux, constantly resituated, momentarily lodged in relationships from which they are as quickly dislodged, inevitably undone', a world of textuality where the focus is always on the reader caught 'in the middest', manipulated, teased, and discovering what Lewis called 'states of the heart', and so challenged to learn our own possibilities. The ever-present threat of learning inadequately or incorrectly is what Spenser embodied in the dangerous, labyrinthine forest; and it is also, paradoxically, embodied in the labyrinthine nature of his text. Goldberg suggests the poem is, in Barthes's terms, an exemplary writable text, one that by its very existence denies the closure which so many of its strategies desire. It is, one might add to Goldberg's claim, precisely this promiscuity of textuality that provides readers with part of the interest of reading *The Faerie Queene*.[11] It is a poem full of stories – and often they communicate at levels below the obvious surface narrative so that their absences are as important as the confused surfaces. The logic of many of the stories Spenser tells is the logic of dream or fantasy, justifiable only in terms of an unacknowledged (or unacknowledgeable) reality that lies outside the narrative and of which the author himself may have been only dimly aware. Hence we can apply what we know of dream structures to reading them. But like all our dreams, they are also collective rather than 'individual'. They are stories that are at once private and intimate and at the same time banal and collective. We would all, however shamedly, recognize our fantasies and daydreams as the products, at least in part, of the commonplace stories and motifs of our own culture –

rags to riches, love at first sight, miraculous meetings, overnight stardom, sexual irresistibility, heroic achievement. We are spoken; or more accurately (echoing Lacan's famous phrase) speakings. However such narratives grow from and return us to our own unconscious desires and insecurities – our desires for and fears of differentiation, our accumulated pleas for security, acceptance, or oneness throughout our lives – they are never only 'ours': they are rooted in the complex demands of race, class and gender that have already interpreted and given language to our earliest struggles – perhaps even our earliest flutterings in the womb, already placed within language by patterns of culturally produced discourses that will name and layer our unconscious.

There is a sense, too, in which Spenser's stories in *The Faerie Queene* are like children's or fairy stories. We tend to tell our fantasies in the narrative modes of our childhood because they once gave us satisfaction and because, as adults, we find ourselves reliving (often out of a sense of compulsion or compensation) the stories of those satisfactions (or their lack) over and over. The 'adventures' into which all the knights and ladies who people *The Faerie Queene* find themselves thrown are projections into the chivalric-romantic terms of the time, of both individual and collective daydreams. Like a modern adolescent imagining him or herself as a movie star (even while glimpsing Hollywood's corruption and superficiality), these adventures are narratives of passions, challenges, and achievements on a grandiose scale.

In this and the following chapters, then, I will attempt to do the impossible, that is provide a summary interpretation that is neither too prolix nor too superficial of one of our literary history's most over-read poems. That is an 'adventure hard' (2. 11. 3) for anyone, and so my focus will be primarily on how the poem illuminates Spenser's literary life.

BOOK ONE: THE LEGENDE OF THE KNIGHT OF THE RED CROSSE

The Book of Holiness takes its reader into the adventures of a young, inexperienced quester, the Red Crosse Knight, identified as St George, the patron saint of England, whose Christian and patriotic significance is made clear from the start:

A Gentle Knight was pricking on the plaine,
Y cladd in mightie armes and silver shielde,
Wherein old dints of deepe wounds did remaine
The cruelle markes of many' a bloudy fielde;
Yet armes to that time did he never wield:
His angry steede did chide his foming bitt,
As much disdayning to the curbe to yield:
Full jolly knight he seemd, and faire did sitt,
As one for knightly giusts and fierce encounters fitt.

                                                    (1. 1. 1)

Yet this striking scene, the Book's opening canto is, typically, pre-
ceded by a Proem that introduces the work and directs its readers to
the perspectives that will help us read aright. He directs us to his
great precedent, Virgil, draws a parallel between the founding of
Rome and England, and reminds us of the historical personage who
is the embodiment of the truth he strives to represent: Queen Elizabeth. He then directly informs his readers of what he sees as the
central significance of his 'literary life': that he is the poet of both the
queen and Protestant England. England is God's chosen nation.
Then Spenser gives us his opening symbolic montage, its details
deliberately chosen to try to deepen the themes announced in the
Proem, and so direct his readers' allegiances to an underlying, explicitly theological, meaning. It contains an insistence on the ideological exclusiveness of Red Crosse's badge, the Protestant emphasis
on struggle and alienation as valuable tests of faith, and (as the canto
unravels) the depiction of Catholicism as Error. Such blatant and
unarguable dualism is, the poem makes clear, not a question un-
necessary dogmatism. In Spenser's view, absolute moral distinctions
are justified by the dangerous world we find ourselves in: our quest
for holiness means that there can be no compromise possible between spiritual perfection, and worldliness. Even if Red Crosse must
seek holiness by questing through the world – which Spenser represents in the perpetual danger and unpredictability of the forest – his
life as one of God's elect demands absolute allegiance. Likewise, his
readers are challenged to lock their wills to his as a demonstration
that they are 'right' readers. Otherwise, they will fall victim to
Archimago, the Book's allegorical representation of the misuse of
metaphorical powers. As Tonkin comments, 'It is Archimago who
causes Red Crosse to *misread* and go astray. In this sense, Archimago

is also *our* enemy, and we also, as readers of Spenser's fiction, must be on our guard against the Wood of Error and the monster in its midst'. The forest into which the knight and lady are led is also a "Wandering Wood of poetry, into which we, as readers, can be 'led with delight,' as Una and Red Crosse are led."[12]

By such a reading, which is certainly 'right', Red Crosse is universalized into a representative of the Christian soul seeking not an earthly ideal but heavenly justification. He is not perfect; the inexperience upon which the opening stanza remarks unfolds as faintheartedness, weakness, foolishness, even apparent betrayals and temporary abandonments of his quest. We are all capable, so the assumption goes, of error and backsliding. Indeed, the final completion of Red Crosse's quest cannot be achieved by his own strength alone, but only through faith and God's grace. He will learn to distinguish true faith from false; true helpers from deceivers; easy satisfaction from difficult triumphs. But intellectually, true to Spenser's Calvinism, Red Crosse's final triumph – putting it in traditional Christian terms, his 'salvation' – is never in doubt. Once elect, the believer will never lose God's grace.

I say 'intellectually', because one of the fascinating aspects of the poem is the way its textuality undermines its ideological purity, even here in the opening book where the poem's polemical intent is at its purest. Poems work by metaphor and suggestion, not statement and dogma; therein lies – as we have seen Spenser knew very well – the central dilemma for the Protestant poet. As Spenser creates the evocative landscape of Faeryland, the more suggestive it is, and the more meanings open up in his readers. The deeper we go into Book One – represented by the mysterious forest as opposed to the open plain on which the action starts – the more problematic become the moral dilemmas. So, increasingly the poem unravels as a series of not just difficult but undecidable choices. Intellectually, they may be easy to make, but the more complex and compelling Spenser makes them, the less clear cut the issues may seem, until quite often it is difficult to tell the true from the false except by the poet's informing us which is which.

Red Crosse's quest is one of increasing complexity, especially once he finds himself cut adrift from his companions and guides, most especially from Una, who stands for oneness, unity of purpose, and truth. The first and easiest battle, with Error, seems clearcut. Error is identified with Catholicism, lies, and deception:

Therewith she spewd out of her filthy maw
   A floud of poyson horrible and blacke,
   Full of great lumpes of flesh and gobbets raw
   Which stunck so vildly, that it forst him slacke
His grasping hold, and from her turne him backe.

Her vomit full of bookes and papers was,
   With loathly frogs and toades, which eyes did lacke,
   And creeping sought way in the weedy gras:
Her filthy parbreake all the place defiled has.

                                   (1. 1. 20)

But what if Spenser's reader does not share his religious certainties? What if he or she was (or is) a Catholic? From Spenser's viewpoint, such a reader is already intellectually and spiritually in error, and a reading that tries to avoid the identification of Error with Catholicism is a reading that is likewise wrong. The poet's goal would therefore be to remind such a reader that he or she needs drastically to examine his state of mortal sin, his or her own state of error, and thereby (Spenser would hope) come to realize that Catholicism is, indeed, Error. But life (and truth) are not as simple as that. And to do Spenser credit, as the poet takes over from the polemicist, so the poem becomes increasingly subtle.

Indeed, after the encounter with Error, the issues are less easily decided. The ambiguity is reflected in the increasing difficulty with which Red Crosse finds his way in a morally murky world of challenge, difficulty, and assault. This process of discovering the untested nature of his commitments culminates in his temptation to suicide, and an even more interesting temptation (especially given Spenser's later disillusion with the world of Elizabeth's court) occurs in the next canto. It is to abandon the quest and flee from Cleopolis, the Earthly City, the city of man, and try immediately to enter the Heavenly City; and finally, the magnificent emblematic stage-piece of Red Crosse's battle with the dragon in the Book's last two cantos.

Spenser's didactic Christian epic, then, starts with holiness, in order to emphasize the fundamental Protestant insistence on man's utter dependence on God's grace. The 'saint', or member of God's elect, does not have the power in himself to earn his or her salvation; he has been chosen by God to be a saint, to quest for and exemplify holiness. On the moral – or what purports to be the psychological – level of the poem Red Crosse is offered as a kind of Everyman figure.

Today, the least convincing of these levels at which the poem operates is precisely this individual or psychological level: Spenser's view of the interiority of human development is, at least in the opening two books, moralistic and mechanistic, simply outdated. It operates by moral commonplaces, represented in the symbolic landscape through which Red Crosse moves. He is a novice, but his armour is old and battered; he continually is confronted with choices where his inexperience is tested, choosing good from bad, and as he falls into greater sense of evil, needing rescue from an outside force. Put in such terms, the world of Spenser's poem may seem commonplace and archaic. We might want to save its relevance by seeing it as somehow 'universal' or 'archetypal', but in terms of showing how we make moral choices in a world more complicated than one populated by black-and-white attractions, it is of little use. It operates with the moral subtlety of a comic book. Red Crosse learns patience, to combat Despair through faith and contemplation. He learns that in order to achieve his quest, he must struggle; that struggle takes place in the world, not in escaping from it; and that it is, at least until the final Day of Judgement, never-ending. We may have such a pattern in our archaic cultural assumptions, but for most of us it is simplistic and childish. We may yearn for such a world, but it was lost when we were three or four years old.

On the 'public' level of the poem, as an allegory of a quest for public or patriotic 'holiness', Book One relies heavily on the chivalric and patriotic associations of the St George legend, and it retains some historical interest. It tells the story of how Red Crosse discovers his identity and vocation as the patron saint of England; his struggle and eventual victory represent what Spenser saw as the final triumph of Protestantism in England and beyond. In the figure of Una, Spenser represents the Virgin Queen of Elizabethan propaganda: she is head of the state and the reformed English church. Her role is that of the unchanging ideal against which Red Crosse measures his failures and his eventual return to true faith. He must give up any attraction to her double – the deceptive figure of Duessa – who stands variously for Mary Queen of Scots, Catholicism and Paganism in general. The betrothal of Red Crosse and Una, anticipated though not consummated at the end of the Book, represents England's final embracing of the true faith, so – on a further theological level of the Book – Red Crosse stands for Christ, Una for the true Church.

Thus, the moral and patriotic levels of the allegory are subordin-

ate to the religious level. Book One dramatizes the great drama of
God's will against evil in the whole Universe, as Spenser saw it.
Between the opening Canto, with its careful setting out of the main
allegorical figures – the knight, the lady, the enemies they meet, the
ambiguous landscape in which they battle those enemies – and the
slaying of the dragon and the completing of the quest, come a series
of episodes, all of which offer a religious perspective on the moral
and poetic drama. Thus to open the initial episodes of error, mistak-
ing, and loss of his companions, Red Crosse's self-disgust and sense
of helplessness leads to further error, represented especially by his
attraction to the false lady Duessa (duality as opposed to the unity
embodied in Una), whose likeness to the true lady is uncanny so that
even night is deceived:

> In that faire face
> the false resemblance of Deceipt, I wist
> Did losely lurke; yet so true-seeming grace
> It carried, that I scarse in darksome place
> Could it discerne
>
> (1. 5. 27)

Throughout the early cantos of Book One, Spenser stresses the
need for divine grace to rescue even the Elect. Una saves Red Crosse
from Despair, confronting him with the promise of salvation: 'In
heavenly mercies hast thou not a part?/Why shouldst thou then
despeire, that chosen art?' (1. 9. 53)

But, in Spenser's Calvinist cosmic scheme, it is not enough that
Una saves him, and that by the latter stages of the narrative, the
knight and lady have been reunited. Salvation has to be earned, even
by the elect: a peculiar aspect of Calvinism and most versions of
Protestantism, at least in the sixteenth-century, stressed both contradictions that only God can motivate and finally save the elect person
and that he (or she) can be punished for not being elect. It is a double
bind of an intensity that might seem ludicrous were it not for the
generations of oppressive schizophrenia it has visited upon men and
women. If, as Freud argued, religion is the greatest of human illusions, its greatness has to be measured as much by its destructiveness as by its comforts.

In the Book's final cantos, these different levels of the allegory
merge. Arthur's victory over Orgoglio and Duessa parallels the triumph of Christ and the Archangel Michael in the Book of revelation,

reinforcing the inevitability of the triumph of good. Red Crosse is shown a vision towards what he assumes will be the end of his quest. He views the New Jerusalem, the goal of all his struggles; overwhelmed by the vision, he wishes to go there immediately:

> O let me not (quoth he) then turne againe
> Backe to the world, whose joyes so fruitlesse are;
> But let me here for aye in peace remaine,
> Or streight way on that last long voyage fare
>
> (1. 10. 63)

But he must remain in the world to wrestle with the greatest enemy, the dragon. He is told that the nearest place on earth there is to the Heavenly City is the seat of Gloriana, and in the 'real' world of history, the world Spenser and his readers inhabit, the closest place is England. As for the knight himself:

> For thou emongst those Saints, whom thou doest see,
> Shalt be a Saint, and thine owne nations frend
> And Patrone: thou Saint George shalt called bee,
> Saint George of mery England, the signe of victoree
>
> (1. 10. 61)

The battle takes three days – representing the three days of Christ's crucifixion and resurrection. He then claims Una. But their union is not final: for the Christian knight, he quest is never over. Holiness is an ideal that, in the world, must always be striven for; it is never to be finally materialized while we are in the world.

These, then, are the main levels of allegory that emerge from the opening Book. At times, one or the other predominates; any particular incident may have multiple significances: Red Crosse's separation from Una, for instance, can represent the abandonment of moral truth, the nation's falling away from religious truth, and from its patriotic duties. The question we might pose is: is it of more than archaic interest today?

I have said that, in my view, Book One involves a highly primitive, moralistic view of the personality. Others may react by saying that it is precisely such a view – one that sees human desires as needing continual (or even recurrent) discipline – that best serves our civilization, and that makes for decency and morality. A minister of the crown in Britain in the 1990s has been quoted as saying that society would be well served by a renewal of a belief in hell fire, and the fundamentalist undercurrent of American politics is all too obvious, seen even in the first 'yuppie' president, Bill Clinton, who in his cartoonist role as 'Slick Willie' might almost have been a Spenserian character. The Spenserian morality is not dead by any means, which makes it all the more important to understand its power as well as its (seemingly obvious) lack of sophistication and (I would argue) its destructiveness. Spenser's opening Book is a powerful and often enthusiastic narrative of such a view of the human personality and how (in his view) it underlies the search for social order and cosmic truth. If we translate 'holiness' as something like 'integrity', then Book One may retain something of its impact, even though such a translation does not do justice to either the strengths and limitations, and especially the sternness of Spenser's view of the human personality.

BOOK TWO: THE BOOK OF TEMPERANCE

Book Two comes down to earth, and focuses on Sir Guyon, the Knight of Temperance, a virtue which is presented in Protestant humanist terms as the means by which human actions may be aligned to virtuous ends through self-control.

Temperance is presented as the civic expression of Christian duty. It is therefore the equivalent in the moral world to holiness in the spiritual. But it is dependent upon holiness, not equal to it. This hierarchy is initially established by Red Crosse's introducing Guyon to his quest. Later he is rescued by Arthur, in an episode recalling Christ's passion, which again stresses the need for spiritual underpinning of the moral life. Gloriana's likeness on Guyon's shield represents the patriotic source of temperance: it shows Spenser's allegiance to what he represented as the ordered judiciousness of the Elizabethan political regime as well the queen's own personal temperance, centered upon her virginity. Of the recurring metaphors for temperance through the book, many are clearly derived from Christianity and repeatedly link the seemingly secular, or at least civic, aspect of Temperance, with the theological. The most obvious is water (a symbol of baptism or rebirth) which calms or moderates the fires of passion. But very curiously for a moral virtue, temperance also seems to depend heavily upon coercion: the palmer's staff, nets, chains and, in the culminating episode of the Book, violent destruction. Indeed, it is especially ironic that Guyon's destruction of the Bower of Bliss should be carried out by direct physical assault, even though it is justified by the Palmer's stern rationalizations. Tonkin writes of Book Two as 'the most "psychological" of the books of the poem',[13] but if so, that simply serves to show the primitivism of Spenser's conception of the interior life of humankind. Temperance is presented as the product of reason, but it is the distinctive Protestant view of 'right' reason where God's will is held to be known to and require obedience from the elect. Book Two therefore often seems didactic, even doctrinaire: it is full of expositions, by Guyon himself, and his constantly nagging companion the Palmer in particular, all designed to establish Spenser's desired 'right' reader.

'Foule Acrasia', the demonic female figure of Book One, reappears and initiates Guyon's quest when he encounters the extremity of Amavia's suicide, brokenheartedly stabbing herself because of the death of Mortdant, her adulterous husband.

> But if that carelesse heavens (quoth she) despise
>   To see sad pageants of mens miseries,
>   As bound by them to live in lives despight,
>   Yet can they not warne death from wretched wight.
>   Come then, come soon, come sweeter death to mee,
>   And take away this long lent loathed light.
>
> (2. 1. 36)

Such extremity and destructiveness would have not occurred, it is asserted, if the principles of godly temperance had been followed. Similar instances of extremity and irrational tragedy follow. Guyon observes and (we are told) learns not only moderation, but also something of equity and pity. To speak of a character in an allegory 'learning' is, of course, a category error: it is we, Spenser's readers, who are supposed to be doing the learning. What we are meant to learn is that the instincts or 'passions' are clearly dangerous and untrustworthy and that ultimately, temperance is underpinned by divine grace. The dark mystery of human irrationality and passion, derived from our fallen state, can be controlled only by higher, divinely sanctioned power. Violence and other kinds of extremity always threaten to break forth. Throughout, the human heart stand for the dangerous and (always untrustworthy) emotional nature of humankind.

At central points, Spenser uses the archaic chivalric practice of private revenge as a metaphor for this potential anarchy. Arthur's intervention in Canto Two indicates that the proper authority for controlling personal violence is the monarch. As Graziani points out, horsemanship (a traditional symbol of control of the passions) is also frequently used to represent control of the animal in humanity. But, ·of course, to base authority in the control of challenges to the status quo, and upon the interventions of divinely sanctioned aristocracy and its symbolic representation, horsemanship, has an undeniable class bias: Braggadocchio's baseness is obvious even to Sir Guyon's horse Brigadore since he cannot ride him properly: 'the "skill to ride" is metaphorical and means that virtue is the proper basis of knighthood, and true nobility', notes Graziani.[14] Braggadocchio's meeting with Belphoebe in canto three demonstrates how he lacks true nobility: he hides under a bush, and then, attracted by her beauty, clumsily gropes at her. But here again, Spenser cannot escape the charge of class bias: the 'true' knight, presumably, has a natural access to beauty, while the newly-honoured upstart who must promote himself does not. Yet when we turn to the Elizabethan court, it is clear that one of the skills for a courtier is, precisely, self-promotion. And among the greatest self-promoters of the court was Spenser's friend and patron Sir Walter Ralegh. While Spenser would in no way have intended Braggadocchio to be seen to be representing Ralegh, to many in the Elizabethan court Ralegh's demeanor would have appeared to be very much that of a Braggadocchio. Within Spenser's abstract scheme, temperance may be easy to define; when we place it in the material world, it turns out to be far more complex.

As the Book develops, the same pattern is repeated. The composure appropriate to temperance is embodied in Medina's rational position as the mean between her two more extreme sisters, whose emotions are seen as representing opposite extremes, hot-blooded impulsiveness and melancholic over-restraint. Canto Four explains anger as lack of control. Temperance, as Spenser wishes to expound it, is not concerned to eradicate human passions so much as to direct them by reason to acceptable ends. These first cantos give us a number of examples of anger and over-reaction. Pyrochles and Cymochles attack Guyon; Furor and Occasion attack Phedon, with Guyon coming to his rescue. Canto Six contains a curious episode. The question it deals with is one with which Spenser wrestled all his career: what place do relaxation, recreation and specifically the pleasure of the arts have in the Protestant ideal of life?:

A harder lesson, to learne Continence
In joyous pleasure, then in grievous paine:
For sweetnesse doth allure the weaker sence
So strongly, that uneathes it can refraine
From that, which feeble nature covets faine.

(2. 6. 1)

In this canto Phaedria represents idle and timewasting consumer-
ism; by contrast, Alma represents the morally profitable reading of
serious works of history and poetry. But there is a hesitation in the
text here, which – given the ideological contradictions emerging in
Spenser's life – is not surprising. 'Merry tales' and the fiction-making
capacity generally are like other passions, capable of exciting responses, readings, that are far from 'right', in Spenser's eyes, such as,
for instance, a reading of Braggadocchio as Ralegh, or (to invoke a
perfectly possible modern reading) of Temperance as the retrogressive reinforcement of the political status quo. In the house – Alma
roughly stands for the soul or the mental and spiritual facilities –
Arthur and Guyon read, respectively, histories of ancient Britain and
Faeryland. The struggle to be temperate in the individual is paral-
leled by the struggle for moderate civil government, which involves
neither a quietist retirement from the world nor violence and ostentation. As Belphoebe comments in Canto Three:

Who so in pompe of proud estate . . .
Does swim, and bathes himselfe in courtly blis,
Does waste his dayes in darke obscuritee
And in oblivion ever buried is . . .

(2. 3. 40)

In the next canto, Mammon shows where the cult of intemperate
self-indulgent material consumption leads. Here we find Guyon
horrified at Mammon's temptation, the ultimate materialist goal that
one might be given all one desired. In the moralistic world in which
Spenser lived, such a temptation ought to be easy to resist. But here
again, the contradictions of Spenser's world outside the poem break
into it. Spenser was living in the shadow of a court and a dominant
class whose life style was increasingly caught up in conspicuous
consumption on the most grandiose scale, and on a national level, he
is writing at the beginning of Europe's vast expansion overseas to
exploit the material wealth and destroy the civilizations of other

lands, including, on however a relatively small scale, that of the Irish. So, when we consider what emerged from the expansionist ideology of Elizabethan England, and how the prosperity and power of England was to be built precisely upon those values of material exploitation that 'temperance' was trying to moderate, we may consider Spenser's values archaic, even nostalgic. The 'real' world, we may say, is not like that; nor was it like that in Spenser's time.

Further, if we consistently refuse to isolate the poem from the conditions of its material production, we should not underestimate the enormous disparities of material wealth and comfort at the time. Material wealth offers us the satisfaction of real pleasures and comforts that enhance, not blight, the lives of real human beings. So again, Spenser's treatment of the 'temptation' of materialism is more interesting when we put it in the context of his time. On the surface, what Mammon presents Guyon, and by extension, the poem's readers, with can be easily repelled: dirt, poison, gloom, ghosts, 'vancorous Despright' are all unsubtle and melodramatic enough for us to get the message. Beneath the repulsive surface, however, real satisfactions lurk – and to do Spenser credit, he does point to them by showing (2. 7. 4) that half-hidden gold does have a power to entice, just as in the Bower of Bliss, the partly visible charms of sensuality do deeply entice the senses. Mammon tempts Guyon with a bride, a comfortable seat, golden apples, fame, a fuller material life, happiness, immortality. These are temptations not to be rejected out of hand.

We live today, traditional Spenserian criticism of this episode often bewails, in an over-materialistic age, where the temptations Guyon encounters have all too easily been accepted and seduced us from truer, 'spiritual' satisfactions. The implication is that we should accept that struggle and difficulty are always worthwhile, that the greatest human achievements are those for which we have to sacrifice mere individual pleasure. Sometimes that may be so: even so relatively trivial a matter as enjoying *The Faerie Queene* takes hard work, the giving up, perhaps, of easier pleasures, and easier poems. But when we take a long historical perspective, we may suspect that the dichotomous, nostalgic thinking that lies behind the conventional rejection of materialism in this episode of *The Faerie Queene* has too often been the embodiment of privileged interests. It is, for instance, of some significance if, relatively speaking, the advocate of material deprivation is a member of a relatively privileged class (or aspiring to belong to one). Much of the history of what passes for our 'civilization' is the history of the struggle for material satisfactions enjoyed and taken as a right by an (though only slowly) increasing minority. It is not that Spenser is being especially hypocritical; it is, indeed, that the urgency with which he depicts his heroes 'temperate' rejection of materialism betrays the unsubtlety and class bias and aspirations of his assumptions.

Guyon, then, emerges from the Cave of Mammon famished, having virtuously rejected Mammon's temptations, and after fainting, receives (by, it is made clear, divine grace) some nourishment. His rejection of Mammon – while dutiful and pointedly ethical – needs a higher motive than worldly virtue affords. Red Crosse tried to rely on his own strength and learned that the strength of being one of the Elect comes only from God; Guyon learns analogously that even the seemingly lesser quest for temperance is also dependent on divine grace. Rescued (as was Red Crosse) by Arthur, Guyon is taken in Canto Ten to the Castle of Alma, where the lesson he (and his readers) are taught is the commonplace Renaissance view that the human body brings together the material and the spiritual, and must be ruled by reason:

> Of all Gods workes, which do this worlde adorne,
>   There is no one more faire and excellent,
>   Then is mans body both for powre and forme,
>   Whiles it is kept in sober government;
>   But none then it, more fowle and indecent,
>   Distempred through misrule and passions bace:
>   It growes a Monster, and incontinent
>   Doth loose his dignitie and native grace.
>
> (2. 9. 1)

And so Spenser brings us to one of the poem's greatest episodes, Guyon's sacking of the Bower of Bliss. Guyon's journey to the Bower marks the culmination of his task to overcome the witch Acrasia. For those readers who find the rest of Book Two heavy (or heady) going, with an all too temperate pace, perhaps far too appropriately reflecting the Book's virtue, the pyrotechnics of the final canto are a rich reward (that very formulation is perhaps a concession to the residual power of the poem's ethic of struggle to salvation through difficulty). The episode is depicted in forty-six extraordinarily evocative stanzas in which Guyon enters the Bower and lays violent waste to it and its inhabitants.

Tonkin writes of the Bower that it is 'the most impressive, and the most oppressive, example of false poetry in the poem thus far'; it is a 'false image of beauty'.[15] An alternative argument, slightly more positive, is that the Bower has the alluring sensuality of a striptease, and Spenser's text (and likely the poet himself) is pulled in contra- ·dictory directions – by the stern moral demands of his didacticism and by the allurement of the seductive sensuality of the poetry. Here, for perhaps the first time in the poem, we can explicitly see the power of the poetry undo the didacticism of its plan. The very violence of Guyon's behavior, hardly compatible with his role as the Knight of Temperance, points to a ruthlessness of authorial closure that seems to surface at key points throughout the poem. The knight's goal is achieved; the power is upheld, but by means of a degree of violence that undermines the moral superiority of temper- ance. As Greenblatt argues, it is as if Spenser's text reveals what the poet (along with the religious and political views he espoused) could not face: the destruction of the Bower articulates his whole culture's 'violent resistance to a sensuous release for which it nevertheless' yearned with overwhelming intensity.[16] Temperance itself is shown as inadequate to the complexities of experience, and the poem is contradicting and teaching (potentially at least) the poet and (cer- tainly) the reader. That clearly is not a verdict with which Spenser would have agreed. The destruction of the Bower is clearly meant to be the culminating justification of the virtue of temperance. It emerges, instead, as a revelation of the allure and plausibility of precisely the opposite of temperance and (even if we point out that the pleasures Guyon rejects and destroys are superficial, even destructive) of the decidedly intemperate means by which, it seems, temperance has to be asserted once its enemies become more than token.

The Bower is described as a kind of earthly paradise, one in the long (perhaps endless) tradition of utopias and earthly paradises in poem, song, or story where, we hope or are promised, we will be happy, fulfilled, satisfied, indulged. In Christianity, as in many other religions, there is a central belief in an earthly paradise somewhere in our mythical prehistory from which we were expelled and to which we wish to return. There are other useful parallels which we might draw. In the psychoanalytic model of the personality, such a paradise is embodied in the womb, or the body of the Mother, the person of the beloved, or even (at least in Freud's gloomier moods) death. From it we were expelled; to it we yearn to return. But there are, so the stories go, false paradises. For the Christian, all earthly paradises are false, except the first paradise from which we are forever expelled, even though we are compelled to search for it, and project our yearning for it upon many aspects of our lives. Re-finding the lost paradise is one of the oldest and most alluring of our stories. The Bower of Bliss takes particular aim at one of our recurring locations for the possibility of such a recaptured paradise – sexuality and sexual experience. For Freud, sex and art are the two great comforts by which we attempt to deal with 'civilization'. The control of the power of art over us is, as we have seen, one of Spenser's great preoccupations, and involves the repression of meanings and suggestions that vary from the 'right'. The control of sex – what Spenser sees as the temperate uses of sex – is built on the repression of and moral direction of desire.

Unlike most of the temptations that have led Guyon to the Bower of Bliss, there is nothing over-easy about the moral issues he faces in the Bower, despite (at key points) Spenser's firm and sometimes over-insistent intentions to provide clear-cut moral perspectives. As Alpers points out, 'the first difficulty the modern reader is likely to have with the Bower of Bliss [is] the fact that most of the enticements held out to Guyon, the attractions that are intended to divert him from his mission, are more alluring than they should appear to the knight of Temperance'. Alpers further points out that it is not simply today's moral relativism that might find aspect of the Bower attractive. The great Victorian and early modern critics Dowden, Ruskin and Yeats also saw the imaginative power of the episode as encouraging precisely the sensual indulgence that the intellectual intent of the poem wishes to chasten.[17] Of course that may indicate that the chaos Spenser feared – and which he projected upon sexuality as he did upon Ireland and Catholicism – is not entirely a modern phenomenon.

At this point, we should not forget the gender politics of such an insistence on the supposed irrationality of sexuality. Guyon, like the other knights, is clearly a fantasy figure into which Spenser projects his idealization of residual superiority of masculine rationality. He looks like a typical male fantasy figure, the kind of hero boys of the time would have dreamed of when they struggled against their real fathers. Men of action and autonomy represent the unfettered projection of the libido or desiring self for fulfillment unhampered by reality. So he has the characteristic male freedoms – military prowess, perpetual movement from one battle or quest to another, just as in another context a romantic male hero (like Mary Wroth's

Amphilanthus, in her romance *Urania*, moves from one woman to the next) and such movement is taken for granted. The romance hero is an intriguing variation not just on a common romance pattern – in Freud's terms, the unfettered male id – but, more accurately, a combination of the dominant male fantasies of Western patriarchy, at once terribly bound to and terribly exploitative of his goal, often as here, represented by a woman, and defining his sense of self not only by the violent overcoming of his rivals, but by his conquest and control of women.

The Bower of Bliss is where Acrasia seduces and overcomes her lovers. It lies, allegorically, between woman's legs. Here the case histories in contemporary psychoanalytic literature are helpful because so overwhelming about the patriarchal obsession with women's genitals as a place of mystery, awe, fear, and (literally) life and death. Men are fascinated with what women have between their legs because they recognize it is powerful, overwhelming. There is an overwhelming sense of awe and fear – it is the curiosity of the obsessed, and that was a degree of dependence on the irrational that Spenser's age could not easily tolerate. It starts as a little boy's fascination, no doubt connected with being born and mothered, and as he (let us hope) matures, it must go through the phases of all those conventional, clichéd associations of mystery, pleasure/pain, risk, danger – all the attributes of the goal or the quest in romance, of course. In a rich psychic development, sight becomes merely the preliminary: the gaze is the most superficial of all the senses, and the reason the immature male is so obsessed with the gaze is that it is the easiest, the least involving. Camille Paglia argues that the obsession which Guyon is trying to control is all really THERE in a woman: the associations are nature breaking through, and so men's fear of women is rooted in something natural, biological, primitive. What lies between is a reminder of birth and death alike. In that, Paglia is certainly a 'right' reader of Spenser's poem.[18]

The effect Spenser wishes to create is built up through an impressively evoked series of preparatory temptations. Some are not difficult to reject. The bowl and cup of wine offered by Genus to Guyon and the Palmer can be (unless one simply needs to relax or be congenial, presumably) rejected easily enough. Guyon momentarily pauses as he sees the women bathing:

> And all the margent round about was set,
>   With shady Laurell trees, thence to defend

The sunny beames, which on the billowes bet,
And those which therein bathed, mote offend.
As *Guyon* hapned by the same to wend,
Two naked Damzelles he therein espyde,
Which therein, bathing, seemed to contend,
And wrestle wantonly, ne car'd to hyde,
Their dainty parts from vew of any, which them eyde.

Sometimes the one would lift the other quight
Above the waters, and then downe againe
Her plong, as over maistered by might,
Where both awhile would covered remaine,
And each the other from to rise restraine;
The whiles their snowy limbes, as through a vele,
So through the Christall waves appeared plaine:
Then suddeinly both would themselves unhele,
And th'amarous sweet spoiles to greedy eyes revele.
                                                    (2. 12. 63–4)

But the depiction of the 'foule' Acrasia, the enchantress who
inhabits the power is more difficult to resist. It is – and Spenser
seems to know much more of this difficult, perhaps impossible,
attempt than he would wish to acknowledge – to detach ourselves
from our desires to find or return to some paradisal world where we
are comforted, made happy, protected, fulfilled:

Eftsoones they heard a most melodious sound,
    Of all that mote delight a daintie eare,
    Such as attonce might not on living ground,
    Save in this Paradise, be heard elswhere:
    Right hard it was, for wight, which did it heare,
    To read, what manner musicke that mote bee:
    For all that pleasing is to living eare,
    Was there consorted in one harmonee,
Birdes, voyces, instruments, windes, waters, all agree.

The jouyous birdes shrouded in chearefull shade
    Their notes unto the voyce attempred sweet;
    Th'Angelicall soft trembling voyces made
    To th'instruments divine respondence meet:
    The silver sounding instruments did meet

> With the base murmure of the waters fall:
> The waters fall with difference discreet,
> Now soft, now loud, unto the wind did call:
> The gentle warbling wind low answered to all.
>
> (2. 12. 70–1)

The very strenuousness here with which Spenser has his hero destroy the bower is a register of the power of what it suggests or stands for in the lives of individual men and women and the collective fantasies that inhabit us, especially in a society where dutiful repression of individual desires was, for the majority of people, seen as the means to social order and salvation. There is a note of grim intemperance in the dismissal of all who have been overcome by the Bower:

> Streight way he with his vertuous staffe them strooke,
>   And streight of beasts they comely men became;
> Yet being men they did unmanly looke,
>   And stared ghastly, some for inward shame,
>   And some for wrath, to see their captiue Dame:
> But one above the rest in speciall,
>   That had an hog beene late, hight *Grille* by name,
> Repined greatly, and did him miscall,
> That had from hoggish forme him brought to naturall.
>
> (2. 12. 86)

BOOK THREE: THE BOOK OF CHASTITY

Despite its title, The Book of Chastity is perhaps the most accessible of the books of *The Faerie Queene* to a modern reader. Like the Bower of Bliss – only in far more detail – it provides us with a means of assessing Spenser's treatment of sexuality and desire in human life. Its central knight is a woman, Britomart; traditionally, the central character of the romance epic is, 'naturally', male. Making the central figure of Book Three a woman raises the question of the extent to which women in the early modern period could share the apparent autonomy and independence embodied in the chivalric fantasy. Just as chivalry and the stereotypes of patriarchal male upbringing generally encouraged men to disguise their forbidden feminine wishes behind a stereotype of male virility – such as represented by chivalry

– so early modern women (and arguably women in patriarchal societies generally) were brought up to disguise their forbidden masculine wishes behind a stereotype of female innocence, weakness and self-sacrifice. As Louise Kaplan notes, the female child proceeds with her 'investigations' into the ways her fantasies fit the world in a pattern that may start out fundamentally similar to the male child's, but 'she endows her discoveries with fantasies that pertain mainly to female development'.[19] Such a development will inevitably occur in historically conditioned forms. This is why *The Faerie Queene* is full of stories of women's desire directed out to heroes; in its most extreme form, this fantasy takes the form of women expecting rejection, even abuse, and then being 'rescued' from their culturally produced underestimation of themselves. This story, so recurring in our cultural history that it often seems 'permanent' or 'archetypal' may involve the apparent superiority of the woman (Una in Book One is a case in point) but the power and agency rests with men. It is the man who rescues her. *The Faerie Queene* enacts this fantasy in Book Three, in story after story, with the heroine finding or putting herself in situations where she is humiliated, molested, or denied her desires, and receiving, in a measure, some perverse comfort that her expectations are thus fulfilled. The classic instance of this is the story of Florimell, in Books Three and Four: she flees from one male 'rescuer' after another; they pursue, often not knowing whether they mean to rescue or capture her. This pattern embodies the destructive and perverse hope projected upon women under patriarchy that in such surrender they will find their elusive own selves by their acknowledged subordination to men – or to traditional patriarchal values.

But an alternative cultural fantasy haunts *The Faerie Queene*, and it makes Spenser's poem surprising and intriguing – if increasingly self-contradictory. The alternative fantasy is that of the mutuality not only of men and women, but of any human beings, of any gender assignment or sexual orientation and – either individually or collectively – might become what Spenser frequently terms 'sovereign' not over but alongside one another. It is a fantasy that has never been accorded primacy in the western tradition, largely because it has never been valorized as a dominant, that is a male, pattern. What men have seemed to embody, and women wanted to emulate, has been the dream of power, autonomy, agency and control. The intersubjective, communal selves we might dream of have been denigrated because men have felt such claims to be threatening to their cherished autonomy and because generations of women have seen any desire for mutuality as involving a sacrifice of their own strivings for that autonomy. Why, asks Nancy Chodorow, must a search for recognition culminate in 'submission, instead of a relationship of mutuality?'[20] That, I will suggest, is a question that occasionally surfaces in Spenser, as it does in Shakespeare, Donne, and on occasion elsewhere in writings in the early modern period. Clearly, the answer lies not primarily in biological conditioning, but in the dominant gender ideologies of our history. But that it enters *The Faerie Queene* at all is a major development in the articulation of an emergent cultural history.

Spenser's third book, then, gives a surprisingly contemporary reading of the quest for what instead of the unpromising label of chastity, we might term integrity in love. It is full of the violence and contradictions of love – obsession, domination, invasion, the multitude of ways by which our dominant traditions of sexual attraction have taught us to express desire. Britomart is taken through a complex process of misprision, naiveté, and over-reaction. She is meant to represent the various aspects of 'femininity,' at least as defined within a patriarchal social formation – sensual attraction, reserve, subordination, motherliness. But what marks a major difference from the first two books is Spenser's allegorical strategies. Where Books One and Two tend to focus on the adventures of a single knight, Book Three is much more polyphonic, a complex opening of mirrors-within-mirrors. Britomart disappears from the main action and is replaced by other heroines – Florimell, Amoret, Belphoebe – who take us into different, more complex, challenges to our experience of desire. Its major allegorical set piece, too, does not directly concern the Book's ostensible heroine: it is a richly evocative description of the Garden of Adonis, the birthplace of the twins Amoret and Belphoebe, and the seed place of all the fecundity of the universe – including (an aspect to which we will return when we look at the remnant of Book Seven) the great enemy, Time. The Book culminates in four of the most impressive cantos of the whole poem – and indeed one of the highest points of English poetry – the story of Amoret's capture by the magician Busirane, her subsequent rescue by Britomart, and (in the first, 1590, version at least) her reconcilement with her lover Scudamour.

The Book opens with a meeting of knights – Arthur, Guyon, Arthur's squire Timias, and Another Knight, whom we learn soon to be a woman, Britomart. The knights fight, Britomart overcomes Guyon, and then all are diverted by the rapid entry and exit of a lady, who we learn is Florimell. According to Lewis, for Arthur Florimell is the shadow of divine glory, or as Tonkin points out, she may be a 'reminder of the difficult path of love in a fallen world'.[21] But she is more subtle than either of those views. All the men chase after her – whether men chase Florimell to rescue or capture her is one of the recurring and wonderfully perceptive ironies of the Book – but at this point at least the possibility of homosexual desire is sternly set aside and Britomart does not. She proceeds alone. Her quest, we learn, is to seek the fulfillment of a prophecy that she will find her true love, the Knight Artegall, and join with him as the ancestors of Spenser's own real life Faerie Queene, Elizabeth. In Canto Four, however, we lose sight of Britomart's quest and return to Arthur and to the young squire Timias in pursuit of Florimell. Arthur learns Florimell's story, Timias falls in love with Belphoebe, and in Canto Six, in one of this Book's two great set pieces, we learn of the birth of Belphoebe and her (slightly) younger twin Amoret – standing very roughly, for idealized non-sexual love and idealized sensual love. In Cantos Seven and Eight, we are told of another of Florimell's narrow escapes, this time from a witch and her son, who in their disappointment at losing their possession of her, create a substitute or what becomes known as the 'false' Florimell. Only in Canto Eight do we return to Britomart, this time in the Castle of Malbecco where she is shocked by the self-indulgent sensuality of its habitants, and finally, in the Book's culmination, in the house of the magician Busirane, where she rescues Amoret.

I have summarized the story-line of the Book because it is both complicated and diverse. Books One and Two are packed with details, episodes and allegorical, but their overall narratives are relatively straightforward. Books Three and Four are far more complicated. Many narrative threads are started and resumed spasmodically in later books, and in some cases not at all. The result is an extremely attractive and often intriguing exploration of the place of sexuality in human experience. In Books One and Two, Spenser's desired formulations may often seem rigid, his moral scheme mechanical and archaic, but the variety of experiences in Book Three and the very fragmentary nature of his presentation of the erotic, make it compelling reading. This is particularly true of Cantos Six, Eleven and Twelve, and in many of the incidental narratives along the way: the stories of Florimell, the attraction of Timias for Belphoebe, or the witty comedy of Britomart's horror at being mistaken for a man by another woman, Malecasta.

> Which whenas none she fond, with easie shift,
>   For feare least her unwares she should abrayd,
> Th'embroderd quilt she lightly up did lift,
>   And by her side her selfe she softly layd,
>   Of every finest fingers touch affrayd:
> Ne any noise she made, ne word she spake,
>   But inly sigh'd. At last the royall Mayd
>   Out of her quiet slomber did awake,
> And chaungd her weary side, the better ease to take.
>
> Where feeling one close couched by her side,
>   She lightly lept out of her filed bed,
>   And to her weapon ran, in minde to gride
>   The loathed leachour. But the Dame halfe ded
>   Through suddein feare and ghastly drerihed,
>   Did shrieke alowd, that through the house it rong,
>   And the whole family therewith adred,
>   Rashly out of their rouzed couches sprong,
> And to the troubled chamber all in armes did throng.
>   (3. 1. 61–2)

Part of the acknowledged complexity of the Book is caused by the interaction of history and mythology of the narrative. In Book Four, Belphoebe sternly rejects her lover, Timias, and it is made very clear that such rejection is seen by the poet as too severe. Belphoebe stands for Elizabeth, Timias for Ralegh, and the occasion allegorized involved Ralegh's secret marriage to Elizabeth Throckmorton, one of the Queen's ladies in waiting, and Elizabeth's subsequent anger and banishing of Ralegh. But in Book Three any special pleading on Ralegh's behalf, merges into the wider moral and cosmic significance of Belphoebe and her sister Amoret. We are given two competing views of love signifying love expressed through the denial of sexuality and love through its affirmation. The intellectual allegiances Spenser upholds necessitates that the former is the superior:

> Her mother was the faire *Chrysogonee*,
> The daughter of *Amphisa*, who by race

A Faerie was, yborne of high degree,
She bore *Belphoebe*, she bore in like cace
Faire *Amoretta* in the second place:
These two were twinnes, and twixt them two did share
The heritage of all celestiall grace.
That all the rest it seem'd they robbed bare
Of bountie, and of beautie, and all vertues rare.

(3. 6. 4)

But it is intriguing that, as in the Bower of Bliss – conventionally, the Garden of Adonis is seen as the 'healthy' counterpart to the Bower – it is the sensual, and the mutable and fragile in human experience which call forth some of Spenser's greatest poetical powers.

Spenser's Garden is a place of origin, the source of all humankind. In a richly evocative narrative, he articulates a myth of the recurrence of birth, death and rebirth: it is 'the first seminaire/of all things, that are borne to live and die' (3. 6. 30). It is the place where Venus brings Amoret to be nourished and sent out into the world. But it is also the powerful articulation of two of Spenser's preoccupations and fears – time and sexuality. The great enemy of the cyclical procreative pattern represented in the garden is, we are told, time:

Great enimy to it, and to all the rest,
  That in the *Gardin* of *Adonis* springs,
  Is wicked *Time*, who with his scyth addrest,
  Does mow the flowring herbes and goodly things,
  And all their glory to the ground downe flings,
  Where they doe wither, and are fowly mard:
  He flyes about, and with his flaggy wings
  Beates downe both leaves and buds without regard,
Ne ever pittie may relent his malice hard.

(3. 6. 39)

Here, as I noted in the previous chapter, is one of our history's greatest commonplaces, one that seemed to strike a resonant chord throughout Spenser's age. By what stories do we explain (or explain away) our existential and commercial awareness of our limitations of the unpredictable and contingent in our lives? How do we account for our one-dimensionality that, as Heidegger put it, we find ourselves thrown into life, into history, into assumptions, material practices and decisions that, we often feel, are not 'ours?' Here, in the

Garden of Adonis, Spenser gives one tentative answer. It is a restate-
ment of an old narrative, one that he will try to transcend in a later,
unfinished Book:

> There is continuall spring, and harvest there
>   Continuall, both meeting at one time:
>   For both the boughes doe laughing blossomes beare,
>   And with fresh colours decke the wanton Prime,
>   And eke attonce the heavy trees they clime,
>   Which seeme to labour under their fruits lode:
>   The whiles the joyous birdes make their pastime
>   Emongst the shadie leaues, their sweet abode,
> And their true loves without suspition tell abrode.
>
> (3. 6. 42)

As I noted in discussing the Bower of Bliss, Freud once asked
what it is we have to draw upon to deal with the seemingly endless
repression and frustration of our desires, and he answered by means
of art and sex.[22] Spenser asks likewise how we deal with mutability,
and the answer he gives is that we see ourselves absorbed into a
beneficent universal pattern that is natural, cosmic, God-given. But
he also hints at something not entirely alien to Freud's answer.
Spenser clearly appreciated deeply the power of art to embody the
stories by which men and women express – or, in Freud's terms,
displace – their anxieties and fantasies. In particular, he knew and
was in turn anxious about the power of art to distort what he believed to be Truth. Likewise, as we see in the Bower of Bliss – and the
whole of Book Three illustrates this – he was both affected by and
suspicious of the similar power of sexuality. These two great forces,
art and sex, come together again and again in *The Faerie Queene* as
subjects of both fascination and anxiety. The garden of Adonis is
therefore a key moment in the poem and in Spenser's cosmology. In
the Garden, the 'art' of the Bower of Bliss is purified in the subtle,
moral and natural sensuality of Adonis:

> Right in the middest of that Paradise,
>   There stood a stately Mount, on whose round top
>   A gloomy grove of mirtle trees did rise,
>   Whose shadie boughes sharpe steele did never lop,
>   Nor wicked beasts their tender buds did crop,
>   But like a girlond compassed the hight,

And from their fruitfull sides sweet gum did drop,
That all the ground with precious deaw dedight,
Threw forth most dainty odours, and most sweet delight.

(3. 6. 43)

Art and sensuality may, even in Spenser's moral scheme, be acceptable to humankind, so long as they can be enjoyed not for their own
selves, but within a whole cosmic order.

Then, as if to acknowledge the fragility of such a vision (before, as
it were, we Malfontian readers can indeed invoke Freud), Book
Three sweeps us back into contingency and unpredictability, in the
moving, often humorous, frequently morally perceptive story of
Florimell. In Cantos Seven and Eight, we are shown Florimell flying
from increasingly threatening circumstances – the witch, the witch's
son, a lascivious fisherman – and then being captured by Proteus.
Even Arthur, the Perfect Knight, joins in the pursuit of Florimell.
What does she stand for? The easy answer is to say something like
the allure of beauty, which draws in even the most dedicated and
morally upright man. But in that gendered word lies the secret of her
appeal. What Spenser embodies in the stories of Florimell is the
masculinist myth of the attraction to what one does not possess,
what escapes, what seems beyond possibility. Such a pursuit is
justified by the extremity of achievement it represents, the ego-
gratification it satisfies, the insecurities it seems to overcome, the
weaknesses it promises to compensate. That whole sequence is one
of the most destructive aspects of what has passed for masculinity in
our culture. Where, real historical women have asked of such a
myth, is the real me? Look at *me*, relate to *me*, not to your need for a
narrative about me that will momentarily satisfy your cravings for
possession or annihilation. What would Arthur do if he captured
Florimell? Spenser does not answer that; he tries to settle the issue in
Book Four when the knights find it difficult to tell the 'true' Florimell
from the 'false', but that solution is too easy.

Part of the sureness of Spenser's storytelling here (not, necessarily, his awareness of all that he was saying) lies in the creation of the
false Florimell. It is the inflatable doll syndrome. By no means simply a kinky pastime, the subject of jokes about Soho, sexshops and
holes in the wall advertising Marital Arts, what underlies the story
of Florimell is a frighteningly accurate depiction of an aspect of how
masculinity has been constructed in our culture. We all, men and
women, straight and gay, construct myths, ideals, expectations about

each other's abilities to satisfy our supposed (and maybe real) needs. We do so when we look forward to romantic meetings or reunions; or when we anticipate coming home to (or going to meet) a wife, husband, or lover; whenever we dream a 'rich and long delight', as Donne put it, about our sexual hopes and fantasies. We often encounter anger, or puzzlement or disappointment in ourselves as much as in the 'other' whom we have tried to thus fetishize. Often the fetishes we treasure, whether inflatable dolls, or the commonplace memories, pictures, pieces of clothing or trinkets of everyday fetishism, seem (and perhaps are) more satisfying than the 'real'. The fetish is controllable. We can accord the fetish enormous power over us, even of death, and still be in control. The false Florimell is the most alluring of all fetishes, our creation of a woman who is 'ours', whom we not only own and control, but whom we men, or the discourses of masculinity that haunt us, created.

Similarly perceptive is Spencer's picaresque story of the Castle of Malbecco, and the story of Paridell's seduction of Hellenore:

> It fortuned as they together far'd,
>   They spide, where *Paridell* came pricking fast
>   Vpon the plaine, the which himselfe prepar'd
>   To giust with that braue straunger knight a cast,
>   As on aduenture by the way he past:
>   Alone he rode without his Paragone;
>   For having filcht her bels, her vp her cast
>   To the wide world, and let her fly alone,
> He nould be clogd. So had he served many one.
>   (3. 10. 35)

In such episodes the power of Spenser's poem – here achieving a level of complexity and multiple significance that was lacking in the first two Books – is wonderfully evident. Book Three's rapid transitions from serious moral exploration to sophisticated cynical comedy are arguably the best sustained writing in Spenser's career and among the most interesting in the history of our poetry.

In the last four cantos, we rejoin Britomart. Amoret, she discovers, has been imprisoned by the magician Busirane, and her betrothed, Scudamour, cannot rescue her. Has he been over emphatic in his male sexuality? Does he represent her fears of sexuality? Can Britomart, herself, a woman, calm these fears? Scudamour, like Britomart's own Artegall, is clearly a fantasy figure into which

Spenser's heroine projects not her 'individual' or 'feminine' ideal of manhood, but something far more sinister. It is, articulated largely unconsciously on Spenser's part, her (and women's) 'natural' assimilation into heroic male values.

Part of the intriguing insight of the end of Book Three is that Spenser articulates something of these contradictions. It is Britomart who must rescue Amoret. She forces her way into the House, and studies a series of images and pageants. What we see enacted is a powerful narrative of a certain pattern of erotic attraction, attachment, and disillusion: Lust, Fancy and Desire, Doubt and Danger, Fear and Hope, Dissemblance and Suspect, Grief and Fury, Displeasure and Pleasure. At the center of the pageant is Amoret, whose heart has been cut out and placed in a silver basin:

> And all about, the glistring walles were hong
>> With warlike spoiles, and with victorious prayes,
>> Of might Conquerours and Captaines strong,
>> Which were whilome captived in their dayes
>> To cruell love, and wrought their owne decayes:
>> Their swerds and speres were broke, and hauberques rent;
>> And their proud girlonds of tryumphant bayes
>> Troden in dust with fury insolent,
> To shew the victors might and mercilesse intent . . .

> Her brest all naked, as net ivory,
>> Without adorne of gold or silver bright,
>> Wherewith the Craftesman wonts it beautify,
>> Of her dew honour was despoyled quight,
>> And a wide wound therein (O ruefull sight)
>> Entrenched deepe with knife accursed keene,
>> Yet freshly bleeding forth her fainting spright,
>> (The worke of cruell hand) was to be seene,
> That dyde in sanguine red her skin all snowy cleene.

> At that wide orifice her trembling hart
>> Was drawne forth, and in silver basin layd
>> quite through transfixed with a deadly dart,
>> and in her bloud yet steeming fresh embayd:
>> And those two villeins, which her steps vpstayd,
>> when her weake feete could scarcely her sustaine,
>> And fading vitall powers gan to fade,

Her forward still with torture did constraine,
And evermore encreased her consuming paine.

                                        (3. 11. 52, 3. 12. 20–1)

Here we need to stand back to look at the significance of these images. Traditional Spenserian criticism has seen, quite rightly, that Spenser's critique of the false Florimell and much of the House of Busirane as a critique of Petrarchism. Behind the witch's creation for her son of a False Florimell and behind the elaborate machinery of the House of Busirane is the laying open of one of the great structures by which we have ordered human desire. The Petrarchan manner was clearly more than a literary fashion; it clearly seized upon something very deep-rooted in Spenser's age's inner life, and given the attention paid to it in Book Three (and, as we shall see, *Amoretti*), we should give it some detailed attention. In chapter six, when we glance at Spenser's sonnet sequence, I shall therefore consider his relation to the Petrarchan manner in some detail and return (as all the men in the poem seem to do) to Florimell.

At the end of this intriguing and richly evocative Book, we have a choice of endings. Or rather, Spenser himself provided an ending for the 1590 publication of *The Faerie Queene*, which concluded with Book Three, and then, as he revised and newly wrote the next three Books for the 1596 publication, he gave us a revised ending. In the first ending, written for the 1590 edition, we are given a rapturous image of the joining together of Amoret and Scudamour in one of the rare moments of mutuality in the Renaissance struggle to find and articulate a satisfying story for the powers of human desire:

> Had ye them seene, ye would have surely thought,
>   That they had beene that faire *Hermaphrodite*,
>   Which that rich *Romane* of white marble wrought,
>   And in his costly Bath causd to bee site:
>   So seemd those two, as growne together quite,
>   That *Britomart* halfe envying their blesse,
>   Was much empassiond in her gentle sprite,
>   And to her selfe oft wisht like happinesse,
> In vaine she wisht, that fate n'ould let her yet possesse.
>   (3. 12. 46)

In the 1596 edition, the book ends before this rapture; the stanzas of mutuality are canceled; the marriage of Scudamour and Amoret postponed until Book Four. In 1590, Canto Twelve, stanzas 43–7, brought the first published part of the *Faerie Queene* to its conclusion. In their celebration of unity through struggle and reconciliation they were an appropriate conclusion – confident, rapturous, serious – to what the poem's later edition would no longer be able to uphold. It is a replete and dignified ending in which Spenser turned to his lovers, and his audience, to exhort: 'Now cease your worke, and at your pleasure play;/Now cease your worke, to morrow is an holy day' (2. 12. 47).

5

A 'world . . . runne quite out of square': The 1596 *Faerie Queene*: Books Four to Six

The Faerie Queene is the ultimate test case in Elizabethan poetry for the ways in which power seeks to control language. It is a poem expressly dedicated to the praise of the queen, her court, and the cultural practices by which the Elizabethan regime established and maintained its power. Spenser accepts his role as that of the Orphic bard, praising, warning, and celebrating the society that not only rewarded but in a real sense created him. Thus his poem's central figure is the queen – as head of the Church as well as the State, triumphing over heresy on the one hand and political dissent on the other, and as the inspiration of the poem itself. The queen's response to the poem, at least to the three books published in 1590, was to reward Spenser with a pension. From Spenser's viewpoint, such a reward was appropriate, an acknowledgment not only of his poetic achievements but of poetry's usefulness as part of the nation's ideological underpinning. More consciously than any other poem in the last two decades of the century, *The Faerie Queene* is 'Art become a work of State', asserting that beneath the contingent world the values of the regime are without contradiction and that when its norms are transgressed, chaos will result. The poem is offered as a microcosm of this truth.

To speak of *The Faerie Queene* as the most magnificent articulation of the Elizabethan court's dominant ideology is, however, as I have been suggesting, a claim that is frequently contradicted by the poem itself. The major characteristic of Spenser's literary life is that, as in the rest of his life, much of the significance of his commitments and actions go far beyond what he could have been aware. His life in Ireland opens up questions of colonialism, imperialism, racism, and how we tend to construct 'other' people. It looks forward to later

136

attempts by the English and to a lesser extent other European powers to dominate technologically less advanced and ideologically less aggressive peoples: in the Americas, primarily, but also, over the next three hundred years, in the Indian subcontinent, in Africa, Australia, New Zealand, in farflung outposts of empire, wherever, it has often been remarked, cricket continues to be played. In short, the significance of Spenser's struggles in Ireland to approximate the life of an English shire – Essex, or Kent, or Surrey, perhaps, or at least close to the court – far surpasses what he could have seen. Likewise, his poem raises the question of how a deeply conservative poet can be surpassed by his own poem so that his readers see the ideological contradictions, not just the ideological mystifications, of his society. What the poem attempts – in the early books buoyantly, in the later ones desperately – is a denial of historical change. *The Faerie Queene* yearns for stasis, wants to project truth as unalterable in the face of unpredictability and, in its manifestation in Elizabeth and her court, as natural, given, and unassailable. It is built therefore on a poetic that tries to avoid debate, to efface all contradiction, and to reconcile all partial truths into a higher harmony or ruthlessly to exclude them as heretical or unnatural. It tries likewise to create a reader who is active but subservient – a loyal participant in the decipherment of emblem, hieroglyph, and allegory that unites poem and policy alike. He or she is interpellated as part of a great celebration of ideological plenitude, just as the Elizabethan courtier was enculturated and socialized by accepting his or her proper place in the court. But just as there was in the court, so in Spenser's poem there is an anxiety that emerges as verbal and narrative contradiction. The pressures and contradictions of the history which it tries to exclude continually seep back into it. Despite its epic claim to speak for the Elizabethan regime, thoughts and actions that were not permitted beyond preserved limits nevertheless enter the poem.

If the three Books of the 1590 *Faerie Queene* seemed to embody a confidence in the interconnectedness of poetry, policy, the ordered universe of Elizabethan ideals as well as its growing expansionism, by 1596, when Books Four, Five and Six were added, the original design for the poem had been seriously compromised; with the structural changes to the poem, the ideological facade of Spenser's allegiances to the Elizabethan regime are increasingly exposed at times, so obviously, indeed, that Spenser himself is acutely aware that something has gone dreadfully awry. The contradictions of the age are reflected in the unfinished and broken nature of the poem itself: Lewis suggested that we speak not of a 'whole' poem at all, but rather of fragments A (1590, Books 1–3), B (1596 4–6), and C (Mutability).[1] Certainly, between the image of mutuality and confidence in the reconciliation of Amoret and Scudamour in the canceled final stanzas of the 1590 edition and the darker late books there are too many contradictions to ignore. The poem encodes many of the real historical conflicts and tensions of its time, dealing with them not (as Shakespeare was already starting to do in the mid 1590s) by juxtaposing and so exploring their rival claims to truth and allegiance, but by trying arbitrarily to displace and condense them to maintain the power of the dominant ideology.

The last decade of Spenser's life, when his epic reached its eventual, though probably not its intended final shape, coincides with an increasing restlessness in the Elizabethan court, with many obvious and many underlying strains upon the economy and the broader social practices of the country – including failing harvests, rural discontent, rising unemployment, increasing inflation, religious intolerance, and outbursts of unusually strong xenophobia directed against Spaniards, Catholics, and (as the plays of both Marlowe and Shakespeare witness) Jews. The 1590s commenced with Spenser's disillusioning return visit to England from Ireland, his impression summarized in the poignant ambiguity of the title of one of his accounts of his visit, *Colin Clouts Come Home Again*. Where was 'home' now? Raymond Williams notes on Sidney's *Arcadia* that the work 'which gives a continuing title to English neopastoral was written in a park which had been made by enclosing a whole village and evicting the tenants. The elegant game was then only at arm's length – a rough arm's length – from the visible reality of country life'.[2] *The Faerie Queene* was planned and partly written at a greater distance from the Elizabethan court than *Arcadia* and part of its intense idealization of the court arises from Spenser's position as an outsider. His visit to the court in 1589–90 must have forced him to see something analogous to the 'visible reality' of which Williams speaks. *Colin Clouts Come Home Again* is Spenser's pastoral recreation of his visit, written as he contemplated both his reception at the court of Gloriana and his continuing celebration of it. One senses from the poem, in Josephine Bennett's words, that 'Ireland had never been "home" to him until he had been part of the court', but Spenser still tries to insist on setting the all too evident corruption of the court in the context of a redeeming ideal. As he contemplates the court's sophisticated barbarism from what had seemed his exile among rude barbarians, he is still confident in his devotion to the Queen (who had, after all, rewarded him with fifty pounds a year). The poem includes some devastating criticism of 'courtiers as bladders blowen up with wynd' and of 'faire dissembling curtesie', but it is emphatic in its praise of the Queen and the 'ring' of those faithful courtiers who like the dead Sidney and his sister, truly reflect their Queen's glory.[3]

Evidently disquieted by what he saw at court, Spenser returned to Ireland. By 1592 his friend and patron Ralegh was in prison and something of his high-risk (and in Spenser's highly partial view, tragically misunderstood) career is reflected upon in Books Four and Six. It was probably completed some years earlier – in *Amoretti* 80, he writes that his poem is 'halfe fordonne', with six books completed. In the last five years of his life he probably did not complete another. That, as well as the changes between the two parts, gives us a clue to the ways even such a loyal upholder of the regime was increasingly dislocated by the world he perceived – though as the ensuing discussion will show, his perceptions are revealing far beyond what he himself knew. The reorganization, revisions and additions that the poem underwent brought out what the early books, in retrospect, can be seen to have largely, though not entirely, repressed – that *The Faerie Queene*, the most ambitious poetic glorification of the Elizabethan regime, could no longer unambiguously celebrate the power which permitted it to exist without revealing the strains and contradictions that were already radically dislocating that power.

It is important to stress the dislocations in the writing and revisions of the poem. Only since the late 1970s, initially in the work of Goldberg, Greenblatt, and Montrose, have we seen the development of any symptomatic reading of the poem that did not try to explain away its dislocated nature. As Tonkin argues, this new 'postmodern' *Faerie Queene* is not entirely the product of our own age and its acceptance of dislocation and constructed subjectivity; the poem's dislocations grow from its historical circumstances. In a sense, they were 'there' from the beginning as much as the dominant reading.[4] It is therefore especially crucial to our understanding of the transition in English cultural life, and not only in poetry, between the death of Sidney in 1586 and the outbreak of the Civil War over fifty years later. Increasingly nostalgic, retrogressive, and disillusioned, it opens for us, in the way the poetry of any transitional period does, the forces which were eventually to shatter the world it celebrates and from which it traced its origins and inspiration. Throughout these three Books, Spenser's desire is clear: to continue to justify the cultural and ideological practices of the Elizabethan court. And yet, as it unfolds, his poem is increasingly fragmented by potent ideological breaks and contradictions. Book Five is particularly revealing: in the opening canto, for instance, Artegall dismisses chivalric reconciliation as an ineffective means of deciding the conflict between Sanglier and his opponent, asserting that 'doubtfull causes' in a world in which 'sinne gan to abound' (5. 1. 11) can be decided only by force. Conflict is settled not by knights acknowledging their places in a hierarchy but by brutal militarism.

BOOK FOUR: THE BOOK OF FRIENDSHIP

The fourth Book, of Friendship, is the most disparate. It has no central hero. While it has some broadly agreed divisions, it is continually complicated by Spenser's continuing many of the polyphonic strands that were started in Book Three, and in some ways Book Four is best seen as a continued outfolding of the previous Book. Yet Spenser probably intended the first two Books to represent a distinction between passionate sexual love and a broader, more disparate realm that includes 'borne brethren . . . deare lovers [and] sworne friends' (2. 1. 24). It thus includes the bonds of family and kinship, which are seen as natural, given by Nature and god; sexual love, which is discovered, desired or visited upon one, often through pain and violence, 'Hate . . . the elder, Love the younger brother' (4. 10. 32); and the concord of resolved conflict that is found in companionship and friendship proper.

The very fluidity of the Book's subject matter is reflected in the fluidity of the stories it tells. Uncannily, the narrative continually undermines, as Goldberg puts it, 'the possibility of fixed character and fixed meaning' in order to focus on the contradictory shapes of desire.[5] Lust, Corflambo, Venus, the false Florimell, and (as the poem seems to move increasingly and uncomfortably closer to the world of Elizabethan politics) the love between Belphoebe and Timias, all unravel as varied, contradictory narratives of the unpredictability and reversals of love. What the Book teaches over and over is that desire is multiple; love and friendship share ambiguous boundaries; relationships slip away from even the best motivated or morally solid principles. This disruptiveness and fluidity in human relationships is reflected structurally in the multiplicity of miscellaneous knights and ladies in continual movement through Book Four, all with their own stories, often interlocking. Spenser continually plays with patterns of conjunction and rupture: Cambell and Diamond each marry the other's sister, thus setting upon examination of closeness and otherness, sympathy and difference. Various lovers get substituted or exchanged for one another. Human beings are repeatedly invited to try to tell true from false. Above all, stories proliferate: they disappear, are renewed, remain unfinished, trail away. In short, part of the story of love and friendship enacted in Book Four is the story of storytelling itself. We are, especially when we consider matters of love and friendship, narrativizing animals: we try to account for the significance of our lives by telling stories. Those stories are given to us by our culture, even though each of us yearns, often fiercely and in defiance of the relatives of historical and cultural production, for the stories to be 'his', 'hers' – to be, as each of us says, 'mine'. Some stories require to be shared, to be 'ours', others, about which we may marvel or of which we are afraid, are 'theirs'. What Book Four shows is how – though we may think we own the stories – it is we who belong to them. Again and again, we see characters caught up in others' narratives. Virtually every canto in Book Four contains some reference to its own telling or to the previous telling of is story. In part, that is simply because as *The Faerie Queene* has proceeded, more and more stories have been introduced, and there is, in Spenser's world view, a need to see stories concluded. Nothing, ultimately, in such a universe as Spenser thought he lived in, can be thought of as open-ended – except, perhaps, mankind's knowledge of what is ordained by God.

So the stories of Amoret and Scudamour, and of Florimell, are given 'happy' endings. But the story of Timias and Belphoebe is left unfinished. Over and over, as these central Books unfold, stories are left, partly or completely unfinished, and even when they are finished, we may not necessarily be told how. In particular is the case with the one story that comes closest to historical event, that of Timias and Belphoebe, which at points become a transparent account of Spenser's view of the relationship between the queen and Ralegh. It is, of course, too simple to say that Timias 'stands for' Ralegh: *The Faerie Queene* is too multiple in its focus to allow for such reductive identification. But in Timias, Spenser seems to provide a very partial interpretation of his friend's relations with the queen. Ralegh, after all, was perhaps the most blatantly manipulative of all Elizabeth's courtiers. Something of his flamboyant role-playing can

be sensed in Timias's relationship with Belphoebe, where he takes
the role Ralegh enacted to perfection in the English court of the
1580s, that of the devoted yet unrewarded servant, 'captived in
endlesse durance/Of sorrow and despaire without aleggeaunce'
(3. 5. 42). But at some point in the second half of the poem, as (most
·probably) Spenser finished and revised his earlier draft of the Book
of Friendship, contemporary events increasingly disturbed him into
taking up the questions of courtly values in ways the first three
books had not anticipated. There are signs that in considering Ralegh's
fall from favor in 1592 Spenser found himself caught between conflicting allegiances, to the queen and to what he perceived as the
injustice of his patron's treatment. In the earlier book, the delicate
ambiguity of Spenser's treatment of Timias's guilt at being taken
with Amoret, 'handling soft the hurts, which she did get' (4. 7. 35),
becomes a delightful comedy. Mistakes of misprision and over-
reaction occur on both sides and Spenser skillfully balances the
seductive sensuality of Amoret with the fierce exclusiveness of
Belphoebe who

> . . . in her wrath she thought them both have thrild,
> With that selfe arrow, which the Carle had kild.
> Yet held her wrathfull hand from vengeance sore,
> But drawing nigh, ere he her well beheld;
> Is this the faith, she said, and said no more,
> But turnd her face, and fled away for evermore.
>
> (4. 7. 36)

The Book's most convincing set piece is probably the wedding of the
rivers Thames and Medway in Canto Eleven.

In this episode, friendship thus becomes a national (even, Spenser
would argue, a cosmic) virtue, as all the rivers of Britain, Ireland,
and across the whole world join together to celebrate the principle of
harmony won from discord and disparateness. Friendship is thereby
presented as concord not merely among people, the creation of
harmonious social relationships out of the potential chaos and dis-
ruption of human interaction, but throughout the natural creation as
well. So, just like the rivers, Belphoebe and Timias are reconciled,
Britomart and Artegal united, Scudamour and Amoret (after many
complications) brought together, and Florimell and Marinell married. But the sense of the unpredictability, even of these perfected
stories, is conveyed in the last lines of the Book, which suggest that

harmony of any kind is never complete, is always to be achieved:

> Right so himselfe did *Marinell* upreare,
>   When he in place his dearest love did spy;
>   And though his limbs could not his bodie beare,
>   Ne former strength returne so suddenly,
>   Yet chearefull signes he shewed outwardly
>   Ne lesse was she in secret hart affected,
>   But that she masked it with modestie,
>   For feare she should of lightness be detected:
> Which to another place I leave to be perfected.
>   (4. 12. 35)

BOOK FIVE: THE BOOK OF JUSTICE

In the fifth Book, the pressure of the Elizabethan regime upon the poem becomes most obvious, and increasingly destructive of the poem's intentions. In Lewis's strong words, 'Spenser was the instrument of a detestable policy in Ireland, and in his fifth book the wickedness he had shared begins to corrupt his imagination'.[6] The Book is deeply concerned, in particular, with the trial and execution of Mary Queen of Scots and the English occupation of Ireland. It is perhaps significant that in the 1970s a number of American critics read Book Five for an 'underlying' universal moral allegory rather than deal with the blatant political issues: their readings were patently ideological, at least in part the product of the Cold War, and so intriguingly attuned to attempts (like Spenser's, not totally deliberate) to cover and mystify awkward political realities. The Book undoubtedly expresses Spenser's unease before the strains of the last decades of the century just as these recent readings register a helplessness before the seeming inexorability of politics.

When he came to England in 1590, Spenser had certainly conceived and possibly finished Book Four – which 'belongs in spirit, design, and even execution, to the 1580s', Roger Sale notes – and parts of Five also were written before Spenser's visit, at a time when he was anxious to defend the principles of Elizabethan power embodied in Grey's tough dealings with what the English, at least, saw as the Irish rebels.[7] From both Book Five and *A View of the Present State of Ireland*, we see how Spenser could be critical of government policy. Yet he was fiercely, even brutally, loyal to its underlying principles, concluding in his treatise that Ireland should be immediately pacified by a massive application of military force. As Helena Shire comments, while Spenser undoubtedly 'knew that the Irish were a language people of ancient culture who had inhabited the island for many centuries, that they were "lettered" earlier than the English, and that their way of life made sense to them', nevertheless, there is no acknowledgment 'whatsoever that the Irish had a right or an understandable determination to persist in their ancestral life-pattern, resisting the presence in the land of foreign overlords, who were intent on subduing them and colonizing the island completely'.[8] Spenser's criticisms of the details of Elizabeth's Irish policy, like his satire on court manners, were frequently harsh but certainly they never called the rights or ideals of the English into question.

To work through Book Five, then, is to see the dislocative power of Spenser's life upon his poem unambiguously and painfully. Lewis's judgement that Spenser's part in England's 'detestable' Irish policy started to 'corrupt his imagination' is perhaps over-stated, but undoubtedly it points to a split of allegiances that had been incipient throughout Spenser's life. Even if we sympathize with Lewis, the degree of determinism in the situation in which Spenser found himself cannot be over-emphasized. On the other hand, he would not have seen it that way. He was deeply committed to the Elizabethan regime, to the Protestant revolution, to the domination of Ireland by English power. But the moral ambiguities of those commitments are starting to betray one of his other commitments, to the moral force of the poet's vocation.

In one sense, the central figure of Book Five is not its Knight, Artegal, who with his servant Talus goes through an often over-obvious allegorical world dealing out very rough, and often ambiguously and over-long justified, justice. It is Elizabeth herself. She is the 'Dread Sovereign Goddess' who represents justice and order. She appears in the Book as the judicious Mercilla, judging (though leaving the final execution to others) Duessa who reappears in the poem to represents Mary Queen of Scots. In an episode in which the giantess Radigund captures Artegall, we get a highly partial view of a series of Mary's interactions with Elizabeth and her government: Elizabeth's aid to the Scots Protestant forces in 1559, Mary's flight to England in 1567, her alleged involvement with the Catholic aristocracy of the North, and her rivalry with Elizabeth.[9]

Spenser makes very clear where his allegiances lie. The justice that Mercilla, Artegal, and (especially) Talus represent is patently ideological, clear representations of Althusser's 'repressive' state apparatuses, the means whereby a regime enforces conformity to its decision about the meanings of 'right' and 'wrong'. When Envy, Detraction and (this and the next Book's great enemy) the Blatant Beast attack Artegall, an uneasiness surfaces, even in the poem itself, that (despite their names, which are meant to signal their 'real' meanings) they have a case – especially when we look at the material details of history, both in Spenser's time and what, subsequently, came through in the tragic history of Ireland. The closest Spenser comes in the *View* to acknowledging any alternatives is to have one of his interlocutors in that treatise acknowledge that the effect of English rule – not the principles, of course – may have been in practice disruptive to Ireland. Book Five – the longest of the work – tries to justify these underlying principles by pointing to the threatened chaos in the whole universe. Unless justice triumphs, and is made to triumph, in very specific particulars, cosmic disorder will result.

Yet in Spenser's universe, Justice presumably does triumph. That belief, after all, is at the core of his religious faith. Despite frequent appearances to the contrary, Justice rules. So, why the anxiety about whether it will do so? The more closely the examples in the Book come to the world in which Spenser was writing his poem, the more we see the answer to that question. The historical references tumble over one another, especially in the final five cantos, as if the poem had to become, perforce, a justification not of underlying principles, but of local, particular policies and incidents in the world of the poem's making. As O'Connell comments, many of these, 'especially those concerned with Ireland, are not likely to strike a modern reader as unassailable examples of justice'.[10]

The Book certainly tries to build its case logically: as a series of incidents illustrating the establishment of law in human affairs, followed by stories illustrating difficult cases in which the principle of the appropriate appellation of law according to circumstances, or 'equity' is illustrated; and finally, the greatest and most celebrated single legal case of Spenser's age – incorporating as it did so many of the regime's most defensive principles and reactions – the trial and condemnation of the Queen of Scots, which is presented in company with a series of allegorized incidents from other arenas of the struggle with Catholicism. So the opening section includes such crimes as murder, assault, robbery, lying, the control of monopolies over tolls; in all cases, the judgments are rendered in order to preserve the status quo. Systems of justice usually serve the powerful, and Spenser was certainly clear about where power (and his allegiances) lay. At times, however, the principles are somewhat compromised by the means by which they are administered: often justice is highly summary, as when Talus carries out the execution of a Giant who, by means of a set of scales (an ironic reference to the symbol for justice itself) has advocated a more democratic distribution of privilege and wealth: Artegall's judgment has not been delivered, but it is obvious what it will be, and so summary justice is the result. The principles of justice, it is assumed, are so obvious that execution is part of the 'natural' order. Equity, which is the focus of the middle cantos of the Book, is the study of the application or adoption of common law to particular cases. It was less tied to precedent and more concerned with the problem of sorting out ambiguous tangles, where the 'natural' lay obscured beneath the confusion of particular cases.

As well as allegorizing both principle and particularities of the Elizabethan legal system – at least as perceived by one of its supporters and beneficiaries – Spenser took the opportunity in Book Five to continue or conclude some of his earlier narratives. Britomart visits Isis Church and learns how her union with Artegall is linked to the union of Justice and Equity, and that, as the allegorical ancestor of Elizabeth, she can rescue her Knight from the capture of Radigund who stands for the allurements and vagaries of foreign law and, specifically, the legal system embodied in the rule of the Queen of Scots. The threat (and attraction) of Elizabeth's cousin and rival is situated very specifically within the struggles of politics: Mary is foreign, a woman, a heretic, an 'other' in a multiplicity of ways. This was not supposedly the identification about which James I and VI – Mary's son and Elizabeth's eventual successor – complained: he objected to Spenser's identification of Mary and Duessa. But in fact, in the figure of Radigund, the otherness of his mother within the cultural nightmares (in a real sense, indeed, the cultural repressed) of loyal Englishmen is also richly brought out.

Having moved from domestic and individual law, to the law of the nation, in its second half, Book Five moves to a defence of the English interests in the international arena. Charitably, one might say that the individual case studies in the early part of the Book are mainly offenses against the lives and property of the 'better sort' and could only be expected from a class-based legal system and hence not out of the ordinary for the age: it would be surprising, after all, to have Spenser supporting the democratization of property or the rights of squatters. Spenser's commitment to the Elizabethan regime is (to say the least) unsurprising. But the more he tries to see eternal principles at work in England's foreign policy, the more partial and contradictory the poem becomes. Part of the difficulty can be measured in the simplification of the allegory. Historical allegory dominates; the dramatization of the multiple aspects of justice is abandoned for a justification of particular political policies. The Spanish, Irish and French are all, by definition, rightful victims of English justice, and we are required simply to agree with the unambiguous judgments. This is poetry as defensive propaganda. No attempt is made at persuasion; the rhetorical mode is that of assertion. As O'Connell comments, when Malengin (guile) is described, it is simply as an Irishman, and his 'capture and destruction by Talus represents Spenser's fondest wish for his adopted homeland':

> Thereto the Blatant beast by them set on
>   At him began aloud to barke and bay,
>   With bitter rage and fell contention,
>   That all the woods and rockes nigh to that way,
>   Began to quake and tremble with dismay;
>   And all the aire rebellowed againe.
>   So dreadfully his hundred tongues did bray,
>   And evermore those hags them selves did paine,
> To sharpen him, and their owne cursed tongs did straine . . .
>
> But *Talus* hearing her so lewdly raile,
>   And speake so ill of him, that well deserved,
>   Would her have chastiz'd with his yron flaile,
>   If her Sir *Artegall* had not preserved,
>   And him forbidden, who his heast obserued.
>   So much the more at him still did she scold,
>   And stones did cast, yet he for nought would swerve
>   From his right course, but still the way did hold
> To Faery Court, where what him fell shall else be told.
>   (5. 12. 41, 43)

Further, as O'Connell notes, 'the episode is grounded on the reader's presumed agreement about Melengin's case, and no attempt is made to persuade us' of the case against him.[11]

At the center of this consistently tough and blatantly ideological view of justice is, therefore, Spenser's allegiance to the queen. Hence the central episode of the Book, at least on the level of the political justification for the view of Justice he is defending – is the court of Mercilla. Sitting with the symbol of English justice, the lion, under her feet, Mercilla is meant to enthrone the justification for the policies the whole Book has allegorized. But the still center of the Book of Justice is a shifting, and somewhat shifty, justification of one particular policy, the execution of Mary. At this crucial point in the Book, it is as if Spenser cannot risk evoking some eternal principle: he returns obsessively to the fascination and, we might suspect, the collective guilt over the execution of Mary. In getting closer to history, Book Five has been unable to escape history's inevitable ambivalence. Nor does the end of the Book restore a note of confidence. Artegall overcomes Grantorto – again probably referring to the defeat of the Irish by his old superior Lord Grey – but that incident has less intensity than the final stages, which describe the surging power of Envy, Detraction and above all, the Blatant Beast.

BOOK SIX: THE BOOK OF COURTESY

When we turn to Book Six, something even more disruptive of Spenser's ideals can be observed. In Book Five, Spenser posed the problem of finding himself, as he must have done so often in Ireland, surrounded by acute contradictions between his ideals and what he saw as social realities. He looks back to the Golden Age and the note of criticism is an unusually sweeping one:

> For that which all men then did vertue call,
> Is now cald vice; and that which vice was hight,
> Is now hight vertue, and so us'd of all
> (5, Proem, 4)

Not surprisingly, therefore, his unease becomes more evident the closer the poem comes to the realities of the Elizabethan court. The gloomy, unresolved ending of Book Five testifies to Spenser's realization that the gap between the actual court of Gloriana and his celebration of it was uncomfortably, perhaps unbridgably, wide. In Book Six, he turns directly to the virtue that did, or should, uphold the life of the court he served and by which, during both his visit to England and in his faithful service in Ireland, he felt so disturbed –

courtesy. He bridges the gap between the two, seemingly very different, Books by having the same monster who thwarts Artegall's quest, the Blatant Beast, appear as the object of Calidore's.

On the surface, The Book of Courtesy invites us to relax with a delightfully leisured, pastoral interlude, and enjoy exciting battles; it promises a civilized contrast with the gloomy brutality of Book Five. Spenser presents courtesy as the manifestation in social relations of those higher virtues he has already treated. Among all the virtues, the poem serenely asserts in its opening, there

> . . . growes not a fayrer flowre,
> Then is the bloosme of comely courtesie,
> Which though it on a lowly stalke doe bowre,
> Yet brancheth forth in brave nobilitie,
> And spreds it selfe through all civilitie.
>   (VI. Proem, 4)

But a poem by a poet whose disquiet at the court had been expressed in *Colin Clouts Come Home Again* could not rest easy with that bland assertion, and throughout Book Six there emerges a deep anxiety about the reality of courtly life. In the 'present age', the Proem continues, courtesy may seem to abound, 'yet being matcht with plaine Antiquitie,/Ye will them all but fayned showes esteeme,/Which carry colours faire, that feeble eies misdeeme'. The mode of criticism in *Colin Clout* had been that of the servant of the court appalled by the court's irresponsibility and superficiality. Here the criticism goes much deeper:

> But in the triall of true curtesie,
> Its now so farre from that, which then it was,
> That it indeed is nought but forgerie,
> Fashion'd to please the eies of them, that pas.
>   (Proem, 4, 5)

The central (if usually absent) figure of the poem has been, to this point, the Queen: and, just as in *Colin Clout* the Lady Cynthia was excluded from the general criticism of the court, so here too Spenser still highlights Elizabeth as the fairest pattern of courtesy, superior to all those of both Antiquity and the present. It is from her that the court derives its being and also what reminders of grace and integrity it retains. Like the virtuous courtiers singled out in *Colin Clout*, the Queen is praised as the fountain, the ocean, the source, of all the 'goodly vertues' which 'well/Into the rest, which round about you ring, Faire Lords and Ladies, which about you dwell,/And doe adorne your court, where courtesies excell'. (6. Proem, 7) But if, as the poem had sadly stated, all contemporary courtesy is 'but fayned showes', 'nought but forgerie', then the apparently excelling courtesy of the present age is mere surface. Similarly, while it is argued that 'vertues seat is deepe within the mynd,/And not in outward shows' and false courtesy is 'a glas so gay, that it can blynd/The wisest sight, to thinke gold that is bras', only eight lines later, the queen herself, the source of the true courtesy, is also described as 'a mirrour sheene', her brightness also serving to 'inflame/The eyes of all, which thereon fixed beene' (6, Proem, 5, 6). Spenser's choice of metaphor and the contradictions of his argument would seem to be produced by his repressed antagonism towards the political oppression of which he was part. Even though such confusions are marginalized, they point to fierce ideological tensions entering into the poem of which Spenser was perhaps not entirely conscious and yet which, by the end of the book, are radically undermining the ideals he is celebrating.

Robert Stillman has persuasively argued for the Book being, in fact, much closer to the realities of Spenser's life in Ireland in the early 1590s than it appears. 'Contemporary criticism of book Six has for too long acquiesced in Spenser's claims to autonomous poetic visions; green worlds are seductive now as then': finding parallels between episodes in the Book and Spenser's analysis of the Irish in the *View*, Stillman suggests that Spenser's acknowledgement that Ireland may be possible to pacify (Artegall's and Talus's view, as it were) but that the true 'civilization' of the conquered land must be undertaken in the material practices, the customs, and ideologically. The apparent move toward romance and escapist pastoral and away from insistent political reference involves a political calculation even more potent than direct physical coercion. There are, indeed, a scattering of references to Ireland – the savages who capture Serena (Canto 8), the Salvage Man, the cannibals – but as Stillman notes, 'the real urgency of Book Six . . . derives from the conceptual power of its mythmaking, not from its infrequent topical allusiveness'. Poetry, once again, is being marshalled in the service of a dominant ideology.[12]

Social text and literary text, social life and literary life, then, forcefully flow into each other. The England that Spenser saw on his visit impinges more directly on the gentle, pastoral landscape of Book Six than might have first been imagined. But there is one characteristic of the Book which opens up Spenser's disaffiliation with his world particularly revealingly. It is the near absence of the original inspiration for the poem: Book Six is the only one in which there is no allegorical representation of the Queen within the narrative. Everything that seems to be undermining the order Spenser had celebrated in earlier books is here embodied in the figure of the Blatant Beast – protean, indiscriminate, and, finally, impossible to enchain. Whether we see the Blatant Beast as detraction, slander, backbiting, or something more general, it stands for a distinctively courtly perversion and one that Spenser saw attacking the court of Elizabeth so successfully that the chosen champion of courtesy, Sir Calidore, pursues but cannot finally defeat it. Presumably, it would have been possible for Spenser to have put an allegorical embodiment in the book finally to defeat or at least counterbalance the Beast. Such a confrontation would have been an assertion of belief in the continuing power of the queen's inspiration. Instead he restricts her presence solely to the Proem and to brief references in later cantos. Even these references are uneasy or obligatory, and show Spenser coming closer than he knew to calling radically into question the ideals on which the court was built.

There are other parts of Book Six where the realities of the 1590s provide a subtext which significantly swerves the poem from its intention. In the story of Timias, which started in Books Three and Four, we saw Spenser dealing delicately with the controversial figure of Ralegh. When Timias reappears in Book Six, the ambiguity is no longer quite so comic or delicate. In Book Six, 3, Spenser attempts to deal, as Ralegh himself was attempting to do, with the queen's anger at his marriage with Elizabeth Throckmorton. Spenser comes down firmly on his friend's side, and blames both the Blatant Beast, the slanderous enemy of courtesy, who 'in his wide great mouth' has seized Serena (6. 3. 24), and the three Knights of Discourtesy, Despetto, Decetto and Defetto, who have attacked and wounded the gallant squire. Like Ralegh himself, Spenser could not face the possibility that his commitment to the court had proved so futile and unrewarding that the court itself was corrupt and destructive; like Ralegh, he could only blame misunderstanding and malice which had, somehow, deceived even the queen.

The world of the late Elizabethan court, then, comes uneasily close to the surface of Book Six, despite the significant absence of the

Queen herself within its narrative structure. Even more disturbing to the apparent serenity of this 'delightfull land of Faery', however, is a pessimism that contrasts radically with the tone of earlier Books. It is prefigured in the Proem to Book Five, where Spenser broods over the 'state of present time' comparing it with 'the image of the antique world', and able to find evidence only for degeneration:

> Me seemes the world is runne quite out of square,
> From the first point of his appointed sourse,
> And being once amisse growes daily wourse and wourse.
>
> (Proem, 1)

All around is the dissolution of human history; only the chosen instruments of justice, like Artegall, stand between mankind and chaos. Implied here is a view of history startlingly different from that of earlier books, where degeneration was seen as only a temporary phase in a pattern of natural replenishment and regeneration. An optimistic, cyclical view of history has been replaced by a view of history as entropic, a view that is stressed even more strongly at the start of Six. There too the antique world's true virtue has been abandoned for 'fayned showes', 'forgerie', and deception, and Sir Calidore's quest, unlike that of any previous hero, has taken him further and further from fulfilment. At the end of the book, the Blatant Beast escapes and 'raungeth through the world againe' (6. 12. 41). The poem's pessimism has become not merely that of a disillusioned, ageing courtier or public servant disturbed by the evident surface corruption of the late Elizabethan court. The end of *The Faerie Queene* records a deeper disillusion, one that links the poem more closely than Spenser (or many of his modern admirers) would like to the generation of cynically quietist, deeply disillusioned, radicals of the 1590s – with the tortured, dislocated writings of Donne, Marston, Greville and Webster, and with the deeply pessimistic Shakespeare of *Troilus and Cressida*. All of these younger men lived into the reign of the son of 'foule Duessa' son's reign, and each had his own, conscious or suppressed, ways of reacting to the pressure of that disillusion. Spenser was to die shortly before the peculiar Jacobean schizophrenia could claim him. What he must have started to experience is poignantly recorded in Book Six.

At the start of the book, the poem turns to define courtesy and thus to set the expected quest in motion. We are told, in a conventional enough starting-point, that 'courtesie' is derived from 'court'. But the terms in which this commonplace is expressed are curiously contradictory: 'Of court it seemes, men courtesie doe call,/For that it there most useth to abound.' 'Seemes' and 'most useth' are more tentative than a wholehearted assertion of the virtue of courtesy might demand. 'Useth' suggests habitual or accustomed expectation as well as a hint of nostalgia; 'seemes' recalls the 'fayned showes' which the Proem has mentioned. Furthermore, Spenser goes on: 'Right so in Faery court it did redound,/Where curteous Knights and Ladies most did won/Of all on earth, and made a matchlesse paragon' (6. 1. 1). The switch to the past tense reinforces the tentativeness of Spenser's discussion of courtesy. Next we encounter a description of his knight of courtesy, and the same ambiguity continues. While Calidore is depicted as 'none more courteous', it is difficult to take the Greek origin of his name (Beautiful Gift) seriously without simultaneously admitting that either Spenser is verging on satire or is interestingly unaware of the contradictions. Calidore, we are told, has 'gentlenesse of spright', 'manners milde', 'gracious speech', 'faire usage and conditions sound', and is shown to be restrained, disciplined, and ceremonious. Yet the emphasis on such characteristics is qualified by Spenser's habitual use of 'seemes' (6. 1. 2) and by the distinctive choice of terms to describe Calidore. To his natural graces, he adds 'comely guize'. While he is 'well approv'd in batteilous affray', yet his 'faire usage . . . purchast' him "place' and reputation. It is difficult to argue that these terms do not undercut any affirmation of courtesy as the triumphant harmonization of opposites.

While Spenser sets up a strong contrast in the Proem between calculated externalized 'showes' of courtesy and the hidden virtues within, as he moves through Faeryland in Book Six, refining and testing his initial definition of courtesy, some revealing contradictions emerge. At the start of the third Canto, the poem qualifies the earlier insistence upon true courtesy lying deep within the mind by asserting that outward manners can in fact be taken as a reliable guide to inward virtue. But now courtesy is said to be bound up with externals, behaving with decorum and bearing oneself 'aright/To all of each degree, as doth behove'. In the fifth Canto, we are assured further that there is always a firm connection between gentle behaviour and noble birth, between external grace and internal virtue, even if it may not be easily discernible. Spenser asserts that Calidore 'loathd leasing and base flattery,/And loved simple truth and stedfast honesty' (6. 1. 3), but the difference between these admirable characteristics and the 'comely guize' and the 'greatest grace' that Calidore 'with the greatest purchast' is not made clear. At one with his age's most conservative moralists, Spenser asserts that a noble, trotting stallion rarely begets an awkward, ambling colt. He seems to be deeply concerned to hold social change at bay and to preserve the traditional standards he clearly saw being eroded in the court of the 1590s. Such contradictions show how the beginning of Book Six simply cannot maintain the moral distinctions on which his exploration of the nature of the court and courtesy needed to be based. Even Spenser himself was perhaps increasingly unable to make such distinctions with his earlier certainty. The world he creates, instead of testing and so refining his chosen virtue, comes increasingly to call it radically into question.

In accordance with the expected pattern of the whole poem, then, Calidore goes off on his quest. It is striking that, embodying a virtue which 'useth' to be found at court, Calidore will eventually find it best manifest in the country. It is also noteworthy that as a knight representing or searching for a distinctively social virtue, courtesy, he goes off alone. His world in fact becomes an increasingly lonely one, dominated by the unpredictability of fortune and the ambiguity of moral choice. 'All flesh is frayle, and full of ficklenesse,' he learns, 'subject to fortunes chance, still chaunging new' (6. 1. 41). The dichotomy between good and evil which is traditionally a central part of the chivalric quest is also missing. Calidore's foe, the Blatant Beast – the savage vilifier of Timias, the adversary who has escaped Artegall's savage hand in Book Five – emerges as a savage parody of courtesy, 'fostred long in Stygian fen,/Till he to perfect ripeness grew, and then,/Into this wicked world he forth was sent'. Such terms recall the nurturing of Amoret and Belphoebe, and the 'infinite shapes of creatures' that are bred in the Garden of Adonis. Indeed, part of the Beast's threat seems to lie in its being uncannily close to the virtue it seeks to undermine: the enemy of courtesy is not an alien force, but a variant of courtesy itself.

The impression that Calidore and his adversaries share a world of common values is brought out in Calidore's confrontation with Maleffort and Briana. Both sides in the battle use the language and the art of courtesy: she accuses Calidore of scorning and shaming the decorum of chivalry by murdering her servants and sends word to her champion Crudor to

> . . . desire that he would
> Vouchsafe to reskue her against a Knight,
> Who through strong powre had now her self in hould,
> Having late slaine her Seneschall in fight,
> And all her people murdred with outragious might.

In similar terms Crudor vows to 'succour her' and in appropriate chivalric manner sends 'to her his basenet, as a faithfull band' (31). In order to stress their shared values, Spenser does not, as he does so often in earlier books, give moral asides to direct his readers' responses. Instead, he stresses Calidore's precipitate entry into the battle. When he sees a knight approaching,

> Well weend he streight, that he should be the same,
> Which tooke in hand her quarrell to maintaine;
> Ne stayd to aske if it were he by name,
> But couch his speare, and ran at him amaine.
>
> (6. 1. 29, 33)

The two combatants are almost indistinguishable as they fight, and when Calidore is finally victorious, he comments upon the dubious outcome in a revealing line, confessing to his vanquished enemy that 'What haps to day to me, to morrow may to you' (41). It is as if they are struggling not in a world of moral absolutes, but for alternate versions of courtesy. Such relativism is a strange departure for *The Faerie Queene* and one that seems contradictory to Spenser's announced intentions.

The episode following, with the squire Tristram, also brings out the ways in which conservatism and moral relativism contradict each other. Calidore's initial hostility to Tristram's 'hand too bold . . . embrewed/in blood of knight' (6. 2. 7) is tempered when he learns of the discourtesy of Tristram's victim, and instead of seeing Tristram's behaviour as discourteous, he accommodates the youngster's behaviour to necessity – 'what he did, he did him selfe to save'. He then enunciates a principle which would seem, logically, to justify the behaviour not merely of Tristram but of Crudor in the previous episode: that 'knights and all men this by nature have,/ Towards all womenkind them kindly to behave' (6. 2. 14). Spenser later tries to smooth out the moral contradictions: Tristram turns out to be of noble birth, the son of 'good king Meliogras' of Cornwall, and so his behaviour is legitimized.

Spenser's difficulty in reconciling his conservative moral absolutism with an increasingly relativistic world comes out particularly in Calidore's need, most intriguing in a knight representing a supposedly inner virtue, to rely on the 'fayned showes' and the values of reputation and appearance which have been indignantly repudiated at the book's start. Calidore (and, in Canto five, Arthur) are perfectly entitled, it seems, to use deceit, subterfuge, and cunning to achieve their ends. What seems to differentiate their true from others' false courtesy is simply success. Perhaps we are just meant to assume that Arthur is by definition right, but if so, an important moral ambiguity surfaces: his methods are difficult or impossible to distinguish from those of his or Calidore's enemies. We are meant to take his virtue for granted even though his actions seem indistinguishable from those of his enemies.

It may be that Spenser was partly aware of the contradictions he was building into his poem. But they undoubtedly articulate a more widespread unease and confusion than his 'intention' knew. We can recognize how such an earnest, committed servant of the Elizabethan court would react to what he saw as the crumbling away of the ideals on which the court was built. But what language did he have to articulate his distress? In what ways could he have articulated the dislocation of the emerging modern subject? What he inevitably falls back on is the residual language of religious renunciation. Yet he did so only as the poem came to what was to be its premature end. In Book One the Red Crosse Knight was given a vision of the Heavenly City, and, overwhelmed by its transcendence even of the Earthly City, Cleopolis, had prayed to be allowed to abandon his quest and enter into the world of eternity. He was sent firmly back into the world to complete his quest, just as Spenser applied himself faithfully to his duties in Ireland. But when, in the middle of Book Six, a similar situation arises in the Blatant Beast's attack on Timias and Serene the temptation of withdrawal from the world arises again. Timias and Serena take refuge with a Hermit, and for once, Spenser creates a character who, although unquestionably embodying what he wants us to see as a signpost towards truth, seems at odds with the ostensible virtue of the poem. He has, he tells them, renounced the court:

> . . . he had bene a man of mickle name,
> Renowmed much in armes and derring doe:
> But being aged now and weary to

Of warres delight, and worlds contentious toyle,
The name of knighthood he did disavow,
And hanging up his armes and warlike spoyle,
From all this worlds incombraunce did himselfe assoyle.

                                        (6. 5. 37)

The terms in which the Hermit is described suggest a restful reward
for many years of devotion to the 'worlds contentious toyle', yet the
cure he prescribes for Timias and Serena – who are still 'young'
(6.5.11) and 'faire' (6.5.39) – is also renunciation of the toil of courtly
strife. He entertains them. His counsel is to 'avoide the occasion' of
their pain, to 'abstaine from pleasure', and 'subdue desire' (6. 6. 14)
– to give over, in other words, the delights of the courtly life. Obviously, the Hermit's advice is perfectly in accord with Spenser's
earlier emphasis that true virtue lies deep within the mind, yet it
does lie uncomfortably beside the active life of courtesy the book has
so far celebrated.

What I have so far highlighted might be described as no more
perhaps than a sense of unease on Spenser's part, most probably
produced by his own experiences in the court, his reaction to Ralegh's
fall from favour, and, simply, his own increasing age and weariness.
From Canto Seven onwards, this unease brings Spenser to focus on
the one commitment to which, it seems, he held even more strongly
than to his political duties – his poetry. As Book Six draws to its
conclusion, the belief in national destiny that lay at the root of his
original choice of the epic written to celebrate England and the court
of Elizabeth seems to falter, and we can see emerging an even greater
contradiction. Unable to celebrate the court and its virtues as unambiguously as he once did, his poem starts to evaluate even its author's role as the celebrant of the queen and her court. The Blatant
Beast attacks not only virtuous and unwary courtiers, but the basis
of the very art that has brought him into being:

Ne spareth he most learned wits to rate,
Ne spareth he the gentle Poets rime,
But rends without regard of person or of time.

Ne may this homely verse, of many meanest
Hope to escape his venemous despite . . .

                                        (6. 12. 40–1)

In this melancholy and somewhat waspish tone, Spenser in fact goes on to conclude Book Six: the forces which threaten society and civility are also attacking the poet and poetry itself, seemingly without restraint.

Therefore how does the poet, whose life has been dedicated to celebrating the court, deal with its rejection not only of the ideals of courtesy on which it is itself founded, but of the poet who would draw them back to those ideals? In the second half of the book, the power and value of poetry in the court become a central subject, and what emerges is a deep unease about the reciprocity of court and poet on which *The Faerie Queene* had been built. While the final six cantos of the book are ostensibly centred on Calidore, they have as an urgent underlying concern Spenser's commitment to the very poem to which he had devoted so much of his life. We can see perhaps Calidore and Colin Clout, who appears in Canto Nine as an embodiment of the figure of the troubled poet, as two aspects of Spenser himself, or more generally, of the court poet.

When we are shown Calidore as the spectator of the stately vision on Mount Acidale, we are aware that as with other doctrinal nodes of the poem, Spenser is focusing with as much intensity as he can on the issues underlying his poem. In this superbly evocative episode, there is inserted a mysterious and striking figure. Besides the ring of dancers on the Mount is the figure of the poet named as Colin Clout. It is one of the most significant touches that Spenser should introduce what amounts to a charmingly deprecative self-portrait at a moment in the poem when the courtly vision seems closest to faltering. It is one of the high points of the whole poem – dignified, passionate, redolent with suggestiveness, and moreover, an episode into which Spenser articulated the centrality of poetry in the service of the state and put most explicitly his anxieties about whether his gesture was either effective or even noticed. As Stillman notes, 'Spenser amasses an impressive, even daunting array of symbolic capital to lend credibility to his idealizing image of courtesy', asserting as so many courtly Elizabethan poems do, that simply 'partake imaginatively in the process' of the unfolding vision 'is to have one's faith awakened in the unity of divine truth as it manifests itself in deliberately marked stages from the mundane to the heavenly and in the poet's capacity to apprehend and represent that unity as timeless, autonomous vision'. [13]

The episode starts by recalling the Book's opening, the terms of which have, as we have seen, become increasingly ambivalent as the adventures have proceeded. The pastoral world, we are told, far transcends the world of courtly vanity, 'Save onely Glorianaes heavenly hew/To which what can compare?' (6. 10. 4). Perhaps Spenser's unease at where his poem is now turning makes him draw attention to this obligatory exception to courtly degeneration. Certainly, the vision Calidore is given on the Mount seems to call into question the value and power of the court. In the centre of the Grace's dance is not the Queen, nor virtuous courtiers, nor an abstract, untested virtue, but Colin Clout's own shepherd lass who 'another grace . . . well deserves to be' (6. 10. 27). There is a brief, though charming, apology for seeming to replace the queen – and yet the transposition has been made. But of course, it is not Colin but Calidore who is the book's central figure and so it is he who breaks into the dance and makes the vision disappear. Interestingly, while Colin may instruct Calidore (and us) on its significance, there is no sense that (unlike the allegorical set pieces in earlier books) the Knight will benefit from the vision he has been given. Instead, he turns back to his devious pursuits and to his quest. Returning to Pastorella, he discovers the fact of her noble parentage and then that she has been captured by brigands.

How do we read this division in the book's culminating scene? It is as if we must choose between Calidore and Colin at this point. Book Six seems to have increasingly revealed contradictions in Spenser's celebration of the court. We might argue that he seems aware of these contradictions to the extent that he can, with some unease, but without apology, project contradictory aspects of his vision into Calidore and Colin Clout. But it is the incompatibility which comes most strongly through in the poem in ways the poet himself which it started. The Beast has infected all estates of society, has been temporarily captured, and in the short-lived triumph of its capture what the knight and his enemy have in common becomes quite explicit. All questions of moral superiority are gone; instead, we have the spectacle of public adulation in which all 'much admyr'd the Beast, but more admyr'd the Knight' (6. 12. 37). The Beast then breaks his bonds and rages through the world again.

6

Mutability and the
Literary Life

'ALL THINGS DECAY'

The Faerie Queene – along with the mysterious Cantos of Mutability, which were published twelve years after Spenser's death – is often seen as the most significant poetic document of its age. This assessment has been based on the poem's celebration of the apparent glories of the 'golden' Elizabethan age. But as we have surveyed Spenser's career, it can be seen that *The Faerie Queene*'s significance may lie rather in its depiction of the crumbling of an archaic world and the opening up of what, for want of a better word, we can term the modern. It is especially crucial to our understanding of the transition in English cultural life, and not only in poetry, between the death of Sidney in 1586 and the outbreak of the Civil War over fifty years later. In part deliberately (and as it grew, increasingly) nostalgic, retrogressive, and disillusioned, *The Faerie Queene* opens for our view the emerging forces which were eventually to shatter the world it celebrates and from which it traced its origins and inspiration. Spenser criticism has rarely confronted this contradiction, preferring to explain away the frustrations, dislocations, and disruptions by searching – probably as desperately as Spenser himself might have – for principles of unity, harmony, and authority that somehow lie 'behind' the shifting intentions and unpredictabilities of the poem and behind the changing shape of his own life. Yet we can see rather a growing fragmentation in the later books – how the binaries and oppositions become more starkly drawn, the quests more difficult to complete.

In the unfinished 'Cantos of Mutability', most especially, Spenser looked back at his career; he sees it as an unpredictable unraveling of his original hopes – 'unraveling' in the contradictory senses of both 'unfolding' and 'undoing, slipping away'. What were probably his final writings – both the Mutability Cantos and the unpublished fragmentary *Note* on English policy in Ireland – show a man who,

160

like Red Crosse, is staring Despair in the face. What perhaps he sees there, in the mirror of Despair, is (again like Red Crosse) himself. The life, literary and other, that Spenser had envisaged as ordered, providential and justifiable was (literally) swept away by the return of Irish insurgents, attacking and laying waste to his domestic contentment at Kilcolman. As he looks in the mirror, he seems to see that much of that life has been shown up as fragmentary, anarchic, disillusioning.

Of course, that is not entirely how Spenser presents it. The bitterness of exile may show through in the ruthlessness of his brief *Note*, but that cryptic memo still unambiguously affirms his commitment to the Elizabethan conquest of Ireland and the extermination of the Irish. Likewise, the Mutability Cantos are a firm affirmation of the external principles he believed lay beneath the changeableness and unpredictability of the universe, the nation, the court, and his life in Ireland. And, it must be said, that through the increasingly turbulent and, given at least part of his reception at court, what must have been the disillusioning years of the 1590s, there were events, and poems, that seem affirmative, life-enhancing, morally and poetically secure. Spenser had become a prosperous landowner; he remarried; and he celebrated what is clearly a growing affection for the Irish countryside and his new wife in a series of evocative poems, including a sonnet sequence, the *Amoretti*, and the celebratory poems on betrothal and marriage, *Epithalamion* and *Prothalamion*. Indeed, he was very busy, poetically speaking, in the 1590s. As well as working on *The Faerie Queene*, and writing new, shorter poems, he was revising older ones for publication. He had become, at least in his own eyes, the senior Elizabethan poet. Perhaps, in retrospect, we can see how mistaken that verdict might have seemed to many newer poets, such as Ben Jonson or John Donne. Spenser was isolated in Munster, far from the court and city, and specifically from the more dynamic literary fashions that were emerging in London in the late 1580s and 1590s were bypassing him – the new, disturbing public theatre, the angry eruption of verse satire, or the fashion for erotic narrative, for instance. In retrospect, we can see a very different world was emerging, one with which Spenser had little contact and less sympathy, an alienation deepened by his exile from his first 'home' in England. But it is also arguable that this newly emergent world is registered, however indirectly, in his poetry. In this final chapter, therefore, I will try to bring together the varied but converging narratives of the last phase of Spenser's literary life. I will deal with the poems of the

1590s outside *The Faerie Queene*, and then turn to that fascinating fragment that (if we are to believe their first publisher) he left in his papers, which we term the Mutability Cantos.

As I noted earlier, the 1591 *Complaints* brought together a number of poems Spenser had written or drafted much earlier in his career. Included in the volume, as well, were a number of miscellaneous pieces written between about 1580 and 1590. These poems, 'disperst abroad in sundry hands', share common concerns: what the printer termed 'like maner of argument in them: being all meditations of the worlds vanitie, verie grave and profitable', above all, the 'trustles' nature of human achievement, and the seriousness of the poetic vocation. Curiously, in the printer's note to the reader, Spenser is still, in 1591, referred to as 'the new Poet', which more than a decade before had been E.K.'s term for him. It is intriguing to speculate, as Crewe and Rambuss have, what different meanings for Spenser's career the revised poems might have had between 1591 and a decade or so before – and also how the whole volume might have received. As Rambuss puts it, we need to ask 'what kind of career gesture is being staged' in a poetically old-fashioned collection that harkens back to the decades before Spenser and Sidney had supposedly transformed Elizabethan poetry.[1]

To readers at the time, in fact, Spenser and his volume might well have seemed an anachronistic reminder of a lost world. We are dealing here with a complex psycho-social phenomenon perhaps peculiar to the modern, post-Spenserian world. Where a person feels him or herself to be defined in large part by reputation within a changing and unpredictable public world rather than by some eternal values or verities, then he or she is likely to feel anxious or threatened by marginalization. When that person feels cut off from what is presented as current, fashionable or powerful, then paralysis or paranoia may result. One aspect of Protestant theology was that to be ostracized or marginalized was proof of virtue. Spenser's beliefs should have inoculated him from such dark fears, even exiled as he so obviously was, outside the court, in darkest Ireland. Indeed, the fear of such marginalization is registered in Spenser's poems. 'The Printer to the Gentle Reader' notes what was no doubt Spenser's own anxiety that the poems were 'disperst abroad in sundry hands, and not easie to bee come by, by himselfe; some of them having bene diverslie imbeziled and purloyned from him, since his departure over Sea' (*SP*, p. 223). Scattered references in the poems themselves complain not only about the follies and betrayals of the world and time, but of the 'meane regard' in which he – 'still wayting to prefer-ment up to climb' (*Mother Hubbards Tale*, ll. 60, 76) – was held. *The Ruines of Time*, written about 1590, for instance, laments Rome's fall, and also bewails the much more loosely felt deaths of the Earl of Leicester and some of his family, including Sidney. Just as Rome's tragedy is in part presented as Spenser's so, as Richard Schell com-ments, 'the poems record the shock of returning to England after a decade's absence', and finding old friends and patrons gone: 'new circles of power provided less hope: Spenser was not so near to their concerns, and he knew that he never would be'. Asking 'where be those learned wits and antique Sages', Spenser is led to a more universal meditation: 'Who then dooth flesh, a bubble glas of breath,/ Hunt after honor and advauncement vaine'. He may claim that 'wise wordes taught in numbers for to runne/Recorded by the Muses, live for ay', but finally the deepest advice the poet can give is: 'unto heaven let our high mind aspire,/And loath this drosse of sinfull worlds desire' (59, 50–1, 403, 685–6). The archaism of the sentiments, which are reflected in the archaism of the poetic forms and styles, betray a broader social statement – the lack of contact with and alienation from the material realities of the post-Armada world. As Rambuss suggests, the volume seems not only to be a diversion from Spenser's epic itinerary, but from 'what that itinerary implies in terms of his role as a poet, his relations to courtly society and his position towards political power in general'.[2] A companion piece, *The Teares of the Muses*, which is difficult to date but was also prob-ably written about 1590, also presents a dispirited view of poetry at the English court. As William Oram notes, Spenser's reading of the English cultural scene laments that the English ruling class has lost its commitment to poetry,[3] asking:

> Whie then doo foolish men so much despize
> The precious store of this celestiall riches?
> Why doo the banish us, that patronize
> The name of learning?
>
> (ll. 147–50)

Spenser bewails the 'ugly Barbarisme,/And brutish Ignorance', and the 'vaine toyes' which 'the vulgare entertaine' (ll. 187–8, 195). Not only are these complaints commonplace, but even by Spenser's own standards, the poetic scene of 1590 was indeed a flourishing one. For the next few years there was an energetic burst of sonnet collections, verse satire, highly popular erotic narratives, and a new

direct energetic poetic in the verse of Donne and Jonson. It is just
that as an outsider, living in Ireland, most of what was happening,
politically and poetically, at the court had passed him by. Spenser
anticipates that tragi-comic figure of the nineteenth and twentieth
centuries of the colonial visiting England and finding that the values
and practices he or she has been solemnly educated to revere as
characteristic of 'Home', have disintegrated before new political and
economic realities. Visits to the 'homeland' are rarely satisfying.
Where has the England one knew and loved gone? Who has betrayed it? Indeed, maybe only back in the colonies – in Australia or
New Zealand or South Africa or what had once been Rhodesia – do
those real English values still seem to be cherished. Fish and chips
become a gourmet dish in Sydney or Victoria, while the English turn
away from New Zealand lamb and prefer pâté. And so the confused
colonials return and ask, as Spenser, as Colin Clout, asked, where
exactly home is, and why the queen isn't doing something about it
all. Since Spenser's lifetime, of course, the queen herself has not
become more central or relevant. And as I suggested in discussing
Book Six, Spenser's queen seems to play a much diminished role in
the later books of *The Faerie Queene*.

Also in *Complaints* – which can be seen as 'a Spenserian sampler',
as Ronald Bond describes it, thus pointing to the poet's need to set a
selection of his poems before a forgetful public – along with the
earlier poems which were discussed in Chapter 3, is *Muiopotmos*,
subtitled *The Fate of the Butterflie*, a mock-heroic satire. *Muiopotmos* is,
Heninger claims, 'Spenser's most successful exercise in Sidney's sort
of right poetry' in which the reference is not historical events but 'the
literary tradition for telling tales'.[4] Like the earlier 'public' poems,
emerging through this more recently composed one are unmistak-
able personal tensions and obsessions – concerns with the value of
the poetic life, the insecurity of the court, the untrustworthiness of
the world, the puzzling changes at court and in England, all connect-
ing to the vast and general betrayal of human life by time:

> So all the world, and all in it I hate
> Because it changeth ever too and fro . . .
> For all I see is vaine and transitorie,
> No will be helde in anie stedfast plight
> But in a moment loose their grace and glorie
>   (428–9, 495–7)

Seen in the context of the 1590s, written by a man living uneasily between his memories of the court and the superficially civilized wilderness of Munster, all these poems hark nostalgically back to an ideal world in which personal and public, piety and policy, might be (or, might once have been) reconciled. Perhaps it never existed. If Spenser had been able to travel back to the England of 1579, say, instead of having to settle for that of 1590, he might have discovered the 'home' he craved. But it has gone, and he has become older, and those iron necessities make for cognitive and philosophical dissonance that pour into the poems of the last few years of Spenser's life. Like the emigrant to New Zealand who, remembering his student days at Cambridge in the 1960s, returns to the England of the Thatcher and Major years and is bewildered because he is no longer at 'home,' Spenser cannot locate where his home is.

In addition to the poems collected in *Complaints*, the late 1580s and 1590s also saw Spenser bring forth a number of separately published pieces. *Astrophel*, which appeared with *Colin Clouts Come Home Again* is another lament, this time for Sir Philip Sidney, destroyed in the defence of Protestant nationalism – at least that is how Spenser mythologizes Sidney's death from complications following a battle wound in 1586 – by a slanderous, cowardly beast, obviously akin to the Blatant Beast of *The Faerie Queene*:

> So as he rag'd emongst that beastly rout,
> A cruell beast of most accursed brood
> Upon him turnd (despeyre makes cowards stout) . . .

Typically, Sidney's death is generalized, as an example of universal frailty, a 'sad ensample of mans suddein end'. Spenser's tribute – interestingly published some years after the spate of poetical tributes to the dead hero shortly following his death – was to be expected for a number of reasons. Like Spenser's patron Ralegh, Sidney was a courtier risking his life for the queen's cause on foreign soil; he had been an early influence and, through his uncle Leicester, associated with Spenser's earlier career. He is, by the time Spenser publishes 'Astrophel', fast becoming mythologized among Protestant intellectuals as a the lost embodiment of an integrity and hope fast fading from the late Elizabethan world – a nostalgia that was to be intensified in the next decades under the reign of James, culminating in Sidney's friend Greville's life of Sidney, which is as much an attack on the Jacobean court as it is a tribute to Sidney.

Some other minor poems of this period require brief mention. *Daphnaida* is a gloom elegy to the wife of Sir Arthur Gorges, which Spenser uses as the occasion to brood on the uncertain nature of the poet's life, and the puzzlement that history should unfold so unpredictably and seemingly so threateningly to the life of virtue and truth. The *Fowre Hymncs* – the first two of which may well have been written a decade or so earlier – were published in 1596. These four poems give quasi-philosophical accounts of Love, Beauty, Heavenly Love and Heavenly Beauty, setting out a doctrine that Books Three and Four of *The Faerie Queene* explore more vividly in interconnected stories. In the *Hymnes*, Spenser is attempting, in Sidney's words, to show 'himself a passionate lover of that unspeakable and everlasting beauty to be seen by the eyes of the mind, only cleared by fate'.[5] The *Hymnes* delineate the process 'whereby the lover is raised from brutish sexuality and prepared for assimilation into Christian charity'.[6] But they lend themselves all too readily to easy oppositions – body and soul, paganism and Christianity – as they do to a simplistic ascension from lower to higher forms of beauty and love. Intellectually, they are a collection of attractively versified clichés, with little sense that real people are involved in the abstractions they celebrate. But the organization certainly makes clear Spenser's consistent regression to traditional moral dichotomies. He sets the poems in a remarkable reversion to the trope of renouncing youth:

> Having in the greener times of my youth, composed these former two Hymnes in the praise of Love and beauty. . . I was moved to call in the same. But being unable so to doe . . . I resolved at least to amend, and by way of retraction to reforme them, making in stead of those two Hymnes of naturall love and beautie, two others of heavenly and celestiall.

Spenser's claim that the first two *Hymnes* were written early may be, Heninger suggests, 'only a pretence . . . to excuse the indiscretions (mild though they are) of . . . sexual passion'.[7] It is not a question of whether Spenser is sincere in his protestations or his assertion that 'many copies' of the earlier hymns 'were formerly scattered abroad', but why he should choose this particular way of introducing them. The early pair of the hymns are more syncretic and open in their use of a mixture of pagan and Christian elements; the later two offer more explicitly a progression from earthly to heavenly based on the commonplaces of Christian theology. Within the poems, the world and God may, however, be seen at least in part as a progression, but Spenser's dedicatory remarks make very clear a more absolute distinction.

Of these poems written in the 1590s, it is *Colin Clouts Come Home Again* that raises most poignantly, and ambiguously, both personal and broader cultural issues over which Spenser must have been brooding incessantly. In particular, it raises the increasingly disturbing issue for Spenser of exactly where 'home' was to be found. In 1589, he went to England with Ralegh; two years later, he finished a retrospective poem about the experience of homecoming. But to which home? By now there are two 'places' (to revert to the metaphor I introduced in Chapter 2) which are, in overlapping senses, 'home' for him. Spenser depicts himself as the poet-shepherd, Colin Clout, and uses the familiar trappings of pastoral to address a number of his friends, acquaintances, and fellow poets. The traditional pastoral ideal of the simple community of shepherds and shepherdesses is, however, given far less emphasis than disharmony, deception, and ostentation. The central figure is presented as the mature true poet – who has grown, as Oram puts it, from the solipsistic shepherd-boy of *The Shepheardes Calender* to a 'priest' of the God of Love. By the end of the poem, he has become a new Orpheus, reaching out to his shepherd followers, transmitting the Beauty above to the World below'.[8]

That, at least, is the way the poem presents itself through the pastoral. But such a scheme hardly fits the ambiguities that emerge from the poem when it is set in Spenser's material world as opposed to the world of pastoral ideals. The poem starts with the question that Spenser must have often asked himself and at times tried to avoid giving an honest answer: 'Colin my liefe, my life, how great a losse/Had all the shepheards nation by thy lacke?' (l. 17). How much, indeed, has Spenser's absence been of any import in the ever-changing world of the court? Within the inner circles of the court, probably none. Spenser, after all, had been a secretary to one of the more embarrassingly brutal English deputies in recent Irish history. And in Ireland he stayed, poor chap. Colin, we are told, is sitting 'at the foote of Mole that mountaine hore . . . by the Mullaes shore' (the Ballhowra Hills to the north of Kilcolman and the river Awbeg respectively); he tells the story of Bregog and Mulla, mythologizing the Munster countryside. He has clearly learnt to love and mythologize his new 'home'. He then moves on to tell the story of Ralegh's estrangement from the queen who, despite her misunderstanding of him, remains the centre of the order and beauty which the shepherds aspire to praise. At this point, Spenser's other 'home', the English court, is praised. What we are presented with is an extraordinary evocation of that colonial nostalgia for 'home', an idealization that will be echoed for hundreds of years, by New Zealanders and Canadians, West Indians and Australians, knowing they are no longer 'English' even though they are still 'of England', and unable to quite let go of the ideal they have brought with them and preserved, even while they are aware that back in England it has been betrayed:

> Both heaven and heavenly graces do much more
> (Quoth he) abound in that same land, then this.
> For there all happie peace and plenteous store
> conspire in one to make contented blisse:
> No wayling there nor wretchednesse is heard,
> No blood issues nor no leprosies,
> No griesly famine, nor no raging sweard . . .
> And Poets wits are had in peereless price:
>
> (308–21)

We are then told of Colin's journey back home: of other poets, noble ladies, his dedication to the queen. Why then, did he leave?

> . . . Why *Colin*, since thou foundst such grace
> With *Cynthia* and all her noble crew:
> Why didst thou ever leave that happie place,
> In which such wealth might unto thee accrew?
> And back returnedst to this barrein soyle,
> Where cold and care and penury do dwell:
>
> (652–7)

This leads to an attack on the corruption of the court, on its profanities and superficialities. The 'home' that Colin had returned to find no longer lives by the values that originally inspired him to go forth into the wilderness as a colonial. The truths that have been abandoned by so many in the court may still live on, even in the Irish wilderness. What do they know of England who only England know?, as Kipling intoned. Cream teas are still a daily ritual in the best homes of Victoria, British Columbia; they play cricket in Jamaica; they still love the royal family in Glendowie, New Zealand.

'LOVE, AND LOVE MY DEAR': SPENSER AND PETRARCHISM

One of Colin's satiric attacks in *Colin Clouts Come Home Again* is that the English court is 'full of love, and love, and love my deare/And all their tale and studie is of it'. *Amoretti*, written in the early 1590s, is Spenser's only venture into the lyric, and it is characteristically moralistic and distinctively unPetrarchan, as if written in part to express his disapproval, or at least his independence, of the current fashion. A sequence of sonnets, it describes the developing courtship of poet and beloved, but its presentation of lover and mistress is far from most of the love poetry that was fashionable at the court from which Spenser had returned. In Sinfield's words, *Amoretti* is an 'unprecedented puritan humanist adaptation of the sonnet sequence to a relationship which ends in marriage'.[9] Indeed, it is written deliberately to distance Spenser from the secularization of the Petrarchan tradition: he turns in effect to the second half of Petrarch's *Canzoniere*, written after Laura's death, and focusing on the unchangeableness of the beloved within the love of God as a model for the unchangeableness of a Christian love. The more characteristic Petrarchan pattern of dominance and passivity, the sadistic/masochistic games in which the two partners may take up quite different roles, are sternly rejected. Spenser does not wish to see the self as fluctuating and always in process. He does not finally wish to view love as disturbing the God-given order of things. *Amoretti* is thus in line with *The Faerie Queene*'s treatment of the moral and cosmic goals of desire: like Books Three and Four of *The Faerie Queene*, *Amoretti* provides a Protestant critique of the persuasiveness of Petrarchan modes of thought and expression.

The sequence is usually read as a fictionalization of Spenser's courtship of his second wife, Elizabeth Boyle. It sets out, occasionally amusingly but in clear moral terms, a pattern of desire that leads not to the Petrarchan impasse of compulsive frustration and idealized hopelessness but to marriage and mutual submission of husband and wife to God's will. Spenser uses much of the paraphernalia of Petrarchism. His beloved is the 'she cruell warriour' who 'doth her selfe addresse/to battell' (11). But although the lover occasionally takes up the expected subservient role, the sequence is firmly articulated as a narrative in which he is the caring superior of traditional hierarchical Christian marriage, and she his respected but subservient helpmate. Rather than being positioned as the idealized inspirer of male masochism, the mistress is even at times lovingly criticized. As Marotti notes, 'Spenser's speaker acts as his beloved's intellectual and ethical superior, a position from which he can comically, but affectionately, condescend to her at various points in the sequence'.[10] The Protestant, ever mindful of God's will and public duty, must subordinate sexual desire to higher goals, and ensure that the woman's sexual threat to rationality is contained. Although the early poems of the collection (those before Sonnet 67) are often light, even occasionally titillating, at the point at which the praise and gentle admonition of the beloved give way to a celebration of Christian marriage, the tone changes. Petrarchan praise is forced into the service of Christian duty: it is acknowledged that the beloved may often be a distraction from higher commitments, which include not only God but also the queen and the poet's own vocation to write the great poem in which he will 'enlarge' the queen's 'living prayses', which is a 'sufficient worke for one mans simple head' (33). So in the latter part of the collection, notably in 80 (where he defends the pleasure of the lyric) the primacy of the queen, the responsibility of a Christian, and dedication to public duty are never compromised by the vagaries of desire.

Of course, Spenser was treading on slightly difficult ground in that increasingly in the later years of her reign, Queen Elizabeth was surrounding herself with the trappings of Petrarchism. Spenser's emphasis on marriage as the holy end of desire is a call to his fellow courtiers, poets and even (though at a distance) to the queen herself to turn to a redirection of desire into piety and national loyalty. *Amoretti* thus has wider implications than simply a critique of Petrarchan love poetry: it is a sign that, at least within the Protestant circle that had formed Spenser's poetical as well as political allegiances, England should stop 'seeing itself as [an] imitation of Renaissance Italy' and rather 'see itself as a Protestant opponent to Catholic Italy'.[11] Just as Ireland and Mary Queen of Scots are, together, a daemonic 'other' to England and Queen Elizabeth, so in the paranoid, dualistic cosmos of the ideology from which Spenser's work grows, Catholicism, the Papacy and rampant promiscuity are the 'other' of the Protestant marriage devoted to the good of the state.

Amoretti provides, then, a stern Protestant critique of the dominant tradition of European love poetry. Spenser himself had, as we have seen, explored this tradition in some depth in *The Faerie Queene*

Books Three and Four. Since his Protestant critique of Petrarchism provides such a recurring strand of his career, and one to which he returns in these crucial last years, it is time now to attempt something of a detailed account of Petrarchism and as why Spenser found it at one so fascinating – and so destructive.

As a starting point, here – with changes that I will discuss below – is a stimulating recent account of the inner dynamics of Petrarchism:

> Petrarchism is theater, the production of a scenario for which characters – in the form of people, parts of people, and nonhuman (including inanimate) objects are cast. The performance is played before an audience, a crucial member of which is the Petrarchan lover himself viewing [himself] performing . . . Petrarchism is a detour that, at best, leads asymtotically to intimacy: it never arrives . . . Petrarchism is centered not upon the partner, but upon the lover . . . The pain and frustration of earlier times live on unresolved, carried within, always a potential threatening force motivating one to resolutions that never quite work, to an undoing never quite done.[12]

This probably would be accepted as an accurate, if incomplete, account of the major dynamics of the Petrarchan tradition as Spenser inherited it. The writer, however, would not easily be recognized as an expert in Spenserian or Renaissance studies – although he was certainly a world authority in his own. In quoting his opinion, I have cheated, but only slightly: apart from a few brief elisions, by substituting the words 'Petrarchism' or 'Petrarchan lover' for the words the writer actually used. What I have given is a quotation from one of the late Robert Stoller's studies of erotic behavior. The words Stoller uses are 'perversion' and 'perverse person'. He goes on to draw conclusions that would also be acceptable (were we not now alerted) as a description of other aspects of Petrarchism. The perverse situation (I restore Stoller's terms, though the reader is invited to substitute for it as we move along) is scripted to help the lover deal with the overwhelming power of the object of his desire. Since her full reality cannot be faced, she can be accommodated by the lover's mind only if she is accorded less than full personhood. He therefore depicts her as the 'possessor of selected parts or qualities only. He anatomizes them. And if even that is too intimate,' he turns from human to 'inanimate objects, such as garments, granting them a certain amount of humanness.' The careful scripting of these erotic scenarios is seen as an 'aesthetic task', undertaken in the spirit of what Castiglione termed *sprezzatura*: the perverse scene is 'most pleasing when it is seamless, when it does not give hints that it was constructed, when it looks as if it sprang full-blown from unconscious depths. If not created spontaneously . . . then it should look as if it was'. Playing at love, the trademark of the Elizabethan court, irritated Spenser when he visited England, but it clearly had, and continues to have, deep-rooted psychological, not merely aesthetic, roots in the culture. Although we may not agree with Spenser's puritanical perspective, his suspicion of Petrarchism as a perverse pattern of behaviour may have been uncannily accurate.

My argument is not (though, curiously enough, this may well be close to Spenser's position) that 'Petrarchism' ought simply to be added to the list of common paraphilia, along with coprophilia, kleptomania and exhibitionism. It is rather that the longevity of Petrarchism was based on the remarkable extent to which it incorporated the major fantasies of patriarchal gender assignments and sexual pathologies. From his distinctive moral perspective, Spenser seems to have been in anticipation of such a judgement: here, for once, I am (partly) in agreement with Paglia, who sees *The Faerie Queene* as 'an encyclopedic catalog' of the 'perversions' of 'Petrarchan stereotypes', akin to 'Krafft-Ebing's *Psychopathia Sexualis*: not only rape and homosexuality but priapism, nymphomania, exhibitionism, incest, bestiality, necrophilia, fetishism, transvestism, and transsexualism'.[13] Beyond the rhetorical conventions of Petrarchism the men and women who were interpellated into it, like the figures in the House of Busyrane in *The Faerie Queene*, Book two, played far more than a set of rhetorical scripts. They were acting out patterns of perversely repetitive strategies that were the outcome of the dominant gender assignments of Western patriarchy.

Historically, Petrarchism was predominantly a male discourse, and its central psycho-cultural trope is, as the episodes referring to Florimell in Books Three and Four clearly show, the quintessential male perversion, fetishism. It characteristically incorporates other typical male perverse strategies, including aspects of both sadism and masochism, exhibitionism, voyeurism, and – at times, catering for more specialist tastes – transvestism, pedophilia and necrophilia. Spenser's critique of his age's dominant system of classifying erotic desire is worth pausing over as we construct his literary life because we all, even today, carry with us the remnants of discursive systems we inherit from our cultural pasts and of which we often have little conscious knowledge or control. In our attempts to make sense of our desires, their unpredictabilities, joys, losses, repressions, and recurrences, necessarily we have recourse to these remnants. We are subordinated to them and steal from them. We construct stories, for ourselves and others, about those acts. It is (maybe) some comfort to know what Freud noted, that unlike other animals, human beings 'are creatures whose sexual lives are governed almost entirely by fantasy', and that the fantasies we, all of us, construct or live out inevitably draw on the narratives through which our earliest, polymorphously perverse yearnings were realized or repressed.[14] As Spenser knew, more than a fashionable literary mode or set of moral commonplaces is at stake here.

Let us look at some of the categories by which Petrarchism organized the surges of human desire. The idolization of the beloved against which *Amoretti* protests, or the pursuit of Florimell and the erotic fetishization of Amoret are, therefore, examples of 'oppression through exaltation', in which the object of idealization is not permitted to be the subject of her own desire. She is 'overvalued', as Freud put it, in order that she can be, the lover hopes, exclusively the subject of his desires. Whenever she does act in relation to her own wishes – predominantly by rejecting him – she is castigated by him as cruel, a beauteous outside framing a heart of stone, or in psychoanalytic terms, the punishing mother figure from whom he is expelled and whom he continues to desire. It is as if she compensates for a deficiency, a lack, in the wholeness of the male lover, thereby putting into question that wholeness and its apparent power. These are precisely the patterns of attraction and repulsion underling Spenser's depiction of Florimell and Busyrane – and they also explain the sternness with which he rejects the seeming idolatry of Petrarchan love in *Amoretti*. Within these compulsively repeated patterns, Petrarchism presented itself as a man's appeal for mercy based on an acknowledgment of fear of discontinuity and helplessness before (or even in the absence of) the cruel, hard-hearted, alluringly yet frustratingly chaste mistress.[15] Her effects on him are like those the child feels in the birth, weaning, and separation/individuation process, or whenever he must leave the comfort of the mother and is thrown alone into the world, yet finding himself inevitably drawn, in reality or fantasy, back to her, puzzled yet reassured by the familiarity of his tortures. She is the all-powerful mother, simultaneously loved and hated, on whose nurturance he is totally dependent, and yet from whom he must break if he is to achieve his (and the gendered pronoun is deliberate) individuation. However much the beloved's absence may be bewailed, it is therefore, paradoxically, both welcome and necessary. The Petrarchan idealization of the beloved is characteristically accompanied by fear of her. When she does respond, the male lover typically finds some way not just to express gratitude and dependence, but to assert his further power. He cannot bear the full presence of the beloved because her claims on him are so overwhelming, and he knows that he must reject her if he is to assert his male autonomy. Hence, I suggest, the popularity of the blazon, the catalogue of a beloved's beauties, of which Amoretti contains a number of examples:

> For loe my love doth in her selfe containe
>   all this worlds riches that may farre be found:
>   if Saphyres, loe her eies be Saphyres plaine,
>   if Rubies, loe her lips be Rubies sounde . . .
>   (15)

If the beloved embodies both the alluring security and the threat of the mother, whom the male desires and rejects, and yet to whom he is inevitably drawn back, he needs to construct a satisfying narrative of this struggle – to justify it to both her and himself. The presence/ absence paradox in Petrarchism is an adult narrativization of Freud's famous fort/da game, in which the child pushes the toy away in order to have the pleasure of having it come back (and also, as the game acquires more potent fantasies, to punish the object for its power over him): 'the vicissitudes of the male in his sexualization lead him to fight from the beginning to escape the temptation of returning to his former fusion with the maternal image, holder of primitive power, the phallic mother, the great nurturing mother.'[16] What is the story that such a lover constructs? Characteristically, as the House of Busyrane so vividly demonstrates, he alleges that it is the beloved's cruelty, not his own desires, that is depriving him of fulfillment. Or, as one of the *Amoretti* puts it:

> In vaine I seeke and sew to her for grace,
>   and doe myne humbled hart before her poure:
>   the whiles her foot she in my necke doth place,
>   and tread my life downe in the lowly floure.
>   (20)

The lover's only means of avoiding the chaos of abandonment is to control her, or at least fold her into a narrative in which she is his. The classic Petrarchan trope is the lover's devotion to the beloved's picture; he constructs his narratives around the stimulation he gains from looking at it or from the mental image he holds as if it were also a picture of her. The thought that she might have her own desires is rarely considered.

This brings me to another of the long-acknowledged characteristics of Petrarchism that is brilliantly illustrated in Book Three of *The Faerie Queene*, the power afforded to sight, specifically by means of the voyeuristic male gaze. Within the Petrarchan system the activity of seeing, as a substitute for (and sometimes a preliminary to) actual physical control is, in Freud's words 'the most frequent pathway along which libidinal excitation is aroused'. Writing on Spenser's emphasis on looking and sight, Paglia sees voyeurism and scopophilia not merely as inherently male (an arguable position, perhaps), but celebrates it as the essence of the 'aggressive eye' of high Western art. The 'sexual character of western seeing' is, she asserts, at the center of our Apollonian triumphs over (female) nature. Stoller argues, on the other hand, that scopophilia is predominantly a gender disorder (that is, a disorder in the development of masculinity and femininity) constructed out of a tradition of hostility, involving 'rage at giving up ones earliest bliss and identification with the mother, fear of not succeeding in escaping out of her orbit, and a need for revenge for her putting us in this predicament'. In Petrarchism the lover's admiring eye attempts to fix the mistress not just as a beautiful object that he wishes to possess, but often as a guarantee against the threat she represents. Recent psychoanalytic studies of scopophilia have seen the gaze as embodying a 'pre-oedipal fear . . . of merging and fixing with the mother', which may be protected against only by incessant watching. Stoller argues that 'sexual excitement will occur at the moment when adult reality resembles the childhood trauma – the anxiety being re-experienced as excitement'.[17] The viewed object is thereby detoxified, relieving the voyeur of his fear either directly or by being projected upon, and so shared with, another. The viewer enjoys closeness without the fear of engulfment. Scopophilic pleasure can be secretive or the man can make sure that the woman 'exhibits': that is, she knows she is being seen and apparently involved in his fears, and her knowledge represents his superego giving permission for his own look/show impulses.

How do these characteristic male strategies for dealing with fears that may seem so basic to our culture's construction of gender become encoded in the Petrarchan attitudes that *Amoretti* encounters and tries to transform into celebrations of Christian love? Surveying the poems that were increasingly fashionable at the English court as Spenser was writing *Amoretti*, we can see how detailed is the focus on the fetishization of the beloved (and we should never forget, when thinking of Spenser's connections with Sidney, of how *Astrophil and Stella* helped direct that fashion). Overwhelmingly, and most obviously in the blazon, the male gaze that is central to Petrarchism is directed, at a woman as the sum of separable parts. The anatomizing of Amoret in Busyrane's ritual is a clear case in point.

At this stage it may appear that I am siding with (and even providing a contemporary justification of) Spenser's ruthless critique of Petrarchism. It is not that the representation of (or gazing at) human bodies or acts in art is inherently wrong. Nor, as Rosalind Coward points out, is it inherently objectionable to gain pleasure from the representation of parts of the body. 'In viewing pictures which we might find pleasurable,' she argues, 'it is often a detail on which we might focus: a certain expression in the eyes, the nape of the neck, the way a hand rests on a part of the body.' It is rather that the predominant codes of patriarchal representation – and, clearly, Spenser is interestingly caught on the boundary of accepting and rejecting this tradition – are overwhelmingly invasive, even violent, requiring the submission of the female body to passivity and fragmentation as a means of controlling the viewer's own fears. 'Every perversion', writes Kaplan, 'is an effort to give some representation to, while controlling, the full strength of potentially murderous impulses, generated by fears of both being controlled and losing access to the person who will serve to control that fear.'[18]

As the story of Florimell demonstrates, Petrarchism is intimately, and inextricably, bound up with the premier male perversion that seeks to come to terms with the fear of the beloved's overwhelming power, fetishism. Clinical studies suggest that the fetishist is usually not trying to victimize or control the beloved, since fetishism is, like Petrarchism itself, directed at the effects of the beloved upon the lover, not the reverse. His goal is rather to find just the right intensity of the beloved's power that he can, for the moment, deal with. If her effects on him become too overwhelming, how much, he asks, can he bear without banishing her? The fetish is the attempted answer to that question. 'A sexual fetish,' notes Kaplan, 'is significantly more reliable than a living person . . . when the full sexual identity of the woman is alive, threatening, dangerous, unpredictable, the desire she arouses must be invested in the fetish . . . fetish objects are relatively safe, easily available, undemanding of reciprocity'. Likewise, the fetishistic narrative is designed to divert attention away from the 'whole story by focusing attention on the detail'. Unlike a real woman, who may (presumably!) have desires of her own, and therefore in patriarchal society, be even more threatening to the supposedly autonomous male, the fetish can be commanded, assigned multiple or contradictory parts, and (except in the masochistic scenario) will not make demands of its own. Fetishes are created as nodes of meaning within the narrativizations of the earliest, most primitive of family romances, the desires to emulate, replace or seduce the parents. They acquire their magical power as part of the primitive fantasy structure of the child contemplating how large, powerful, and irresistible his or her parents seem. In adult life, fetishism 'entails a displacement of sexual desire away from the whole identity' of the beloved to some accessory, they (or chain of substitutes for them) may be reactivated and often enormously elaborated in adulthood, their origins long lost under the accretions of later narratives. Kaplan comments: 'the extravagant sexual theories of little boys may be outgrown and forgotten but they are never entirely given up. They are repressed and temporarily banished from consciousness but persist as unconscious fantasies that are ready to return whenever there is a serious threat, imagined or actual, to a man's hard-earned masculinity.'[19]

Fetishism, though rarely discussed as such, has in effect long been noticed as a major ingredient of Petrarchism, and the episode in which the witch originally creates the false Florimell for her distraught son vividly displays and stands aside from it. Fetishes, of course, may be anything that the erotic imagination imbues with metonymic power – shoes, clothing, pets, portraits, locks of hair, odors, sounds. The clinical literature is full of stories of the bizarre, banal, outrageous, and ordinary in this most widespread of male paraphilia, as, indeed, is the Petrarchan tradition. It is as if the lover can deal with a woman best – or, as he would put it, when he most admires her – only when he can aestheticize her, when her beauty and desirability are a compliment to him, and the power of her physical presence no longer a threat. The witch's son uses, to employ a photographic metaphor, a freeze-frame, capturing her for all time, not as true to life, but true to what he can bear to in relation to the ways he has learnt to depict women and their effects on him. His move, from the real Florimell to the fetish, is precisely the reverse of Orlando's determination in Shakespeare's *As You Like It* to move from the world of fantasy to the world of the real: 'I can live no longer by thinking' (5. 2. 50).

Another standard trope of Petrarchism is that of rejection; the lover's mistress is absent, unkind, loves another, has a cold heart that denies her fair outside; he himself has no peace and yet is continually at war; he burns and freezes. There is, as the vivid procession in the House of Busyrane makes clear, a strong strain of masochism involved in the Petrarchist pose. The peculiar script of masochism is the pleasure taken in delayed gratification, in the pain of denial and waiting: the masochist 'waits for pleasure as something that is bound to be late, and expects pain as the condition that will finally ensure (both physically and morally) the advent of pleasure'.[20] Masochism involves assigning to the other the absolute power of forbidding pleasure – in the case of male masochism, giving the all-powerful mother the power of the Law to rule absolutely, at least within the script he laid down, his life and death. Perhaps that is why so much of the destructiveness of desire as Spenser anatomizes it in Books Three and Four deal with procrastinated fulfillment, and why his sonnets are sternly based on the celebration of his own marriage, which is finally place not within the context of unfullfilled desire, but Christian duty:

> So let us love, dear love, lyke as we ought,
> love is the lesson which the Lord us taught.
>
> (68)

'Epithalamion' is likewise in this vein, a critique of Petrarchism and an affirmation of a taditional Protestant view of marriage. It was written as a tribute to Elizabeth Boyle, whom Spenser married in 1594, most likely on 11 June, the Feast of St Barnabas. An epithelamium is a public poem of celebration; in this poem, Spenser links his own individual affection to cosmic and natural patterns. It is a rich, learned, evocative and complex poem, showing that Spenser was most engaged when bringing philosophical or theological ideas into verse, and celebrating Christian sanctioned rites as manifestations within time of God's control and purpose. Just as the wedding day enacts an ordered sequence of time from sunrise to sunset, so the poet's own life and new marriage must be understood within God's control of the temporal. At the end, the poet prays:

> That we may raise a large posterity,
> Which from the earth, which they may long possesse,
> With lasting happinesse,
> Up to our haughty pallaces may mount,
> And for the guerdon of theyr glorious merit
> May heavenly tabernacles there inherit,
> Of blessed Saints for to increase the count
>
> (417–23)

To tie up this miscellany of celebratory poems, 'Prothalamion' deserves some mention. It was written on the occasion of the double betrothal of the two daughters of the earl of Worcester. It is a celebration of the calm and harmony that, within the ideology of aristocratic marriage, such an occasion should bring. It is Spenser being the appropriate servant of the dominant ideology of the regime. Yet into the poem he inserts many personal references, mentioning the 'discontent of my long fruitlesse stay/In Princes court, and expectation vayne/Of idle hopes' (6–8). The wistful pastoral atmosphere, embodied in the refrain, 'Sweete Themmes runne softly, till I end my Song' is juxtaposed with such personal references, as if something darker is haunting the poet's public tributes. Spenser mentions his own and not merely the bridal part's ties to London, his recollections of Leicester, his new devotion to the rapidly rising earl of Essex, and (of course) to the queen. The poem is a fascinating revelation of some of Spenser's major roles throughout his life: the poet celebrating the values and ceremonies of the ruling class, the marginalized and ambivalent man.

'WITH HIS SCYTH ADDREST': THE CANTOS OF MUTABILITY

In 1609, the publisher Matthew Lownes issued 'TWO CANTOS OF MUTABILITIE: Which, both for Forme and Matter, appeare to be parcell of some following Booke of the FAERIE QUEENE, UNDER THE LEGEND OF Constancie.' Are the Mutability Cantos indeed part of a new Book, perhaps the central or core stanzas? A separate poem? A conclusion to the whole poem, written perhaps when

Spenser realized he would never finish it? And can we be sure that the canto numbers are Spenser's? What evidence is there for Lownes's identification of a Book of Constancy?

Regardless of intention, the effect of the Mutability Cantos is that of reassessment, not just of *The Faerie Queene* but Spenser's whole poetic career. They provide us with a perspective, from the mid 1590s, of his literary life and the various shapes it had taken. The likely date for Spenser's working on the cantos is 1595, since an event in that year seems to be referred to. Read separately, they are a poetically rich, straightforward allegorical account of what Spenser and his age clearly saw as a major philosophical (and experiential) issue, how to find 'permanence' or 'eternity' in a world that was increasingly changing and unpredictable. They show Spenser's poetry at its most accessible. There is a sustained narrative that varies in tone from the amusing to the profound of the goddess Mutability claim to replace Jove as supreme heavenly deity. That is followed by a presentation of her argument before Nature who gives final judgment – even while admitting the strength of her case – against Mutability. As a counter narrative, we are told a charming story of how Faunus' bride Molanna helped to let him see the goddess Diana naked, and how he is punished for his presumption.

What is especially impressive about the poetic power of the Mutability Cantos is the way Spenser moves confidently from local, almost pictorial, settings to the mythological and cosmic. The sense of place is especially impressive. Despite their philosophical ambitions, the Cantos are among the closest places in which Spenser comes in his literary life to his material life. His evident affection for his newly adopted land permeates the poem. Arlo Hill, around which the narrative of Nature's judgment on Mutability moves, is a mountain visible from Kilcolman. At the same time, the pastoral setting of Spenser's own estates is connected to Eden, to the possibility of a renewed paradise, and to the visible and invisible order of the universe. Mutability's case is based on the obvious attraction and liveliness of the changes not just in human affairs but in the course of the seasons, months, and days. Mutability stands for the attractiveness of the material world, which includes even the heavens themselves. The power of change – which, intellectually, Spenser wishes to resist – is given its most attractive presentation precisely because it is rooted in his life in Ireland, on his estate, newly married, seemingly prosperous and secure.

When the Cantos are seen in the context of the rest of *The Faerie*

Queene, however, a somewhat more ambiguous meaning emerges. Earlier in the poem, in the Garden of Adonis (3. 6) there had been an attempt to turn history to myth by showing how the universal changes of nature had an underlying principle of stability. The Garden is the source 'of all things, that are borne to live and die'. And yet it is dominated by the figure that recurs so powerfully in Elizabethan mythology, Time. Time is the arbiter of human life, the destroyer of youth, beauty, and the rude challenger to the order of human society. Time, we are told

> . . . with his scyth addrest,
> Does mow the flowring herbes and goodly things,
> And all their glory to the ground downe flings . . .
> All things decay in time, and to their end do draw.
> (3. 6. 39, 40)

The Elizabethans saw 'time' and 'mutability' as more than mere philosophical categories, and the Mutability cantos provide us with an opportunity to take stock on what was clearly an obsession for Spenser throughout his life. Time is an absolute psycho-physical continuum – as when we speak of past, present, future, hour, season, year. Yet time also embodies the more subjective sense of our often very different senses of its passing: flowing, speeding, dragging, wasting. What Spenser and his age realized to an unusual extent, was that our awareness of time cannot easily be separated from its being, as it were, part of our own existence. Newton claimed that 'absolute, true, and mathematical time, of itself and from its own nature, flows equably without relation to anything external', but this is not time as it seems to affect our inmost being, our anxieties or desires. 'Time', as Shakespeare's Rosalind notes in *As You Like It*, 'travels in divers paces with divers persons.' Perhaps because we are never separated from the mystery of our own beings, our awareness of time and change can never be satisfactorily expressed in objective, scientific terms. Although, as Hans Meyerhoff observes, 'succession, flux, change . . . seem to belong to the most immediate and primitive data of our experience', and 'the question, what is man, therefore invariably refers to the question of what is time', it seems nevertheless that human beings in primitive societies demonstrated their awareness of time largely by elaborate attempts to unmake it, particularly by their participation in recurring myths and rituals which were designed to abolish or transform its effects. For such societies, 'time is recorded only biologically without being allowed to become 'history' – that is, without its corrosive action being able to exert itself upon consciousness by revealing the irreversibility of events'. What was alone real for such societies was the sacred which is timeless and the reality of life depended on man's participation in expressions of this timeless world. It was in the higher religions, especially Judaism, that time and history were first made the object of conscious reflection outside the area of myth and ritual and associated with its slipping away and especially with the anxiety of death, an anxiety which, as Paul Tillich points out, is not necessarily tied to the moment or details of death, but rather with the uncertainty of having to die sometime in the future, and having to live through each moment with this anxiety.[21]

Is this anxiogenic association of time as change that makes the slipping away of time such a persistent subject of song, meditation, poem, and philosophy? As A. N. Whitehead put it. that 'all things flow' is the first vague generalization which the unsystematized, barely analyzed, intuition of civilization produced. It is the theme of some of the best Hebrew poetry in the Psalms; it appears as one of the first generalizations of Greek philosophy in the form of the saying of Heraclitus; in Anglo-Saxon thought it appears in the story of the sparrow flitting through the banqueting hall of the Northumbrian king. Many modern writers, living in an age where the concept of a transcendental realm complementary to time seems to many minds to have effectively disintegrated, have still been deeply aware of the pressing need to find a way to give meaning to the seemingly irresistible flow of time towards death. From Kierkegaard onwards, indeed, an influential tradition of modern philosophy has dwelt on the radical temporality of man's life as a dominant and pressing factor of existence.[22] Explicitly for such writers, and perhaps experientially for most twentieth-century Western men and women, what is most real is the profane, the temporal, the absoluteness of time. But even if an uneasiness about time as a 'problem' recurs through much, if not all, of human history, it seems that certain epochs have been more deeply concerned with time than others. This seems to have been true of the late sixteenth and early seventeenth-centuries. In England, Elizabethan and Jacobean literature gives widespread signs of a particularly acute concern with the nature and meaning of time which is connected with a profound, if gradual, intellectual revolution.

What, then, did Spenser understand by 'time'? There are two

main, interconnected senses. First, time is an abstract category or continuum of experience, as when philosophers speak of Time as opposed to Eternity, as in the remark of the sixteenth-century Huguenot theologian Philippe de Mornay: 'what greater contraries can there be, than time and eternitie'.[23] Second, there is time in the sense of the passing of moments, the inevitable mutability and change men perceive in their lives, as evoked by Shakespeare's Sonnet 60: 'Like as the waves make towards the pebbled shore,/So do our minutes hasten to their end.' What distinguishes Spenser's attitudes to time are the philosophical or more precisely the theological contexts into which such observations are put. First, as we have repeatedly seen, Spenser has an insistent preoccupation with 'mutability', the sheer fact of change in life, the threats it seems to pose to human security and permanence and the consequent problem of finding permanent values in an ever-changing world. Second, Spenser consistently treats change as the relationship between time and a non-temporal, transcendent Eternity, traditionally expressed in Christian theology by the doctrine of Providence. Mutability thus could mean insecurity, change, decay, the ceaseless wearing-away of life. It is vividly represented in Spenser's Titanesse:

> What man that sees the ever-whirling wheele
> Of Change, the which all mortall things doth sway,
> But that therby doth find, and plainly feele,
> How MUTABILITY in them doth play
> Her cruell sports; to many mens decay?
>
> (7. 6. 1)

Without change and death, Nature could not fulfill its regenerative purposes. What matters is not that individual creatures are inevitably subject to transience, but that through all change, the universal and God-given natural principles of procreation and fertility continue. The principles of the universe are 'eterne in mutabilitie'. This is the commonplace doctrine that Spenser confidently mythologizes in the Garden of Adonis in Book Three.

In the Mutability Cantos, Time reappears as the demi-goddess, Mutability, who challenges the power of the gods and claims to be the single universal principle. In building the central episode of this unfinished Book of Constancy around this issue, Spenser is putting his finger precisely upon the one of the key emergent philosophical contradictions of the early modern period. Some modern scholars have pointed out Spenser's affinities with avant-garde philosophers, such as Giordano Bruno, in this book. In one of Bruno's dialogues, *The Expulsion of the Triumphant Beast*, Fortune (like Spenser's Mutability) argues for the god's recognition of change as an autonomous principle of the universe. But if any ideas from Bruno are referred to here, they are invoked only to be rejected. The Lucretian law that all things are powerless to resist time is firmly set in the contexts of the natural creative order and the explicitly Christian perspective of God's eternity. For Bruno, mutability is a discovery of liberation and creativity.[24] For Spenser, however seductive Mutability appears, she is the enemy and must be rejected. Mutability's claim is that both heaven and earth are subject to change:

> For, who sees not, that *Time* on all doth pray?
> But *Times* do change and move continually.
> So nothing here long standeth in one stay:
> Wherefore, this lower world who can deny
> But to be subject still to *Mutabilitie*?
>
> (7. 7. 47)

In Spenser's poem, Time and its power are placed in the context of a larger purpose: the more Mutability demonstrates the facts of change, the more it is obvious that Nature includes Mutability in itself, that change and death are part of a universal order – just as the Elizabethan regime itself must be seen as unchanging and constant, centred, in Ralegh's words, on the queen, the 'Lady whom Time hath forgot'.

In the final stanzas of this fragment of two cantos and two disconnected stanzas, Spenser explicitly invokes the orthodox Christian framework, in which time is transcended by an eternal realm which

> . . . is contrayr to *Mutabilitie*:
> For, all that moveth, doth in *Change* delight:
> But thence-forth all shall rest eternally
> With Him that is the God of Sabbaoth hight:
> O that great Sabbaoth God, graunt me that Sabaoths sight.
>
> (7. 8. 2)

So, at least, is the argument of the Mutability Cantos. Its fragmentary nature makes it difficult to see it unambiguously as a coherent whole or as a continuation of the rest of the poem. Many aspects of the cantos continue the concerns of earlier books but there are many which do not fit. As Marion Campbell notes, 'for all their affinities with the rest of the poem, what the Mutability Cantos offers us is not so much a recapitulation as a reversal, or at least a dislocation of our experience of the world of *The Faerie Queene*'. The stance of the narrator is one such dislocation: he is 'clearly shaken by the tale he tells and he finds himself unable to proceed with his customary confidence and objectivity'.[25] Even more telling is the apocalyptic note in the final cantos in which the poet turns back to his poem and, in effect, rejects the poem itself.

There is an irony in the poem's final fragments that may turn a reader back to that point in Book One where the Red Crosse Knight was enjoined not to turn his back on the world but to pursue his quest to the end. There, he did so in part to enforce the reader also to pursue a quest for the principles of holiness, temperance, love, friendship, justice, and courtesy upon which the poem's vision would be built. Yet, as the poem proceeded and we read on, those virtues became increasingly blurred. The Mutability Cantos likewise show an uneasiness before the terms they propose. The two great adversaries, Cynthia (representing the status quo) and Mutability, both appeal to the same 'sterne' principles (7. 6. 12, 13) and even when they turn to Jove for judgment, he has no firm means of distinguishing between them. As Jove and Mutability face each other, it is also difficult to distinguish their speeches as if, in Miller's words, by the end of these two encounters there is no hierarchy remaining except by the force of assertion. As we saw in Book Six, the poet has to step in himself to show the truth. But here he does so in such terms that the poem itself is rejected. Throughout, part of *The Faerie Queene*'s energy has been built upon its author's firm intentions, and the clash between those intentions and the multiplicity and deferrals of the poem itself. As Richard Neuse puts it, 'The *Faerie Queene* opens up what Elizabeth and her regime tried to prevent, a public space for debate'.[26] Now, in the Cantos of Mutability, the despair of the poem to affirm a final truth finally surfaces explicitly. Just as Sidney, at his death, was to ask for his 'toys' and 'vanities' – the products of his literary life – to be destroyed, so Spenser is, in effect, rejecting his whole poem. The final stanzas concede the failure of his undertaking: they look back and see that as the poem has developed, there are secretly proliferated contradictions which break the poem apart. Spenser might well have attributed it to mutability or the fall, but in the final stanzas of the poem as we have it, Nature vanishes, the world is dismissed, and so is poetry. What remains is an absence that undermines what Spenser has devoted his whole life to make present in his poem.

Set in the context of sixteenth-century poetry (and even if we look ahead and acknowledge the presence of Renaissance England's other great epic, *Paradise Lost*), *The Faerie Queene* can be seen as the last attempt to decipher the world by affirming as natural, given, and eternal the secret resemblances and hierarchy behind its plethora of signs. It attempts to create a reading of nature, society, man, and poetry as an interconnected network of harmony and hierarchy, the whole recognized and valorized by each individual part – only to find that each part breaks into its separate world. At the poem's end, left with only his words, he discovers that they too have lost their divine resemblance. It is as if Spenser sensed how language could no longer function as marks of a divine order.

If we say, as I have asserted, that *The Faerie Queene* is unquestionably the 'greatest' poem of the period and one of the two or three long masterpieces in English poetry, what do we mean? Clearly not that it is united, or finished; or that its vision is noble, coherent, let alone 'true'. Spenser's poem is one of the most fascinating in all our poetry, at once one of the richest and emptiest poems, one to which readers can return endlessly because it is an encyclopedia of the ways ideology and textuality interact, and of the processes by which languages intersect and rewrite one another. There is a deep longing for meaning and stasis in *The Faerie Queene* which is contradicted at the deepest level by its own being. It attempts to transform history into culture, culture into nature, and to fix that which inevitably changes in stasis. As such it epitomizes all that the Elizabethan court itself likewise tried and failed to do. Spenser's poem may be described as 'great' on two main counts. First, like the society which produced it, it could not remain faithful to the desires which motivated it, and the more those were asserted to be natural and true, the more their falsity and the naked power on which they rested, is revealed. *The Faerie Queene* is thus a rich and fascinating articulation of a complex and fascinating cultural formation. Second, as a text (as, to be precise, textuality, as the stimulus to seductive and multiple readings), it remains intriguing, perplexing, rich, unmistakably a great work of poetry. In major ways it participates in the construction of modern ideologies, to the extent that he can be seen giving imaginary solutions to real problems which are part of our historical inheritance.

Indeed, *The Faerie Queene* offers those imaginary solutions over and over again, often missing the underlying issues, those which (as I have suggested) struggle on the margins of the text to be heard – and some of which, often generations, even centuries, later have struggled successfully to find a voice.

In 1598 Spenser returned, clearly in some anguish to England. He may have been ill; he certainly was distraught, disillusioned, appalled that his apparent stability as an English planter, official and patriot had been swept away by the resurgent Irish. He died only a few months later, early in 1599, aged about forty-eight. His admirers have, in effect, argued that the material life he had constructed may have been destroyed; but that his literary life has triumphantly lived on. From the Christian renunciation, even despair, of the 'unperfit' final canto of the Mutability Cantos, that may not be how Spenser himself saw it. For once, I suggest, we might want to side with virtually all his critics.

7

Envoi

A 'literary life' is obviously related to what we conventionally term 'biographical criticism,' by which an author's work is in some sense explained by means of reference to his or her life. But our understanding of the terms *biography, author, criticism* and *work* have, of course, radically shifted their meanings since the time, starting perhaps in the early nineteenth-century, when the inextricability of an author's life and writings seemed unquestionable. Between Coleridge's famous reading of Wordsworth's poems as a revelation of his personality, experience and philosophy, and today lie major intellectual and experiential paradigm shifts that make any naive association of biographical origin or conscious authorial intention archaic and quaintly nostalgic. In writing this literary life of Spenser I have tried to take note of these shifts to present what I believe to be a more complex picture of the career of a major writer, and in doing so have necessarily moved into realms of knowledge and speculation – social history, psychoanalysis, ideological analysis – that call into question the determining function of the author and yet take his (or her) 'inner life' seriously.

For despite my desire to go beyond the residual limits of biographical criticism, I hope that a recognizable life has emerged from the previous chapters. Like all of our lives, it took shape not only consciously but unconsciously, articulating and being written by historical movements wider than any individual can hope to control or even know. We are all thrown into worlds we did not create or choose, and our lives are mixtures of seeming determinism and apparent agency. All men and women live out multiple histories, multiple stories of desire, achievement, loss, possibility and impossibility. Re-reading *The Faerie Queene*, itself an encyclopedia of such stories, brings home the realization that we do so within many and contradictory narratives we have inherited from pasts which we did not ourselves create, and yet which give us, often without our being aware that we are being incorporated within them, the only narratives we know. As we mature, we start to create what we fancy to be our stories. One of the great, encouraging illusions of the liberal post-Renaissance West has been that the stories we are held by are, indeed, 'our' stories, just as one of the most powerful and confusing disillusions of the twentieth-century – articulated by Darwin, Marx, Freud, Foucault and many others – has been that they are not 'ours' at all, that we are never fully aware of the range of stories from which we might choose, and that we are, in many ways far beyond our understanding, let alone control, always already chosen by 'our' stories. A century after the invention of psychoanalysis, we are still living in the uneasy and often schizoid condition of both willing ourselves to construct individual dreams of autonomy, independence, agency, and also still discovering, some of us daily, how many of those stories lie in wait for us, always already told for us, sometimes without our knowing. Spenser is certainly one of those who, more skillfully than most, put into reverberating words his versions of some of the most powerful stories of our history. He is one of the great story tellers of our literature (a term which might usefully be used to refer to those stories that are written down and read over and over precisely because they are repeatedly haunting). Of course they are not Spenser's 'own' stories any more than those we tell are ours.

A literary life is also, in its small way, a story. In this final chapter, then, I want to pause over some of the elements that have made up the strands of my story of Spenser's life. The conventional answer to the question 'what went into the making of Spenser's literary life?' is those movements of events in the late sixteenth-century which I have already surveyed. But that is only half the story. All interpretations, all stories indeed, include much that readers and tellers themselves bring to their readings and tellings. My literary life of Edmund Spenser has brought a number of methodological issues to the fore, which have emerged precisely as I found it impossible to construct a literary life objectively, without the involvement of my own stories – and those of criticism and the reading of 'literature' in the late twentieth century.

Today, any reading of a literary life (the texts that make it up and of the broader culture that surrounds and produces those texts) must grapple with the methodological (and wider political) issues raised by a variety of revisionist historicisms that have dominated Renaissance and early modern studies since the 1980s, including the so-called New Historicism, Cultural Materialism, Psychoanalysis and Feminism. All these approaches to literary theory (including biography) and critical praxis have shown how any consideration of literary and related texts must be inseparable from concerns with the locations and forms by which power and desire flow through society's dominant institutions, including the family, religion and politics. The differences as well as the overlappings are worth pausing over briefly. New Historicism has tended, as does Helgerson's reading of Spenser, over which I paused in chapter one, to focus on texts as parts of a network of cultural forces, what Greenblatt terms 'a shared code, a set of interlocking tropes and similitudes that function not only as the objects but as the conditions of representations'.[1] In the New Historicist view, a cultural formation like that of late Elizabethan England is bound together, almost like a conspiracy within which individual texts and individual subjects alike are both imprisoned and legitimated. Like the various versions of 'old' Historicism, which it wants to supplant or supplement, although asking a wider range of questions, New Historicism characteristically sees the past as 'other', and resists, not always successfully (or in my view, always wisely) the appropriation of earlier texts by those concerns. It wants to put texts from the past back into their history. Thus the New Historicist approach to Spenser, such as Helgerson's, gives us a richer and more provocative context in which Spenser's life can be set than the contexts earlier historicist critics and biographers provided. But it is still (or, at least is claimed to be) rooted in Spenser's own time – a more complex depiction of an earlier age rather than a depiction of how how our readings of Spenser are produced in part out of the questions of our own time.

By contrast, Cultural Materialism has focused more on growing points and contradictions within society, and so on the question of something before which, as I have shown, Spenser, like many other Elizabethans, was very uneasy – the matter of historical change. Cultural Materialism endeavors to see texts as reproduced in the context of struggles in *our* history rather than simply produced in theirs and available to later readers for their perusal in those terms. Cultural Materialism has been especially concerned with individual subjects' desires to resist institutional power rather than, as is more characteristic of New Historicism, its apparent seamlessness. It has been especially concerned with marginal groups, like women, witches, the disenfranchised poor, and on conflict among class factions that may generate social change, rather than on what has been more the concern of New Historicism, the dominant groups of a culture – in the case of the early modern period, primarily the monarch and the male aristocracy. Feminism, also characteristically reading the past as part of a project to account for the present and to change the future, has drawn our attention to the neglected and vital force of gender in the construction of subjectivity, characteristically arguing that gender assignments and relations between the sexes are a primary aspect of social organization. Psychoanalysis – derived from, though in its most interesting manifestations, sharply deviating from Freud, especially on the matter of the social construction of gender, identity and the unconscious – has directed our attention to the mechanisms by which our 'conscious' behavior has it origins in forces and assumptions that may lie deeply embedded in our socialization, childhood patterns, even (some, including Freud himself, argue) our biology.

The point of this brief taxonomy of some current critical modes is that the issues they have raised, sometimes in conflict, sometimes as allies, have transformed the writing of literary and cultural history: we can no longer speak of 'the text' and its 'historical background', or of an 'author' with the confidence we could a generation, even a decade, ago. Specifically, Fredric Jameson has argued that not since Freud have we been able to take the notion of a life for granted; we can no longer write biography as if the shape of a life were a given.[2] Hence this literary life is written, unabashedly, unavoidably, from the present. But two additional issues require some more detailed consideration. The first of these is the use of psychoanalysis in historical studies and as a key in the construction of a literary biography. Another recurring aspect of what we somewhat uneasily term 'literature' is that it exists on the boundary, at least in part of its production, between the conscious and the unconscious – the latter term being understood to apply as a metaphor applicable to both individual subjects and cultural formations. Part of the pleasure of poetry, especially when it looks to be dealing with or based upon incidents in the poet's life, is that it plays deliciously across the boundary between fantasy and 'reality', creating a to-and-fro friction of tantalizing desire to know and actualize. Likewise, the writer of a literary life must venture, however tentatively, into the difficult terrain of probing the psyches, as it were, of both a person long dead and a society long gone. So, in writing about human subjects long dead, how do we get some sense of their inner lives?

The seduction of psychoanalysis for the writer of a biography – or, indeed, any cultural history that takes the inner lives of its subjects seriously – is precisely that it concerns itself with such a problem, with finding ways of articulating and setting out in narratives what Juliet Mitchell terms 'the material reality of ideas both within, and of, man's [*sic*] history . . . the ideas that people hold and live by'.[3] Since the turn of the century, psychoanalysis has tried, variously and contradictorily, to decipher and model the ways by which the habits and seeming laws of human societies have been internalized in what Freud ambiguously named as the unconscious. At the very least, its charting of the boundaries of the biological and the cultural provides us with rich metaphors for the latent content behind compulsive patterns of individual and social behavior and for the ways recurring fantasies surface in language and other cultural practices. If, to adapt Deleuze and Guattari's formulation, 'the unconscious is a desiring-machine and the body parts, components of that machine', cultural historians and literary biographers probing the textual manifestations of human behavior can usefully ponder both theoretical and clinical studies in psychoanalysis and related fields, including developmental psychology, family therapy and psychotherapy. But they need to do so not only in the classic Freudian areas of the manifestation of desires in dreams and fantasies, or in the common second-generation Freudians' focus on patterns of separation/individuation and object relations, but in ordinary material details of a subject's life: in the material places lives took shape and were lived out, in modes of political or familial conflict, in habituated feelings, in poetry – in short, in both 'individual' or 'personal' desires and the underlying trans-personal patterns that structure them. Such a level of analysis helps us to articulate what John Brenkman calls 'a socially grounded theory of subjectivity', thus locating ideology, as Jane Gallop puts it, within the 'desiring body', tracing the narratives of history where we all experience them, in our bodily experiences   as human subjects.[4]

   To root the seductive categories of psychoanalyis within lived realities of place and person, relationships, and interactions is to move out of the universalism to which Freud and many of his followers have been so prone and thus heed Jameson's crucial warning: 'Always historicize'.[5] It is a warning that psychoanalytical criticism has, indeed, not always heeded: historical concerns have rarely entered psychoanalysis except in the most idealist manner. One of the dangerous seductions of psychoanalysis is that, like any theory of existence tempting one into universalism, it offers a model for explaining why nothing can be done about the human condition. But one of the hopes it offers is that it may, however clumsily and tentatively, give us a way of linking the ideas and ideologies that swirl around us with the material and emotional details of our lives. It also affirms (perhaps the most profound thing it offers) that we are story-telling animals: we are continually telling and retelling, starting and trying to finish stories; continually finding that stories we started are being finished by other people, or being totally re-written. Spenser has at times played something of a villain's role in this book; nonetheless he remains one of our most compelling tellers of stories, and for that reason alone we need to pause before we condemn him. Psychonanalysis has been called the 'talking cure'; the reading of literature, the telling and retelling of its stories, and its greatest storytellers, may equally deserve that compliment.

A second methodological issue, related to the first, and one that throughout has complicated my construction of this literary life, is the place of the biographer or cultural historian in the history he or she constructs. The primary subject of this book, Edmund Spenser, lived on the shifting and ill-defined boundaries of two historical worlds: one that seems in so many of its material and emotional details unquestionably alien to most of us, and another that is frighteningly familiar. In part that is why the whole early modern period has proved so fascinating to us in this century – not because, simply, it contained 'great' writers, like Shakespeare, or Donne, but because it has seemed to provide a contradictorily dim and searchlight-bright mirror for our own time. We live in manty of the long shadows thrown by the age of Spenser. His life and career therefore raise not merely 'historical' questions, but questions about the contemporary presence of history, and perhaps questions about what is permanent, or at least recurring – and why – in our individual and shared histories. It is, incidentally, one mark of difference between our world and his (perhaps, for some of us, between our world and our parents' worlds!) that the questions and narratives of 'permanence' or 'universals' or 'essentials' in human life used to pertain predominantly to beneficent, providential stories of the ends and purpose of the universe; now they are predominantly questions and narratives of our conditioning, our social construction, even our biological and psychological makeup. Paradoxically (some would say tragically), because we live by a plurality of contradictory narratives, we are often able to combine and recombine fragments of our different histories and make some attempts at stories that we feel to be 'ours'.

Some other, very confident, words of Freud's occur to me here: in constructing this literary life, like Freud reconstructing a case history, 'I have restored what is missing, taking the best models known to me from other analyses; but like the conscientious archeologist I have not omitted to mention in each case where the authentic parts end and where my constructions begin'.[6] But how to tell that? Just as Freud's construction of his famous case-histories are, at least in part, stories of himself, so this history of Spenser is, in what I acknowledge to be in an untrivial sense also, in part, *my* history. To return to a methodological point I made in the first chapter, each of us brings a distinctive, even if always changing, repertoire, conscious and unconscious, to our reading and interpretative experiences. These repertoires are not purely 'personal', simply the product of our 'subjective' ego-identities or 'individual' preferences, ambitions, or goals. When we read, and write, we put these repertoires into play. And because it is therefore *from* a distinctive place and *for* distinctive goals, reading has, implicitly or explicitly, a utopian (or distopian) dimension: ultimately it is our own visions of the future that determine how we view the past. The most engaging readers, I submit, are those who are most engaged with such a vision and who wrestle to make it a part of the stories they tell.

While not all of our particular repertoires – whether specifically 'literary' or more general – are strictly relevant to a publicly articulated discussion in a literary life where the primary focus is, by definition, another person, it is therefore foolish to imagine that one's own beliefs, assumptions and goals about such ideologically charged issues as class, gender, race or agency should (or even can) be excluded from discussion. In his recent study of manhood in the American Renaissance, David Leverenz has similarly noted how his readings are bound up with his own involvement with gender role reversals that called into question the dominant ideologies of American maleness; Jane Gallop has likewise recently affirmed her need to 'make connections between my work' and 'my memories, my sexuality, my dreams'. In *Sexual Personae*, a book I continue to read with a mixture of anger and fascination and with which I argue throughout this study, Camille Paglia makes clear the connections between her ethnic background and her celebration of Western masculinism, which she sees so triumphantly exhibited in *The Faerie Queene*. Stephen Greenblatt's recent collection of essays, *Learning to Curse*, analyses the autobiographical impulses in his writing. And, in a moving preface to *The Country and the City*, Raymond Williams, whose words over many years have stirred my own conscience, speaks of finding himself caught on the boundaries between the contradictory worlds whose history is charted in his book. This study is likewise about its author's struggles with the issues, or at least their historical consequences, that its ostensible subjects contended with.[7]

The case history that is (or should be) the classic warning to any interpreters of other human subjects is of course Freud's analysis of 'Dora'. Reading his patient as the sometimes helpless, sometimes duplicitous, victim of her own desires, Freud neglected to ask what part he himself played in her analysis. In view of his insistence on reading Dora's story against the grain, the analyst's seemingly neutral stance provokes not only the question he asked – where was Dora in all of this? – but rather: where was Freud? What is the stake of the observer, the analyst, the reader, the critic, in the analysis he or she offers? As we all consider our possible continuities with Spenser and his time, I wonder whether it is possible for us to say what we 'really' want to know from our reading? Freud was unable to recognise what he himself had so brilliantly described: the inevitable interaction of analyst and patient, reader and text. Such a process suggests that reading – and constructing a literary life – is precisely the interactive process that psychoanalysts term transference and counter-transference. Why is Freud attracted to Dora? He won't admit it, but of course he is since he decided to write about this failed case so many years after its failure. Why do we find ourselves drawn over and over to certain stories? Is this a fascination with narrative – with seeing a life take shape? Just wanting to see the narrative take shape? Is it a form of voyeurism and counter-voyeurism?[8]

In the case of Spenser, I am trying to describe the cultural practices in which he was implicated, but my own commitments and, no doubt at times, contradictory positions in relation to the ideological contradictions of my own time are not irrelevant. They are not simply part of my 'approach' or 'methodology', but part of my subject – what I am writing about, not only what I am writing with. I write as a middle-aged white male, working in the late-twentieth century academy, whose background is not just the alienation and restlessness of the international academic, but specifically Britain and its late Empire (a distant part of which I was born and grew up in), as well as North America. Imperial power (of different kinds), gender and class contradictions, the deracination of the academic intellectual, even the repeated return-of-the-repressed all too characteristic of middle age, are parts of the repertoire which I bring to this study, and which match all too easily with parts of Spenser's. Many of these factors are only of marginal relevance, but some – given the earlier discussion of Spenser's career and writings – are central. Roland Barthes remarks that we study what we love and hate: I am conscious of a fascination with Spenser and some of his writings for a variety of contradictory and intense reasons. In particular, I was born – 'interpellated', as Althusserians (in this case, I think, with stunning accuracy) are wont to say – into the system of class, racial, and gender hierarchies that constituted the late British Empire. I thus acquired a seemingly instinctive colonial cringe before the very vestiges of the once dominant ideological apparatuses of monarchy, aristocracy, class discrepancies, and imperialism which play such a large part in this book. It is a picture, I suggest, both tragicomic and yet peculiarly positioned in relation to the histories that produced it to be able to offer some insights into the equally tragicomic, seemingly deterministic yet random, lurches of our shared history.

For this parenthetical discussion to be of more than therapeutic value, it needs to articulate not 'subjective' but a broadly shared set of contradictions that will allow other readers to enter into the dialogue (or rather polylogue, since there are many voices involved). What writing this history (or story) has brought home to me has been that the ideological contradictions in which I am caught as a subject of a complex though by no means unique history have been, over and over, part of the history I share with Spenser. Such continuities force us to face not the naive matter of 'identifying' with a person or fictional character, or effecting the very real historical differences between his time and ours, but rather the question of continuity and difference with the past and, even more important, the question of our own futures. In that tentative utopianism, this is unapologetically a book with an agenda, trying to provide a glimpse of past struggles in order to help create another world in which real people, not just abstract 'human subjects', can play a multiplicity of roles with, in, and as one another, accepting and reveling in difference by making it more familiar.

And yet, admittedly, contradictorily, this book also looks back and records a fascination with the otherness of a man who struggled to leave his mark on a world that is also long gone. That realization may lead to nostalgia as easily as to determination; to fantasies of the past as readily as of the future. We must realize that however hard one stares at the records, manuscripts, buildings, or even the poems Spenser wrote, we can never capture the 'reality' of his inner life. We can only tell tales. We are all, in the stories we live out and tell, over and over, to ourselves and each others, tellers of tales. As the analyst (and story-teller) Louise Kaplan, mulling over the connection between Emma Bovary and the real-life struggles of twentieth-century readers to make sense of their lives, literary and other, including (no doubt) herself, puts it:

> The crochet needle moves forward, steadily enlarging old patterns and creating new ones. In the process of creating something new, every so often at some crucial juncture the needle reaches back to pull in earlier stitches and patterns, integrating some facet of the old into a new pattern of organization. Whatever was created earlier can always be given new meaning, and some of what is created later will always bear the influence of earlier patterns.[9]

Notes

The place of publication, unless otherwise noted, is London.

FQ: *The Faerie Queene*, ed. A. C. Hamilton (1977).
SE: *Spenser Encyclopedia*, ed. A. C. Hamilton et al. (Toronto, 1990)
SP: *The Yale edition of the Shorter Poems of Edmund Spenser*, ed. William A. Oram et al. (New Haven, 1989).
SpN: *Spenser Newsletter*.
SSt: *Spenser Studies*.

CHAPTER 1: THE CONSTRUCTION OF A LITERARY LIFE

1. C. S. Lewis, *English Literature in the Sixteenth Century Excluding Drama* (Oxford, 1954), pp. 358–64.
2. Humphrey Tonkin, *The Faerie Queene* (1990), p. 1.
3. Malcolm Evans, *Signifying Nothing: Truth's True Contents in Shakespeare's Text* (Brighton, 1986), p. 256.
4. Janet MacArthur, *Critical Contexts of Sidney's Astrophil and Stella and Spenser's Amoretti* (Victoria, BC, 1989), pp. 8, 16, 19.
5. Richard Helgerson, 'The New Poet Presents Himself: Spenser and the Idea of a Literary Career', *PMLA*, 93 (1978), 893.
6. Thomas Nashe, 'Preface to Greene's Menaphon', in *Elizabethan Critical Essays*, edited by G. Gregory Smith (Oxford, 1904), I, p. 318; George Puttenham, *The Arte of English Poesie*, ed. Gladys Doidge Willcock and Alice Walker (Cambridge, 1936), pp. 25, 38, 42. For the poet as secretary, see Richard Rambuss, *Spenser's Secret Career* (Cambridge, 1993), p. 72.
7. Richard Helgerson, *Self-Crowned Laureates: Spenser, Jonson, Milton, and the Literary System* (Berkeley, 1983), p. 60; Rambuss, pp. 4, 6, 9.
8. Margaret Mahler, Fred Pine, and Martin Bergman, *The Psychological Birth of the Human Infant: Symbiosis and Individuation* (New York, 1975).
9. *SpN*, 12 (1981), 50.
10. Simon Shepherd, *Edmund Spenser* (1989), p. 20.
11. Shepherd, p. 21.
12. *SE*, pp. 668–71.
13. Derek Attridge, *Well-Weighed Syllables: Elizabethan Verse in Classical Metres* (Cambridge, 1974), p. 113.
14. See G. L. Hendrickson, 'Elizabethan Quantitative Hexameters', *Philological Quarterly*, 28 (1949), 237–60; Mary E. I. Underdown, 'Sir Philip Sidney's Arcadian Eclogues: A Study of his Quantitative Verse' (unpublished doctoral dissertation, Yale, 1961); William A. Ringler, Jr. 'Master Drant's Rules', *Philological Quarterly*, 19 (1950), 70–4. The para-

graphs on quantitative verse are adapted from my study, *Mary Sidney Countess of Pembroke* (Salzburg, 1979), pp. 121–8.

15. *Elizabethan Critical Essays*, I, pp. 89, 99.
16. Jonathan Goldberg, *Sodometries: Renaissance Texts, Modern Sexualities* (Stanford, 1992), p. 76; Robert C. Evans, 'Literature as Equipment for Living: Ben Jonson and the Politics of Patronage', *College Literature Association Journal*, 30 (1987), pp. 379–80.
17. S. K. Heninger, Jr., *Sidney and Spenser* (University Park, 1989), pp. 10–11.
18. Rambuss, p. 7.
19. Floya Anthias and Nira Yuval-Davis, *Racialized Boundaries: Race, Nation, Gender, Colour and Class and the Anti-Racial Struggle* (1992), pp. 2–4, 14, 40–51.
20. Lewis, p. 349.
21. Edward Said, *Culture and Imperialism* (New York, 1993).
22. Raymond Williams, *What I Came To Say* (1989), pp. 74–84.
23. Sir Philip Sidney, *Defence of Poetry*, in *Miscellaneous Prose of Sir Philip Sidney*, ed. Katherine Duncan-Jones and Jan van Dorsten (Oxford, 1973), pp. 78, 79.
24. Alan Sinfield, *Literature in Protestant England* (1983), p. 23.
25. Philip Greven, *The Protestant Temperament: Patterns of Child-Rearing, Religious Experience, and the Self in Early America* (New York, 1977), p. 5.
26. For the discussions of the appropriateness of English as a literary language, see *Elizabethan Critical Essays*, I, p. xiv; Puttenham, p. 4; Roger Ascham, Preface to *Toxophilus*, ed. Edward Asker (Westminster, 1895), p. 14; William Caxton, quoted by Vere L. Rubel, *Poetic Diction in the English Renaissance from Skelton through Spenser* (New York, 1941), p. 1; William Hawes, *The Pastyme of Pleasure*, edited W. E. Mead, *EETS*, 6, 73 (1928), pp. 917–18; *English Poetry 1400–1580*, edited by William Tydeman (New York, 1970), p. 5; Tottel, p. 2.
27. D. B. Quinn, *The Elizabethans and the Irish* (Ithaca, 1966), p. 26; Stephen Greenblatt, *Renaissance Self-fashioning from More to Shakespeare* (Chicago, 1980), p. 177.
28. Shepherd, pp. 60–4, 69.
29. Jonathan Goldberg, *Sodometries: Renaissance Texts, Modern Sexualities*, op. cit.
30. Margot Heinemann, *Puritanism and Theatre* (Cambridge: Cambridge University Press, 1980), p. 214; Philip Massinger, *The Bondman*, ed. B. T. Spenser (Princeton, 1932).
31. *Sexual Personae: Art and Decadence from Nefertiti to Emily Dickinson* (New York, 1991), p. 173.
32. Paglia, p. 7; Freud, 'Civilisation and its Discontents', *The Standard Edition of the Works of Sigmund Freud*, ed. and trans. James Strachey et al.
33. Klaus Theweleit, *Male Fantasies, Volume I: Women, Floods, Bodies, History*, trans. Stephen Conway; *Volume II: Male Bodies: Psychoanalyzing the White Terror*, trans. Erica Carter and Chris Turner (Minneapolis:

University of Minnesota Press, 1988, 1989), I, p. 276; II, p. 9. See also Barbara Ehrenreich, introduction to *Male Fantasies*, I, p. xii.

34. Goldberg, *Sodometries*, pp. 17, 19, 23; Alan Bray, *Homosexuality in Renaissance England* (London, 1988).

35. David Lee Miller, *The Poem's Two Bodies: the Poetics of the 1590 Faerie Queene* (Princeton, 1988), p. 223.

36. Richard C. McCoy, *The Rites of Knighthood: the Literature and Politics of Elizabethen Chivalry* (Berkeley, 1989), pp. 23–4; William Segar, *The Booke of Honor and Armes*, ed. Diane Bornstein (Delmar, NY:, 1975), pp. 89–90; John Nichols, *The Progresses, Processions, and Magnificent Festivities of King James the First* (New York, 1968), III, pp. 392–3; Maureen Quilligan, 'Lady Mary Wroth: Female Authority and the Family Romance', in *Unfolded Tales: Essays on the Renaissance Romance*, ed. Gordon M. Logan and Gordon Teskey, (Ithaca, 1989), pp. 274–8; Paglia, p. 173.

37. Theweleit, I. p. 213; Jessica Benjamin, *The Bonds of Love: Psychoanalysis, Feminism, and the Problem of Domination* (New York, 1988), p. 135.

38. Frye, *The Secular Scripture: a Study of the Structure of Romance* (Cambridge, Mass, 1976), p. 161.

39. Theweleit, *Male Fantasies*, I, pp. 162, 166, 192.

40. Coppélia Kahn, *Man's Estate: Masculine Identity in Shakespeare* (Berkeley, 1981), pp. 12, 20, 55; Louise Kaplan, *Female Perversions: The Temptations of Madame Bovary* (New York, 1991), p. 107; Paglia, pp. 10, 19, 173; Freud, *Standard Edition*, XI, p. 108.

41. Paglia, p. 172.

42. *SE*, pp. 101, 409.

43. W. W. Robson, 'Spenser and The Faerie Queene', in *The Age of Shakespeare*, ed. Boris Ford, revised edition (Harmondsworth, 1982), p. 120; Paglia, p. 170.

44. Shepherd, p. 119.

CHAPTER 2: THE POET'S THREE WORLDS

1. Louis Althusser, *Lenin and Philosophy and Other Essays*, trans. Ben Brewster (1971), pp. 142–3.

2. Edward Hyde, Earl of Clarendon, *The History of the Rebellion and Civil Wars in England* (Oxford, 1849), I, pp. 5, 10.

3. Edward W. Said, 'Travelling Theory', *Raritan*, I. 3 (1982), 62; Michael Foucault, 'Prison Talk' in *Power/Knowledge: Selected Interviews and Other Writings, 1972–77*, ed. Colin Gordon (New York, 1980), p. 39.

4. Roy Strong, *Splendour at Court* (1973), pp. 19, 21.

5. Sir Henry Wotton, *The Elements of Architecture* (1624), p. 6.

6. Puttenham, pp. 50, 60, 61, 137–8.

7. Frank Whigham, 'The Rhetoric of Elizabethan Suitors' Letters', *PMLA*, 96 (1981), 882. See also the same author's longer study, *Ambition and Privilege: The Social Tropes of Elizabethan Courtesy Theory* (Berkeley, 1984).

8. Rambuss, p. 72; Puttenham, pp. 45–6.
9. See Steven May, *The Elizabethan Court Poets* (Columbia, Mo., 1990).
10. Puttenham, pp. 137–8, 186, 298–300.
11. Rambuss, 9, 12, 14, 29.
12. *SE*, p. 535; Goldberg, *Sodometries*, p. 40.
13. Greenblatt, *Renaissance Self-fashioning from More to Shakespeare*.
14. Raymond Williams, *Marxism and Literature* (London, 1977), pp. 121–7.
15. This paragraph draws on: Raymond Williams, *The Long Revolution* (1961), pp. 48–71, and 'Literature in Society', in *Contemporary Approaches to English Studies*, ed. Hilda Schiff (New York, 1977), pp. 36–7; Terry Eagleton, 'Text, Ideology, Realism', in *Literature and Society: Selected Papers from the English Institute*, ed. Edward W. Said (Baltimore, 1980), p. 156; James H. Kavanagh, '"Marks of Weakness": Ideology, Science and Textual Criticism', *Praxis*, 5.1 (1982), 31.
16. *SE*, p. 235.
17. *SE*, pp. 160–4.
18. *SE*, p. 458.
19. See Kim Hall, 'Acknowledging Things of Darkness: Race, Gender, and Power in Early Modern England', unpublished dissertation, University of Pennsylvania, 1990. I owe this reference to Susan Green, of the University of Oklahoma.
20. Richard Berleith, *The Twilight Lords: an Irish Chronicle* (New York, 1978), pp. 140, 142, 175, 176; Michael MacCarthy-Morrogh, *The Munster Plantation: English Migration to Southern Ireland 1583–1641* (Oxford, 1986), pp. 2, 20–1, 26–7, 14–15.
21. Rambuss, p. 25.
22. *SE*, pp. 405–7.
23. *SE*, pp. 713–15.
24. *View*, ed. Renwick, pp. 62–3.
25. Ciaran Brady, 'Spenser's Irish Crisis: Humanism and Experience in the 1590s', *Past and Present* 111 (1980), 35.
26. MacCarthy-Morrogh, pp. 202–7; Berleith, p. 224.
27. Rambuss, p. 25; Brady, 17.
28. Berleith, p. 225.
29. Anthias and Yuval-Davis, p. 38.
30. Berleith, p. 225.
31. Rambuss, p. 98; *SE*, pp. 30–5; Berleith, p. 225.
32. *SE*, pp. 111–12.
33. Mary Ellen Lamb, 'Apologizing for Pleasure in Sidney's *Apology for Poetry*' (unpublished paper); Sidney, *Defence*, pp. 92, 97, 101, 105.
34. Paglia, p. 171.
35. *SE*, pp. 173–7.
36. A. Leigh DeNeef, 'Rereading Sidney's Apology', *Journal of Medieval and Renaissance Studies*, 10 (1980), 186; Margaret W. Ferguson, *Trials of Desire* (New Haven, 1983), p. 146.
37. Ralph Lever, *The Arte of Reason* (London, 1573), foreword; Richard Mulcaster, *The First Part of the Elementarie*, ed. E. T. Campagnac (1925), p. 172: Thomas Nashe, *Works*, ed. E. D. McKerrow (1958), II, p. 61.

38. Hamilton, p. 15.
39. A. Leigh DeNeef, *Spenser and the Motives of Metaphor* (Durham, NC). 13, 61, 144.
40. A. Kent Hieatt, Short Time's Endless Monument (New York, 1960), pp. 81–2.

CHAPTER 3: THE MAKING OF A PROTESTANT POET

1. John N. King, *English Reformation Literature: The Tudor Origins of the Protestant Tradition* (Princeton, 1982), pp. 16, 209.
2. Sidney, *Defence* pp. 81, 109, 120.
3. Sidney, *Defence*, pp. 78, 79–80.
4. S. K. Heninger, Jr, *Touches of Sweet Harmony: Pythagorean Cosmology and Renaissance Poetics* (San Marino, 1974), p. 382.
5. Jon A. Quitslund, 'Spenser's Amoretti VIII and Platonic Commentaries on Petrarch', *Journal of the Warburg and Courtauld Institute*, 36 (1973), 258.
6. King, p. 319.
7. Coburn Freer, *Music for a King: George Herbert's Style and the Metrical Psalms* (Baltimore, 1972), p. 60.
8. Ascham, in *Elizabethan Critical Essays*, I, p. 20.
9. Helgerson, *Self-Crowned Laureates*. See also Helgerson's *The Elizabethan Prodigals* (Berkeley, 1976).
10. *SE*, pp. 30–5.
11. Rambuss, pp. 19–21.
12. *SE*, p. 330.
13. Calvin, *Commentary on Galatians*, trans. T. H. L. Parker (Edinburgh, 1965), p. 99; Calvin, *Institutes*, I. xviii. i; Arthur Dent, *A Sermon of Gods Providence* (1611), sigs. A6r–A7r. For Augustine's view of time and providence, see *Confessions*, XI. x–xxviii, 597–638; *City of God*, XII. xiii–xix, 452–60. For a detailed treatment of the Augustinian philosophy of time, see Herman Hauser, 'St. Augustine's Conception of Time', *The Philosophical Review*, 46 (1937), 503–12.
14. Puttenham, pp. 26, 38.
15. See Louis Montrose, 'Celebration and Insinuation: Sir Philip Sidney and the Motives of Elizabethan Courtship', *Renaissance Drama*, n.s. 8 (1977), 3–35; 'Of Gentlemen and Shepherds: The Politics of Elizabethan Pastoral Form', *ELH*, 50 (1983), 415–20.
16. Heninger, *Sidney and Spenser*, pp. 307–9.
17. Goldberg, *Sodometries*, pp. 72–6.
18. Sidney, *Defence*, p. 93.

CHAPTER 4: 'CONSORTED IN ONE HARMONEE'

1. Jonathan Goldberg, *Endless Worke* (Baltimore, 1981), p. 27.
2. For the letter to Ralegh, see *FQ*, pp. 737–8.
3. Tonkin, p. 35; Goldberg, *Endless Worke*, pp. 9, 21, 77.
4. Quoted by Rosemary Freeman, *Elizabethan Emblem Books* (1948), p. 2.

5. Puttenham, pp. 186–8.
6. Isabel MacCaffery, *Spenser's Allegory: The Anatomy of Imagination* (Princeton, 1976), p. 9.
7. Donald Cheney, review of Goldberg, *Endless Worke, SpN,* 13, no. 2 (1982), 35.
8. Goldberg, *Endless Worke,* p. 76, n. 1; Maureen Quilligan, *The Language of Allegory: Defining the Genre* (Ithaca, 1979), p. 35; Terry Eagleton, *Walter Benjamin or Towards a Revolutionary Criticism* (1981), pp. 10, 22.
9. Michael Murrin, *The Veil of Allegory* (Chicago, 1969), p. 168; Quilligan, pp. 29, 31.
10. Sidney, *Defence,* pp. 92, 93.
11. Lewis, p. 380; Goldberg, *Endlesse Worke,* p. 77.
12. Tonkin, p. 63.
13. Tonkin, p. 87.
14. *SE,* pp. 263–70.
15. Tonkin, p. 107.
16. Greenblatt, *Renaissance Self-Fashioning,* pp. 157–92.
17. *SE,* pp. 104–7.
18. Paglia, p. 9.
19. Louise Kaplan, *Female Perversions: The Temptations of Madame Bovary* (New York: Doubleday, 1991), pp. 88, 174.
20. Nancy Chodorow, 'Gender, Relations and Difference in Psycho-analytical Perspective', in *The Future of Difference,* ed. Hester Eisenstein and Alice Jardine (Boston, 1980), pp. 3–19.
21. Tonkin, p. 115.
22. Freud, 'Civilisation and its Discontents', *Standard Edition,* XXI, pp. 111, 112, 114. For an alternative view to Freud's, see Richard E. Leakey, *The Making of Mankind* (New York, 1981).

CHAPTER 5: A 'WORLDE . . . RUNNE QUITE OUT OF SQUARE'

1. Lewis, pp. 378–9.
2. Williams, *The Country and the City* (1973), p. 33.
3. Josephine Bennett, *The Evolution of 'The Faerie Queene'* (Chicago, 1942), p. 157.
4. Humphrey Tonkin, *SpN,* 23, (1992), 22–3.
5. Goldberg, *Endlesse Worke,* pp. 9, 76, no. 1.
6. Lewis, p. 349.
7. Roger Sale, *Reading Spenser: An Introduction to 'The Faerie Queene'* (New York, 1968), p. 162.
8. Helena Shire, *A Preface to Spenser* (1978), p. 51.
9. Donald V. Stump, 'The Two Deaths of Mary Stuart: Historical Allegory in Spenser's Book of Justice', *S St* 9 (1991), 81–105.
10. *SE,* pp. 280–3.
11. *SE,* pp. 280–3.
12. Robert E. Stillman, 'Spenserian Autonomy and the Trial of New Historicism', *English Literary Renaissance,* 22 (1992), 305, 307, 310, 311, 313.
13. Stillman, 310–11.

CHAPTER 6: MUTABILITY AND THE LITERARY LIFE

1. Jonathan Crewe, *Hidden Designs: the Critical Profession and Renaissance Literature* (New York, 1986), p. 55; Rambuss, p. 84.
2. *SP*, p. 381; Rambuss, p. 86.
3. *SP*, p. 265.
4. Heninger, *Sidney and Spenser*, pp. 362–3; *SP*, p. 218.
5. Sidney, *Defence*, p. 77.
6. Heninger, *Sidney and Spenser*, p. 330.
7. Heninger, *Sidney and Spenser*, p. 332.
8. *SP*, pp. 522–3.
9. Sinfield, p. 66.
10. Arthur F. Marotti, ' "Love is not Love": Elizabethan Sonnet Sequences and the Social Order', *ELH*, 49 (1982), 417.
11. Reed Way Dasenbrook, *Imitating the Italians: Wyatt, Spenser, Synge, Pound, Joyce* (Baltimore, 1991), p. 83.
12. Stoller, *Observing the Erotic Imagination* (New Haven, 1985), pp. 31–2.
13. Paglia, p. 189.
14. Freud, 'Three Essays on Sexuality', *Standard Edition*, VII, p. 171.
15. See e.g., Leonard Forster, *The Icy Fire* (Cambridge, 1968), Appendix 1; Theweleit, *Male Fantasies*, I, p. 284.
16. Raquel Zak de Goldstein, 'The Dark Continent and its Enigmas,' *International Journal of Psychoanalysis*, 65 (1984), 187.
17. Freud, 'Three Essays', *Standard Edition*, VII, p. 156; Paglia, p. 242; Stoller, *Observing the Erotic Imagination* (New Haven: Yale University Press, 1985), pp. 31–2. See also Charles W. Socarides, 'The Demonified Mother: A Study of Voyeurism and Sexual Sadism', *International Review of Psycho-Analysis*, I (1974), 192–3 and David W. Allen, *The Fear of Looking or Scopophilic-Exhibitionist Conflicts* (Bristol, 1974), esp. pp. 40–1.
18. Rosalind Coward, 'Sexual Violence and Sexuality', *Feminist Review*, XI (June, 1982), 17f.; Kaplan, p. 125.
19. Kaplan, pp. 35–54. See also Freud, 'Three Essays on Sexuality', *Standard Edition*, VII, p. 171.
20. Freud, 'Three Essays on Sexuality', *Standard Edition*, VII, p. 171.
21. Sir Isaac Newton, *Mathematical Principles*, trans. Florian Cajori (Berkeley, 1934), p. 6; Hans Meyerhoff, *Time in Literature* (Berkeley, 1955), pp. 1–2; Mircea Eliade, *Cosmos and History*, trans. Willard R. Trask (New York, 1959), pp. 74–5; the whole chapter, pp. 51–92, is relevant here; see also S. G. F. Brandon, *Time and Mankind* (1951), p. 23; Paul Tillich, *Systematic Theology*, I (1953), p. 215.
22. A. N. Whitehead, *Process and Reality* (Cambridge, 1929), p. 295.
23. Philippe de Mornay, *A Woorke concerning the trewnesse of the Christian Religion*, trans. Sir Philip Sidney and Arthur Golding (1587), p. 139.
24. For detailed treatment of Bruno's connections with Spenser, see G. F. Waller, *The Strong Necessity of Time* (The Hague, 1976), chapter 3.
25. Marion Campbell, 'Spenser's Mutabilitie Cantos and the End of *The Faerie Queene*', *Southern Review* (Adelaide), 15 (1982), 53.
26. Richard Neuse, *SpN*, 14 (1983), 49.

CHAPTER 7: ENVOI

1. Stephen Greenblatt, *Shakesperian Negotiations* (Berkeley, 1989), p. 86.

2. Fredric Jameson, *The Political Unconscious* (Princeton, 1980), p. 9.

3. Juliet Mitchell, *Psychoanalysis and Feminism* (London: Allen Lane, 1974), p. xxii; *Woman's Estate* (Harmondsworth: Penguin, 1971), p. 167.

4. Gilles Deleuze and Felix Guattari, *Anti-Oedipus: Capitalism and Schizophrenia*, trans. Robert Hurley, Mark Seem and Helen R. Lane (Minneapolis: University of Minnesota Press, 1983), chapter 17; John Brenkman, *Culture and Domination* (Ithaca: Cornell University Press, 1987), pp. 143, 196; Jane Gallop, *Thinking through the Body* (New York: Columbia University Press, 1988), p. 132.

5. Jameson, p. 70.

6. Freud, 'On the Universal Tendency to Debasement in the Sphere of Love', *Standard Edition*, XIV, pp. 188–9.

7. David Leverenz, *Manhood and American Renaissance* (Ithaca: Cornell University Press, 1989), pp. 7–8; Gallop, *Thinking through the Body*, p. 7.

8. See e.g., Hannah S. Decker, *Freud, Dora and Vienna* (New York: Free Press, 1990; *In Dora's Case*, ed. Charles Bernheimer and Claire Kahane (New York: Columbia University Press, 1985); Riccardo Steiner, 'Dora: "La Belle Indifference", or 'Label(le) in Difference', in *Desire*, ed. Lisa Appignanesi (London: ICA), pp. 9–13.

9. Kaplan, p. 53.

Select Bibliography

The place of publication, unless otherwise noted, is London.

BACKGROUND AND METHODOLOGICAL STUDIES

Althusser, Louis. *Lenin and Philosophy and Other Essays,* trans. Ben Brewster, 1971.

Anthias, Floya, and Nira Yuval-Davis. *Racialized Boundaries: Race, Nation, Gender, Colour and Class and the Anti-Racist Struggle,* 1992.

Dollimore, Jonathan. *Radical Tragedy.* Chicago, 1984.

———. *Sexual Dissidence: Augustine to Wilde, Freud to Foucault.* Oxford, 1991.

Frye, Northrop. *The Secular Scripture: a Study of the Structure of Romance.* Cambridge, Mass, 1976.

Gates, Henry Louis, Jr., ed. *"Race", Writing, and Difference.* Chicago, 1986.

Greenblatt, Stephen. *Renaissance Self-fashioning from More to Shakespeare.* Chicago, 1980.

———. *Shakesperian Negotiations.* Berkeley, 1989.

———. *Learning to Curse.* Chicago, 1991.

Kaplan, Louise. *Female Perversions: The Temptations of Madame Bovary.* New York, 1991.

Nandy, Ashis. *The Intimate Enemy: Loss and Recovery of Self under Colonialism.* Delhi, 1983.

Stoller, Robert. *Observing the Erotic Imagination.* New Haven, 1985.

Theweleit, Klaus. *Male Fantasies, Volume I: Women, Floods, Bodies, History,* trans. Stephen Conway; *Volume II: Male Bodies: Psychoanalyzing the White Terror,* trans. Erica Carter and Chris Turner. Minneapolis, 1988, 1989.

Williams, Raymond. *The Country and the City.* 1973.

———. *Marxism and Literature.* 1977.

———. *What I Came To Say.* 1989.

HISTORICAL AND LITERARY HISTORICAL STUDIES

Berleith, Richard. *The Twilight Lords: an Irish Chronicle.* New York, 1978.

Goldberg, Jonathan. *James I and the Politics of Literature.* Baltimore, 1983.

———. *Sodometries: Renaissance Texts, Modern Sexualities.* Stanford, 1992.

Helgerson, Richard. *Self-Crowned Laureates: Spenser, Jonson, Milton, and the Literary System.* Berkeley, 1983.

———. *The Elizabethan Prodigals.* Berkeley, 1976.

Javitch, Daniel. *Poetry and Courtliness in Renaissance England.* Princeton, 1978.

King, John N. *English Reformation Literature: The Tudor Origins of the Protestant Tradition.* Princeton, 1982.

Lamb, Mary Ellen. *Gender and Authorship in the Sidney Circle.* Madison, 1990.
Lewis, C. S. *The Allegory of Love.* Oxford, 1936.
———. *English Literature in the Sixteenth Century Excluding Drama.* Oxford, 1954.
———. *The Discarded Image: An Introduction to Medieval and Renaissance Literature.* Cambridge, 1964.
MacCarthy-Morrogh, Michael. *The Munster Plantation: English Migration to Southern Ireland 1583–1641.* Oxford, 1986.
McCoy, Richard C. *The Rites of Knighthood: the Literature and Politics of Elizabethan Chivalry.* Berkeley, 1989.
Montrose, Louis. 'Celebration and Insinuation: Sir Philip Sidney and the Motives of Elizabethan Courtship', *Renaissance Drama,* n.s. 8 (1977).
———. 'Of Gentlemen and Shepherds: The Politics of Elizabethan Pastoral Form', *ELH,* 50 (1983).
———. '"Shaping Fantasies": Figurations of Gender and Power in Elizabethan Literature'. *Representations,* I (1983).
Murrin, Michael. *The Veil of Allegory.* Chicago, 1969.
Paglia, Camille. *Sexual Personae: Art and Decadence from Nefertiti to Emily Dickinson.* New York, 1991.
Quilligan, Maureen. *The Language of Allegory: Defining the Genre.* Ithaca, 1979.
———. *Milton's Spenser: The Politics of Reading.* Ithaca, 1983.
Quinn, D. B. *The Elizabethans and the Irish.* Ithaca, 1966.
Said, Edward. *Culture and Imperialism.* New York, 1993.
Sinfield, Alan. *Literature in Protestant England.* 1983.
Strong, Roy. *The English Icon.* 1969.
———. *Splendor at Court.* Boston, 1973.
Waller, Gary. *English Poetry in the Sixteenth Century* 1986; second edition, 1993.
Wayne, Don. *Penshurst: The Semiotics of Place and the Poetics of History.* Milwaukee, 1984.
Whigham, Frank. 'The Thetoric of Elizabethan Suitors' Letters,' *PMLA,* 96 (1981).
———. *Ambition and Privilege: The Social Tropes of Elizabethan Courtesy Theory.* Berkeley, 1984.

STUDIES OF SPENSER

Brady, Ciaran. 'Spenser's Irish Crisis: Humanism and Experience in the 1590s', *Past and Present* 111 (1980).
Cain, Thomas. *Praise in 'The Faerie Queene'.* Lincoln, 1978.
Campbell, Marion. 'Spenser's Mutabilitie Cantos and the End of *The Faerie Queene'*, *Southern Review* (Adelaide), 15 (1982).
Dasenbrook, Reed Way. *Imitating the Italians: Wyatt, Spenser, Synge, Pound, Joyce.* Baltimore, 1991.
DeNeef, A Leigh. *Spenser and the Motives of Metaphor.* Durham, NC, 1990.
Evans, Maurice. *Spenser's Anatomy of Heroism.* Cambridge, 1970.
Goldberg, Jonathan. *Endlesse Worke.* Baltimore, 1981.

————. *James I and the Politics of Literature*. Baltimore, 1983.

Hamilton, A. C. *The Structure of Allegory in 'The Faerie Queene'*. Oxford, 1961.

————. ed. *Essential Articles for the Study of Edmund Spenser*. Hamden, 1972.

————. et al., eds. *Spenser Encyclopedia*, Toronto, 1990.

Helgerson, Richard. 'The New Poet Presents Himself: Spenser and the Idea of a Literary Career', *PMLA*, 93 (1978).

Heninger, S. K., Jr. *Sidney and Spenser*. University Park, 1989.

————. *Spenser's Images of Life*. Cambridge, 1967.

Lewis, C. S. *Spenser's Images of Life*. Ed. Alastair Fowler. East Lansing, 1967.

MacArthur, Janet H. *Critical Contexts of Sidney's Astrophil and Stella and Spenser's Amoretti*. Victoria, BC, 1989.

MacCaffery, Isabel. *Spenser's Allegory: The Anatomy of Imagination*. Princeton, 1976.

Miller, David Lee. *The Poem's Two Bodies: The Poetics of the 1590 Faerie Queene*. Princeton, 1988.

Quilligan, Maureen. *The Language of Allegory*. Ithaca, 1979.

Rambuss, Richard. *Spenser's Secret Career*. Cambridge, 1993.

Sale, Roger. *Reading Spenser: An Introduction to 'The Faerie Queene'*. New York, 1968).

Shepherd, Simon. *Edmund Spenser*. 1989.

Shire, Helena. *A Preface to Spenser*. 1978.

Shore, David R. *Spenser and the Poetics of Pastoral: A Study of the World of Colin Clout*. Kingston, 1985.

Spenser, Edmund. *The Faerie Queene, ed. A. C. Hamilton* (1977).

————. Oram, William A. et al., eds. *The Yale edition of the Shorter Poems of Edmund Spenser*. New Haven, 1989.

————. Works: Variorum Edition (10 vols, Baltimore 1932–58; reprinted 1966).

————. Smith, J. C., and De Selincourt, E., eds, *Poetical Works* (3 vols, Oxford, 1909–10).

Stillman, Robert E. 'Spenserian Autonomy and the Trial of New Historicism: Book Six of *The Faerie Queene*'. *English Literary Renaissance*, 22 (1992), 299–314.

Stump, Donald V. 'The Two Deaths of Mary Stuart: Historical Allegory in Spenser's Book of Justice', *Spenser Studies* 9 (1991), 81–105.

Tonkin, Humphrey. *Spenser's Courteous Pastoral: Book Six of 'The Faerie Queene'*. Oxford, 1972.

————. *The Faerie Queene*. 1990.

See also the *Spenser Newsletter* (1968–   ).

Index

209